The Great Tastes of
CHINESE COOKING

Jean Yueh

The Great Tastes of
CHINESE COOKING
Contemporary Methods and Menus

Times
BOOKS

Published by TIMES BOOKS, a division
of Quadrangle/The New York Times Book Co., Inc.
Three Park Avenue, New York, N.Y. 10016

Published simultaneously in Canada by
Fitzhenry & Whiteside, Ltd., Toronto

Library of Congress Cataloging in Publication Data
Yueh, Jean.
  The great tastes of Chinese cooking.

  Includes index.
  1. Cookery, Chinese.   2. Food processor cookery.
I. Title.
TX724.5.C5Y824   641.5'951   78-20674
ISBN 0-8129-0808-2

Manufactured in the United States of America

To my husband, Eric,

and our son, Ted,

who are my best food tasters and critics.

Without their enthusiasm

and constant support,

this book would not have been possible.

Acknowledgements

My deep appreciation and thanks to Irene Rich for her encouragement, her invaluable editorial suggestions, and her superb and sensitive skills in clarifing and strengthening my writing.

I am grateful to Anne Collings for her thoughtful and constructive guidance, and her aid and skills in helping to test the recipes in this book.

Many thanks to Roger Yeu for providing the transliterations, and Rosemarie Hausherr for her unique and skillful photography.

A special salute to Elaine Martin for her compassionate, witty, and always apt advice.

I cherish the many happy hours I shared together with all my students. Their continued enthusiasm has inspired me to write this book.

Contents

Introduction

During the past twelve years, my teaching approach has evolved into a philosophy of Chinese cooking which combines modern Western technology with classical Chinese recipes so that the best of East and West meet in a happy gourmet marriage.

To achieve this, I teach Americans to adopt the basics of centuries-old Chinese cooking and adapt these same principles to Western life styles. But throughout my cooking classes, there was always one common complaint: "I just love Chinese food, but the preparation, chopping, and cutting take so long!" And since the aesthetic appeal of each Chinese dish usually depends on the uniformity of the cut food, cutting *is* an important aspect of Chinese cooking. So much so, that Chinese chefs traditionally spend years mastering this technique.

Now you can easily understand why for years I kept searching for a machine that could replace the hand-chopping, slicing, and shredding in Chinese recipes. And this is what I've discovered in the food processor, for with the advent of this machine vegetables and semi-frozen meat can be sliced or shredded in seconds. (Semi-frozen meat is much easier to slice and shred.)

With this in mind, I've developed recipes of Chinese dishes for this book which involve chopping, mincing, pureeing, slicing, shredding, mixing, and kneading. Dishes containing ingredients that are cut into cubes or diced are not included, since the processor does not perform these tasks. However, cutting and dicing are usually not as time-consuming as the chopping, slicing, and shredding called for in so many Chinese recipes.

Along with the detailed instructions on the use of the food processor in Chinese dishes, the book also gives the basic principles and techniques of Chinese cooking. Below are other features of the book:

o The emphasis of this book is on simple and no-fuss Chinese cooking that is practical for the American life style.

o It is filled with ideas and tips for easy everyday dishes that can be ready for short notice serving.

o The chapter on Menu Planning gives different themes for easy entertaining with menu suggestions and timetables using plan-ahead and cook-ahead techniques.

o A collection of best-loved regional dishes and national favorites—from the very simple (with ingredients available in the supermarkets) to the more fancy and exotic recipes.

o Recipes are written clearly and explicitly, with step-by-step instructions, so that even a beginner can use them with confidence.

o Dishes are introduced with enticing descriptions and serving suggestions for use as one-dish meals.

o Complete listing of preparation and cooking time.

o Ingredients are listed in chronological order and in one vertical column, so the reader can check the needed ingredients at just a quick glance.

o Recipes are planned in the most efficient way with a preparation sequence that minimizes washing of food processor parts.

o Dishes are indicated that can be frozen, made in large quantities, partially or completely cooked ahead.

o Substitutes are suggested for ingredients you may not have on hand.

o Information is included on buying, preparing, and storing ingredients.

o Detailed information is listed for storing and reheating cook-ahead dishes.

o Optional time-saving techniques for use of the microwave oven and its applications to Chinese cooking are included.

o No monosodium glutamate is used in any of the recipes.

o Only lean cuts of meat and chicken breasts are used in the recipes, which are ideal for low-cholesterol cooking.

o Metric equivalents for all measurements are included.

Another attractive feature of the food processor is that it cuts down hand labor tremendously. For instance, when a recipe in a Chinese cookbook calls for ground meat, classically it would have been hand-chopped. But the grinder lacerates the meat and gives it a different texture. The food processor, however, can achieve almost hand-chopped textures of coarse, medium, and fine degrees—and it does it in just a few seconds.

It is truly a delight for anyone who enjoys cooking to be able to chop their own meat. And the biggest advantage is that they know exactly what goes into the chopped meat—a most worthwhile asset for those who want to reduce or restrict their intake of animal fat.

Pork, for example, is the most important and commonly used red meat in Chinese dishes. We have infinite varieties of chopped pork dishes, for this flavor is much more delicate than that of ground beef. Supermarkets don't usually have ready-ground pork, and many do not grind pork at just any time of the day. If they do, it usually contains a lot of fat. So, by chopping your own meat in the processor, you get more value for your money.

Another time-saving bonus of the processor is that the seasoning mixture can be combined at the same time that the meat is being chopped. This saves another preparation step and another bowl to wash. I was also delighted to discover that this chopped meat mixture which was mixed by the food processor has a lighter texture than the same meat mixture which was traditionally mixed by hand. Traditionally, light texture is achieved only by adding a good portion of pork fat, so there's another plus health factor when using the processor!

One other time-saving use of the food processor is in the making of bread and pastry dough. In fact, the machine kneads the dough for Mandarin pancakes and the wrappers of egg rolls, wontons, and dumplings in less than a minute. And once you become familiar with the processor, you can adapt your own favorite Chinese recipes—or start experimenting. I hope you find as much enjoyment as I did in using the food processor in new ways for new things.

This book is written for busy people who want fast, healthy, delicious, and authentic Chinese food. It's achieved by merging modern technology with centuries-old cuisine.

A NOTE ON THE TRANSLITERATION OF CHINESE CHARACTERS

The English title of each recipe is accompanied by the Chinese characters used to describe the dish and a transliteration, or romanization, in our alphabet. The system used here is the one recently adopted by agencies of the People's Republic of China, the United Nations, and the United States Board of Geographic Names, and is called Pinyin (which means "transcription").

Since Chinese is not written with an alphabetic script, but with ideograms—in effect, drawings—that convey meaning but do not express sound, it has been difficult to devise a phonetic system that converts that sound of Chinese characters into those of English. As many as twenty systems had been developed to transliterate Chinese, but it is generally agreed that Pinyin provides a closer approximation than any of the others. Readers pronouncing the Pinyin romanizations will hear words that most closely approach the Chinese dialect historically known as Mandarin. While the Chinese government is fostering Pinyin in an effort to standardize speech, the reader should be aware that the recipes in this book come from many regions in which a variety of dialects are traditionally spoken. Therefore, the pronounciation provided here may not be the one used in the place of origin of a given dish and, indeed, may not be intelligible to residents of that area. For example, a reader ordering a dish in a Cantonese restaurant from a Cantonese-speaking waiter will not be understood if this system is used.

What Pinyin does do for the cook using this book is to offer an *idea* of the Chinese name of a dish in much the same way that a French cookbook will let the chef know that a Parisian veal stew is called *blanquette de veau*.

Since Pinyin uses some letters, such as "q" and "x," that are not readily interpreted by the English speaker, a guide to pronounciation follows:

a Vowel as in *far*
b Consonant as in *be*
c Consonant as in *its*
ch Consonant as in *church,* strongly aspirated
d Consonant as in *do*
e Vowel as in *her*
f Consonant as in *foot*
g Consonant as in *go*
h Consonant as in *her,* strongly aspirated
i Vowel as in *eat* or as in *sir* (when in syllables beginning with c, ch, r, s, sh, z, and zh)
j Consonant as in *jeep*
k Consonant as in *kind,* strongly aspirated
l Consonant as in *land*
m Consonant as in *me*
n Consonant as in *no*
o Vowel as in *law*
p Consonant as in *par,* strongly aspirated
q Consonant as in *cheek*
r Consonant as in *right* (not rolled) or pronounced as z in *azure*
s Consonant as in *sister*
sh Consonant as in *shore*
t Consonant as in *top,* strongly aspirated
u Vowel as in *too,* also as in the French *tu* or the German *München*
v Consonant used only to produce foreign words, national minority words, and local dialects
w Semi-vowel in syllables beginning with u when not preceded by consonants, as in *want*
x Consonant as in *she*
y Semi-vowel in syllables beginning with i or u when not preceded by consonants, as in *yet*
z Consonant as in *zero*
zh Consonant as in *jump*

The Great Tastes of
CHINESE COOKING

The Food Processor

TOOLS OF THE MACHINE

Steel Blade: Chops, minces, and purees cooked and uncooked meat, poultry, seafood, nuts, and vegetables. Mixes food and sauces. Makes pastry dough, and kneads dough for Mandarin pancakes, bread, and wrappers of egg rolls, wontons, and dumplings.

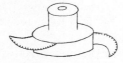

Medium Serrated Slicing Disk: Slices vegetables and partially frozen raw meat and poultry. Cuts partially frozen raw meat and poultry and some vegetables into julienne strips.

Medium Shredding Disk: Shreds vegetables, but the shreds are too fine for stir-frying.

Plastic knife: Mixes eggs, light batters, and sauces.

Optional Tools Applicable to Chinese Cooking:

Fine Serrated Slicing Disk: It slices vegetables and partially frozen raw meat and chicken paper-thin. Cuts some vegetables to $^1/_{12}$-inch/1½-cm thick strips.

French Fry Cutter: This disk cuts vegetables into sticks about 2 inches/5 cm long and ¼ inch/¾ cm thick.

Julienne Disk: It cuts vegetables into $^1/_{14}$-inch¾-cm thick strips. The shreds are too fine for most stir-fry dishes.

Wide-Mouth and Long-Neck Funnels: These are useful for adding liquid ingredients. The long-neck funnel can be used for slicing a single carrot or a sausage.

GENERAL TIPS

1. *Safety First:* Always wait until the disk or blade has *stopped spinning* before removing the cover of the beaker. Use the pusher when slicing or shredding. To adjust food in the feed tube, use chopsticks or small wooden tongs rather than your fingers.

2. To avoid washing beaker unnecessarily, work from *dry* to *wet* foods. The recipes in this book are designed in such order. Mince the vegetables first as they need a dry beaker. You can then slice or shred the other ingredients, or chop and puree the meat and poultry.

3. *For easiest cleaning,* wash each part of processor immediately after using.

SPECIAL TECHNIQUES ON USING THE FOOD PROCESSOR

Chopping and Mincing Vegetables (Steel Blade)

1. On/off turns: This means a quick twist in turning the machine on and then off *rapidly.* The machine works so fast that the contents must be checked after 1 or 2 on/off turns to see if the desired result has been achieved. Otherwise, you can end up with a puree. Whether food is coarsely or finely chopped is regulated by the number of on/off turns and the total processing time.

2. For mincing and chopping vegetables: The beaker and the blade should be dry to get the best results.

3. To chop *soft vegetables:* Cut them in 1-inch/2½-cm chunks. Celery should be stringed. Cucumber should be seeded to reduce liquid. To get

more uniform results, do not overcrowd the beaker, putting no more than 2 cups/½ L in at one time.

4. To chop *hard vegetables:* Cut carrots, turnips, etc., in 1-inch/2½-cm chunks. Start the machine, and drop pieces through the feed tube. Chop to the desired size.

5. To mince *ginger and garlic:* Cut ginger into a ½-inch/1½-cm cube. Peel garlic, leaving it whole. Start the machine first, then drop garlic and/or ginger through the feed tube and leave machine on until they are finely minced. The beaker and the blade should be dry before starting.

6. To chop *onion:* Peel and cut into quarters. For more uniform results, chop one onion at a time. Onions will get watery if too many of them are chopped together.

Slicing Vegetables (Medium or Fine Slicing Disk)

1. For uniform slices, cut off a flat end of your vegetable and cut to a length so it is shorter than the feed tube. (Use the pusher as a guide to the length and the width of foods to be sliced.) Place cut vegetable in the feed tube with the flat side down.

2. To be sure of getting round slices from vegetables like *carrots* and *scallions,* wedge the vegetables in bunches tightly and vertically in the feed tube to keep them upright. Or, for a single carrot, insert the carrot in the long-neck funnel and slice.

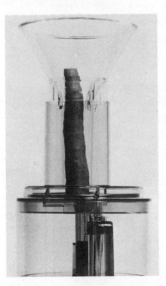

3. When slicing single vegetables like *cucumber* or *zucchini,* place it against the right side of the feed tube wall to get round slices. When shopping for these round vegetables, look for those with a diameter not bigger than 1½ inches/4 cm (so it can go through the feed tube without trim-

ming). This will save you time, and untrimmed slices will look so much prettier. Or, with the larger vegetable, you may squeeze and press it into shape to fit the feed tube before slicing.

4. The feed tube is slightly larger at the bottom than at the top. Some vegetables may be too large to go through from the top, but can be inserted through the bottom of the feed tube.

Shredding Vegetables (Medium or Fine Slicing Disk)

Vegetables shredded with the medium shredding and julienne disk are too fine for most Chinese cooking. To get julienne strips, one would use either the medium or fine slicing disk. The medium slicing disk is used in most of the recipes.

1. For *onion:* Cut ends off and then cut onion into lengthwise halves or quarters to fit the feed tube. Place it vertically in the feed tube using moderate pressure on the pusher.

2. For *bell pepper:* Cut ends from the pepper. Remove seeds and membrane. Cut lengthwise into quarters or into 2-inch/5-cm sections. Wedge them vertically in the feed tube and slice.

3. The medium slicing disk does not give satisfactory results when shredding *scallions.* This is better performed by hand. However, if you have a fine slicing disk, you can get finely shredded scallions by first cutting scallions into 2-inch/5-cm lengths, and then placing them horizontally in the feed tube. Use very light pressure in the pusher to slice.

4. To get julienne strips for vegetables like *carrots, cucumbers, zucchini, turnips, potatoes,* and *bamboo shoots,* cut them in 2-inch/5-cm lengths or the largest size that will fit the feed tube horizontally. Process with the slicing disk. Remove vegetable slices from the beaker and reprocess. This time hold cover upside down by the feed tube; insert and hold the pusher by the same hand about 1 inch/2½ cm lower than the bottom of the feed tube so it forms a 1-inch/2½-cm deep cup. Using the other hand, place stacked slices on edge, with longer edges touching the bottom of the pusher. Stack more slices until they are very compact in the tube, so they will not fall out.

Replace the cover on the beaker. You can now fit one or more stacked vegetable layers through the top of the feed tube. Apply light pressure on the pusher to slice.

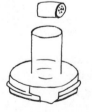

5. Use the fine slicing disk only when very fine shreds of vegetable are desired.

Slicing Meat and Poultry (Medium or Fine Slicing Disk)

The slicing and shredding of the meat and poultry is for many the most tedious and time-consuming aspect of Chinese cooking, for the actual cooking time is usually only a few minutes. But now the food processor can slice partially frozen meats and chicken in few seconds, greatly reducing the preparation time of many stir-fried dishes.

1. The medium slicing disk is used for most purposes. The slices made from the fine serrated slicing disk are too thin for stir-frying, but are very good for a Mongolian fire pot—the Chinese version of fondue cooking.

2. All meat and chicken should be *sliced across the grain,* whether the slicing is done by hand or by the processor. This will produce more tender meat after stir-frying—a very important aspect of Chinese cooking. So when you prepare the meat for freezing and slicing, bear in mind that the meat should be placed flat side down in the feed tube with the grain of the meat muscle running perpendicular to the slicing disk.

3. Meat and chicken should be cut in the largest possible pieces to fit the feed tube, using the pusher as a guide. Then freeze cut pieces on a baking pan until firm enough for slicing.

Approximate Partial Freezing Time for Slicing:

1½-inch/4-cm thick meat—1½ hours
1-inch/2½-cm thick meat—1 to 1¼ hours
Chicken breast—¾ to 1 hour

Or you can freeze boneless chicken breast and feed tube-sized meat pieces, and store in the freezer for future use. Just before using, weigh out the right amount for partial thawing.

Approximate Partial Thawing Time for Slicing:

Room temperature 68°
1½-inch/4-cm thick meat—1¼ hours
1-inch/2½-cm thick meat—45 minutes
Chicken breast—25 minutes

Room temperature 74°F/23°C
>   1½-inch/4-cm thick meat—45 minutes
>   1-inch/2½-cm thick meat—20 minutes
>   Chicken breast—15 minutes

Preheated 250°F/120°C oven
>   1½-inch/4-cm thick meat—13 minutes
>   1-inch/2½-cm thick meat—10 minutes
>   Chicken breast—5 minutes

Microwave oven (on High)
>   ¾ pound meat—55 seconds
>   1 whole chicken breast—30 seconds

As you can see from the list above, microwave ovens cut the thawing time to less than a minute.

To get the best result in slicing, proper defrosting time is important. If the meat is too frozen, you will get slices too thin to be of any good for stir-frying. On the other hand, if it is over-defrosted, you will not get neat slices from the processor. The list above will give you a guideline. Your ovens and your room temperature may be different, so time may vary somewhat, but after a few trials, you'll find the optimum time. Also take into account that your kitchen temperature may vary from season to season. *I find it very helpful to set a timer as a reminder,* after the meat or chicken is removed from the freezer. In this way, the food will not over-defrost. Meat should still be very firm, but you should be able to insert the point of a knife all the way through the meat. *So be sure to test the meat with a knife before slicing with the processor. Use the slicing disk to slice only what you would expect to slice with a sharp knife.*

To slice meat: Using the slicing disk, place partially frozen meat flat side down in the feed tube (or cut a flat bottom edge) with the grain of the meat muscles perpendicular to the slicing disk, and slice. Expect the machine to make more noise than usual.

To slice chicken: After the chicken breasts are partially defrosted, cut the pieces crosswise across the grain into halves so they will be shorter than the feed tube. Pack the breasts cut side down in the feed tube (or with cut side parallel to the slicing disk) and process with the slicing disk. Expect the machine to make more noise than usual.

Shredding Meat and Poultry (Medium Slicing Disk)

1. Cut and freeze meat and chicken as you would for slicing. It is easier to shred meat if it is about 1½ inch/4 cm thick or thickest to fit the feed tube. However, I have shredded 1-inch/2½-cm thick flank steak without any difficulty. The larger chicken breast is thicker, and therefore is easier to shred.

2. Fresh meat and chicken should be partially frozen; frozen ones should be partially thawed to the proper firmness for slicing.

3. To get julienne strips, use the medium slicing disk and slice the meat or chicken across the grain. Then quickly remove the still partially frozen slices from the beaker. (It is important to work quickly, for the meat will not shred neatly if the slices are defrosted.) Hold the cover upside down by the feed tube; insert and hold the pusher by the same hand about 1 inch/2½ cm lower than the bottom of the feed tube so it forms a 1-inch/2½-cm deep cup (from the bottom of the feed tube). Using the other hand, place stacked slices on edge, with longer edges touching the bottom of the pusher. Stack more slices until they are very compact in the tube, so they will not fall out. (See the illustration for shredding vegetables.)

Replace the cover on the beaker. You can now fit one or more stacked layers through the top of the feed tube. Apply light pressure on the pusher to slice.

Chopping and Mincing Meat, Poultry, and Seafood (Steel Blade)

One of the most useful aspects of the food processor is the chopping. You can make the exact kind of chopped meat you want—coarsely or finely chopped, lean, medium, or fat with the texture you would get only from traditional hand chopping. Many Chinese dishes which use coarsely chopped meat are more tasty and have better texture than meat from the grinder, for the grinder lacerates the meat. Another great convenience with the food processor is that it can chop the smallest amount of food efficiently. Some Chinese recipes call for only 2 to 4 ounces/60 to 115 g of chopped meat; the grinder will not produce such a small amount, and even a small block of 4 ounces/115 g of frozen ground meat would take about an hour to be completely defrosted at room temperature. The processor can chop partially frozen meat cubes. Usually, by the time they are chopped, the meat is also thawed. So now you can produce any amount of chopped meat—from freezer to finished state—all in about 12 minutes, and only in 4 minutes when using a microwave oven to thaw the meat.

1. Use on/off turns. Whether food is coarsely or finely chopped is regulated by the number of on/off turns and the total processing time. The machine works fast, so remember to check the contents after 1 or 2 on/off turns to see if the desired result has been achieved, or you may end up with a puree.

2. Use food cut in 1-inch/2½-cm cubes for chopping. If meat is to be chopped, be sure to remove coarse membranes and gristle before or after processing, for the food processor rejects them.

3. For more uniform texture of coarsely chopped food, use only 1 cup/¼ L to 1½ cups/3½ dL of food for each batch (1 cup/¼ L meat weighs about ½ pound/225 g). However, you can process 2 cups/½ L of food in the beaker if the food is to be finely chopped.

4. Add marinade and seasoning ingredients with the 1-inch/2½-cm cubes during chopping. This will eliminate the step of combining these ingredients with the chopped food later on, and also give the mixture a lighter texture for making balls and patties.

5. To *chop partially frozen 1-inch/2½-cm cubes of meat,* follow these easy steps for *partial defrosting.* (Meat should be defrosted until the point of a knife can be inserted all the way through the meat cubes before processing.)

a. Weigh the exact amount of meat cubes needed, spread them out on a plate or a tray at *room temperature.* After *20 to 30 minutes,* they can be processed.

b. To defrost them faster, spread the frozen meat cubes on a plate and put them in a *preheated 250°F /120°C oven* for *10 minutes,* then process.

Or put the frozen meat cubes loosely together in a sealed plastic bag. Immerse the bag in a bowl of *tepid water,* and in *10 minutes* the meat can be chopped.

6. If you have a microwave oven, you can save more time on thawing. Time for completely thawing the 1-inch/2½-cm meat cubes in a microwave oven (at a "High" setting):

½ pound/225 g 1-inch/2½-cm meat cubes: about 50 seconds

1 pound/450 g 1-inch/2½-cm meat cubes: about 1½ minutes

7. If you find your machine vibrates too much when chopping the partially frozen meat:

(a) Chop ¼ pound/115 g of meat at a time or,

(b) Start the machine, then drop the meat cubes through the feed tube. Chop to the desired size.

HOW TO BUY AND STORE FOOD FOR USE IN THE FOOD PROCESSOR

On a not-so-busy day, or when chicken breasts, pork, or beef are on sale, stock up. Cut and prepare them for freezing with the processor use in mind.

This may seem like a tedious task, but you'll soon find it is very handy to have a variety of pre-cut meat in the freezer all the time. In the long run, they can save you many trips to the supermarket. And it may just be the lifesaver for those impromptu meals (see Meals on Short Notice, page 33). It is always a good rule-of-thumb to have pre-cut frozen meat on hand for Chinese cooking, even if you don't have a processor. Remember, it is much easier to slice and shred meat when partially frozen, whether it's done by hand or machine. That's a practice I used long before the food processor was invented.

Cut meat into the largest size that will fit the feed tube for slicing and shredding. (Use the pusher as the guide.) The small pieces left from cutting can be used for chopping. You also should have a good supply of meat cubes for chopping meat. Freeze the cut meat in a baking pan by placing the pieces in rows without touching each other. The cut meat can be frozen in layers, provided each layer is separated by plastic wrap, so you can separate the pieces individually after they are frozen. Then put them in tightly sealed plastic bags. Label each kind of meat separately and clearly, with dates, so you use the older ones first. If you have them weighed and packed into ¾ to 1 pound/340 to 450 g units, be sure to label the packages (for example: Pork for slicing May 1, ¾ pound/340 g). In this way, you can identify them easily in the future.

Beef for Slicing and Shredding

Any cut of beef which can be roasted or broiled may be used for stir-fry cooking.

Flank Steak: Cut crosswise across the grain to 3½ inches/9 cm long or slightly shorter than the feed tube. Then cut lengthwise to 2 to 2¼ inches/5 to 5¾ cm to fit the width of the feed tube. After freezing on a baking sheet, put them in a well-sealed plastic bag for freezer storage. Among the various cuts of beef, flank steak is the one that contains the least fat.

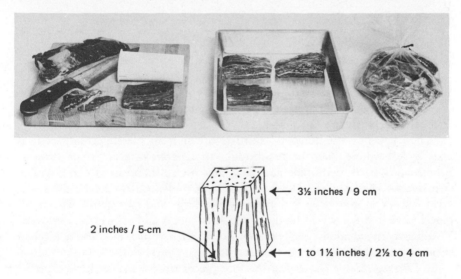

Beef Roast: Remove all visible gristle, fat, and hard membranes (for the processor will not slice through them). Proceed as with flank steak, cutting crosswise across the grain to 3½ inches/9 cm long and then lengthwise to about 2-inch/5-cm wide pieces. Actually, here you can cut the beef thicker, about 1½ inches/4 cm or as thick as possible to fit the feed tube. (The thicker pieces are better for making meat shreds.) Freeze them in a baking pan, then wrap them in a well-shaped plastic bag for freezer storage.

Pork Roast: You can use either pork loin or pork butt. Pork butt is more juicy but has a lot of fat, ligaments, and waste. Pork loin is more readily available in the supermarkets and has less waste, but is also more expensive.

Remove all the visible gristle, fat, and hard membranes. Prepare the chunks as you would with beef roast.

Pork Chops: If you only want a small amount and do not want to buy a whole roast, you can buy double-thick pork chops. Remove the bones. Cut into 1½ × 2-inch/4 × 5-cm chunks or the largest size that will fit the feed tube. Again, the grain of the meat muscle should be perpendicular to the slicer. Freeze them in a baking pan, then wrap them in a well-sealed plastic bag for freezer storage.

Lamb for Slicing and Shredding

Leg of Lamb: Remove all visible gristle and hard membranes; prepare the chunks as you would beef roast.

Chicken Breast (Skinned and Boned) for Slicing and Shredding

1. *Boning chicken breast:*
a. Using a kitchen shear or knife, cut and remove the skin.
b. Cut through the meat along the ridge of the breast bone. Then cut and free the meat from the bottom part of the rib cage.
c. Pull and detach the flesh from the bone.
d. Repeat with the other half.

When you buy the boneless, skinless breast from the supermarket, it is usually left whole. Cut in the middle to separate the two half breasts. Remove any hard membrane and fat. Since each half breast is composed of two layers—the large piece and a small layer underneath—detach the small layer first. You now have four pieces—two large and two small. The small pieces have a small white tendon, which is tough and should be removed. To remove the tendon, grasp the end of it with your hand, use a kitchen shear or a small knife to scrape against it, then gently pull the tendon out.

2. *Freezing chicken breast:* Lay the four pieces from a whole chicken breast side by side, without overlapping, on a piece of plastic or freezer wrap, then wrap them up and freeze on a baking sheet or flat surface. If you are doing several breasts at one time, wrap each breast individually. Stack the packages one on top of the other, and put the whole stack in a well-sealed plastic bag, then freeze on a flat surface. Most recipes require one breast, so defrost as you need them. I used this freezing method even before the processor was invented, when I would slice the breast by hand.

3. For *chicken shreds,* the larger breast (about 1 pound or more with bone and skin on), which is thicker, will be better for shredding.

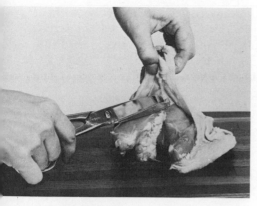
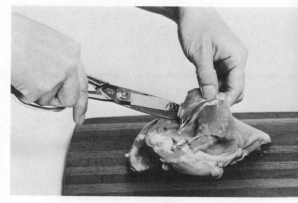
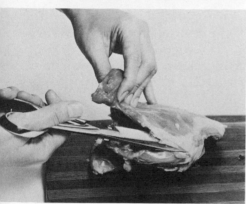

To bone a chicken breast: Cut and remove the skin; cut through the meat along the ridge of the breast bone; cut the meat from the bottom part of the rib cage; pull the flesh from the bone.

4. The Chinese do eat other parts of the chicken besides the breasts. We are using the breast here because it is easier to slice and shred by the food processor. Also for the aesthetic appeal of the Chinese food, white meat looks much prettier than the dark meat in dishes that have chicken puree, chicken shreds, and chicken slices. Chicken breast is also lower in saturated fat than is dark meat.

Beef and Pork for Chopping

    Beef—use beef round or any boneless beef roast
    Pork—boneless pork roasts such as pork butt and pork loin, or pork
           chops (bone removed)
    The food processor will not chop gristle or hard membranes, so remove them from the meat, and then cut meat into 1-inch/2½-cm cubes. If you buy beef round that is already cut in pieces, you should remove the plastic wrap and cut the larger pieces into 1-inch/2½-cm cubes.

To stock up for future use, freeze the meat cubes individually (without touching each other) in a baking pan. You can freeze them in layers, provided each layer is separated by plastic wrap. Transfer the individually frozen cubes to a well-sealed plastic bag for freezer storage.

When you are ready to cook, just weigh out the right amount and defrost to the desired degree for chopping.

HOW TO STORE FOOD IN FREEZER
FOR USE WITHOUT THE FOOD PROCESSOR

Meat for Slicing and Shredding

They can be cut as you would for use in the food processor to 2 × (1 to 1½) × 3½-inch/5 × (2½ to 4) × 9-cm pieces (see illustration on page 11). Or cut them along the grain of the muscle to 2-inch/5-cm wide pieces. Most recipes call for ½ to ¾ pound/225 to 340 g of meat, so cut them to convenient sizes for freezing.

Freezing Chicken Breast

Prepare as you would for use with the food processor.

Meat for Chopping

To store meat for future grinding or hand-chopping, prepare and freeze as you would for use with the food processor. To store ready-ground meat, freeze it in ¼-pound/115 g portions. In this way they will defrost faster, and several recipes called for only ¼-pound/115 g of meat.

TO CHOP FOOD BY HAND

1. *Meat, chicken or shrimp:* You can use ready ground meat or use a grinder to grind the food, or hand chop with a Chinese cleaver or a sharp knife. If the food is to be mixed with other ingredients in the food processor, just mix them by hand in a mixing bowl.

2. *Vegetables and nuts:* Hand chop or mince them with a Chinese cleaver or a sharp knife.

SLICING AND SHREDDING FOOD BY HAND

Hand slice vegetables or meat with a Chinese cleaver or a sharp knife. Slice partially frozen meat or chicken to 2-inch/5-cm long and ⅛-inch/½-cm thick slices, making sure they are sliced across the grain. For shreds, cut slices to ⅛-inch/½-cm thick strips.

Slicing food by hand.

PUREEING CHICKEN AND FISH

Use a blender to do the job as in Chicken Velvet (page 153), Chicken Velvet Corn Soup (page 200), and Fish Balls (page 166).

Utensils and Equipment

It is not necessary to have special utensils to cook Chinese food, since any well-equipped kitchen usually has all the needed items on hand.

WOK

A wok is one of the most versatile cooking utensils ever conceived. It can be used in many ways: to stir-fry; to deep-fry; to steam; to braise; and to poach; as well as to smoke. Because of its curved bottom, it makes the best possible use of even the smallest amount of oil. Thus, it can efficiently cook a very small amount of food as well as a full recipe.

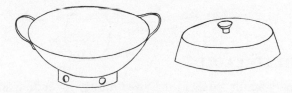

A cast iron wok is recommended over woks made of stainless steel or aluminum, for it distributes heat more evenly; it also heats and cools more quickly. A 14-inch/35-cm wok is most practical for common use. However, if cooking for one or two persons, a 12-inch/30-cm wok is quite sufficient and lighter.

A new iron wok comes with a layer of industrial grease to protect it from rusting. Be sure to wash it first with hot water and detergent, dry it thoroughly, and heat over medium heat. With a paper towel, spread a thin layer of vegetable oil over the entire inside surface of the wok; heat for a few minutes, then rinse with hot water and dry thoroughly. Repeat the oiling and heating process two more times, then the wok is ready to use. Do not be alarmed by the formation of black rings after seasoning and cooking, for, in fact, the blacker the wok gets, the better it cooks. After cooking, while the wok is still warm, use a hard or bamboo brush to scrub it clean with hot water, avoiding the use of hard detergent. The wok should be heated and dried after each washing to prevent rusting. Oil it occasionally while the wok is still new.

If you do not have a wok, a heavy skillet can be used. Some people actually prefer a skillet for electric stoves. To use a wok efficiently on an electric stove, you should heat the wok very hot and until the electric coil is red hot, then add and heat the oil, before adding the ingredients. If the heat is too high or if the food starts to burn, remove from the heat for a few seconds or cook on a second burner with medium heat. If it is cooking too slowly, place it back on the high burner. Always watch the heat, and do not hesitate to adjust the heat to insure proper cooking.

The wok usually comes as a set with a cover and a ring. For stir-fry cooking, it is better to use the wok without the ring for maximum heat. For steaming and deep-frying, it is much safer to put the ring underneath to stablize the wok. The cover is only used for slow cooking and steaming.

LONG-HANDLED SPATULA

It is convenient for stirring and turning food in the wok. However, a Western spatula or a long-handled spoon can be substituted.

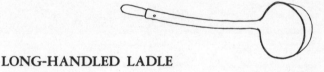

LONG-HANDLED LADLE

In the ordinary family kitchen, it is used mostly for ladling soup and liquid. It is not essential if you already have a soup ladle.

STRAINER

The Chinese strainers come in all sizes. An 8-inch wire strainer with bamboo handle is quite handy for deep-frying. It can be washed in the dishwasher. However, one can use a slotted spoon in place of the strainer.

CLEAVER

Chinese cleavers come in different sizes and are made of different metals. The stainless steel ones are rust-proof and easier to take care of. The carbon steel ones are easier to sharpen to a fine edge for better cutting. The light-

weight cleavers are for slicing and shredding; the heavy-weight ones can be used to chop through bones. Carbon steel knifes will rust, so they should be wiped dry after using. A sharper knife is a safer knife, so sharpen the cleaver frequently with a sharpening stone, usually sold in hardware stores and housewares departments.

Any good and sharp Western knife can be used in place of a cleaver, as can any Western-style meat cleaver chop through bones. A good kitchen shear can cut through poultry bones easily.

STEAMER

Steaming is an important cooking method in China. The traditional steamers come in all sizes and are made of bamboo. They are made to be set onto woks containing boiling water. It is an ingenious design: They come

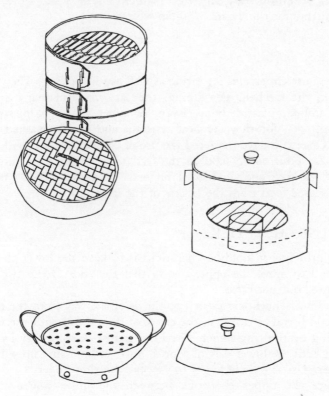

in separate layers, with each layer fitting on top of the other, so several dishes can be steamed at once on the same burner, thus saving fuel and cooking surface. They are attractively made, and food can be served directly from them.

Modern aluminum steamers also come in layers and with a pot underneath for boiling water. They don't have the ventilation system that the bamboo steamers have, so more water will be collected in the dish during steaming.

To improvise, one can use a large pot or a roaster. Use a short can (such as a small water chestnut can) or two cans for the roaster. Have both ends of the can removed, then place a rack on top of the can or cans. Fill water at least 1 inch below the rack and place food on the rack. Cover the pot and steam the food over boiling water. It is important that the dish containing the food be at least 1 to 2 inches/2½ to 5-cm smaller in diameter than the pot, so there is plenty of room for the steam to circulate while cooking.

There also are aluminum perforated steaming trays available now, designed to fit right into the wok. Food with or without a dish is placed on the tray. Fill the wok with water at least 1 inch below the tray, then close it with the dome-shaped cover of the wok and steam. Buy a 12½-inch/31½-cm steaming tray for the 14-inch/35-cm wok, or a 10½-inch/26½-cm tray for the 12-inch/30-cm wok.

CHOPSTICKS

The Chinese use chopsticks for eating as well as for cooking. They are indispensable in the kitchen. For dining, they are made of many different materials—bamboo, plastic, bone, ivory, or silver. For cooking, we use bamboo chopsticks, for they are heat resistant and can be washed in the dishwasher. Once you have mastered the use of chopsticks, you will find it most useful for positioning food in the feed tube of the food processor, since they work like one's extended fingers. They can also be used to transfer and scrape food from the beaker of the food processor.

HOW TO USE CHOPSTICKS

The basic principle in holding chopsticks is to keep the lower chopstick stationary, and to move the upper one so that the ends of the two chopsticks will meet but not cross.

1. Hold the lower chopstick about two thirds of the way from the thinner (or the round) end. Place it in the crook of the thumb with the thinner part resting on the ring finger. Keep the chopstick stationary by pressing down with the lower part of your thumb, and pressing up with your ring finger. Use the little finger to support the ring finger.
2. Then place the upper chopstick between the index finger and the

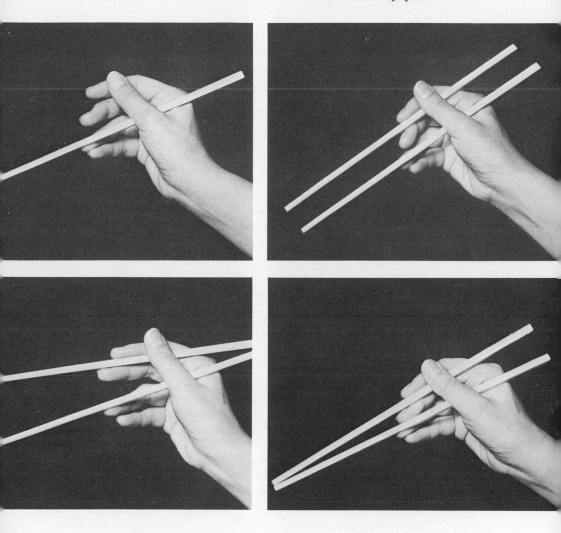

thumb. Place your middle finger below this chopstick in a position very similar to holding a pencil for writing. The two chopsticks where the thumb cuts across should be about an inch apart. Keep the ends of the two chopsticks even at all time.

3. Now you can widen the space between the ends of the two chopsticks by pushing up the upper chopstick with your middle and index fingers.

4. And to have the ends of the two chopsticks meet together, so you can pick up and hold food, you press the upper chopstick down with your middle and index fingers.

This is, however, not the only way to hold chopsticks. Try whatever is most comfortable and easy for you.

THE MICROWAVE OVEN

The microwave oven is not a necessity for this cookbook. However, if you already have one, it's handy, and saves a great deal of time in defrosting food and heating precooked items.

But remember, this is a precise cooker, so exact timing is important in order to achieve the best results. When in doubt, it is always better to undercook and not to over-defrost the food. After all, you can always cook it longer if needed. Some food like bread that is overheated in microwave ovens becomes inedible.

The timing chart below is a guideline for use of the oven at a "High" setting. Your microwave oven may be different, and since some ovens have different settings, time may vary somewhat. Also, the cooking time depends on volume: *heating time increases* in proportion to the amount of food. Use utensils recommended for the microwave oven.

Applications of Microwave Ovens to Chinese Cooking

1. It partially defrosts meat and poultry for slicing, shredding, and chopping in less than or about 1 minute.

2. It's excellent for heating precooked boiled rice and noodles. (Heat them in a covered serving bowl.)

    1 cup/¼ L cold precooked rice takes about 1 minute to heat.

    2 cups/½ L cold precooked rice take 2 minutes to heat.

    2 cups/½ L frozen precooked rice take 4 minutes to heat.

    4 cups/1 L cold precooked noodles take about 2 minutes to heat.

3. It's great for heating precooked fried rice and soft-fried noodles.

4. It does a good job warming breads, but do not over-heat breads, as they will get hard and dry.

    1 Pita bread—heat for 30 seconds.

    1 frozen Pita bread (on a plate covered with plastic wrap)—heat for about 1 minute.

    1 frozen steamed bread (on a plate covered with plastic wrap)—heat for 2 minutes. (4 × 2 × 1½-inch/10 × 5 × 4-cm bread)

5. It's the best way to heat up precooked or leftover stir-fried dishes; also marvelous for family members who are late for dinner.

    ½ pound/225 g meat with vegetables on an uncovered platter—heat for 2 to 3 minutes, stirring once during heating.

    1 pound/450 g stir-fried ground meat on an uncovered platter—heat for 3 to 4 minutes, stirring once during heating.

6. It also cooks or reheats meat balls and shrimp balls.

7. It speeds up the drying time of the bread for shrimp toasts to less than 10 minutes. (Drying time by air takes 2 days, and drying time in a warm oven takes 1 hour.)

8. It shortens the cooking time for the chicken breast as is used in Hacked Chicken in Spicy Sauce and Noodles in Sesame Sauce, Szechuan-style.

THE KITCHEN SCALE

Anyone who does a substantial amount of cooking will find a kitchen scale very useful. To ensure satisfying results from the recipes in this book, all measurements should be carefully followed. A few ounces more or less of meat, poultry, or seafood will make the dish either too bland or too salty. A scale is almost indispensable, and certainly a worthwhile investment.

THE HOT TRAY

Hot trays are not necessary items, but they are very good for keeping cooked Chinese food warm before or during a meal. They are most useful for buffet dinners.

Chinese Cooking Methods

STIR-FRYING

Stir-frying is one of the most unique cooking methods in the world. Interestingly, the new French cuisine is adapting this ancient Chinese technique to their dishes. Their new cuisine stresses freshness of the ingredients, with vegetables crisply undercooked. In this way, the flavor comes not from the rich sauces but from the natural juices of the raw material.

About 90 percent of the Chinese restaurant dishes are done by stir-frying, so this is the cooking method most Americans are familiar with. It is also their favorite way of Chinese cooking.

It is easy to understand, for stir-frying is so different from their own cooking. In stir-frying ingredients are cut to small pieces of bite size. All the preparation can be done ahead, and cooking time is very short—usually less than 5 minutes. In fact, dexterity is an important factor. It tastes best when served immediately after cooking.

Because of the short cooking time, and now with the aid of a food processor, preparation time is reduced to a fraction of the normally required time. Stir-fry dishes are very convenient for busy people, especially for those who work and have unpredictable hours. Therefore, I have included many popular stir-fry dishes in this book.

To achieve successful results, one needs to first understand the principles of stir-frying. The ingredients used should always be cut to uniformly small pieces, or else they will not be cooked evenly. In most dishes, meat plays the leading role: its size and shape determines the size and shape of the other ingredients. If the meat is in shreds, the other ingredients will all be in shreds of similar size. And if it is in slices, then the rest will be in slices. Vegetables and meat (or chicken and seafood) in the dish are usually cooked separately, allowing for the difference in cooking time for the different kinds of food. They are usually combined at the end, with a sauce mixture to complete the dish.

To avoid that last minute panic, and because the cooking is very fast, it is important to *have all ingredients ready* and to have *read through all the cooking steps before heating the oil*. To facilitate this organization, I have included a "Have Ready Before Cooking" column in the stir-fried recipes, so there's no need to stop during cooking to search for a misplaced ingredient. The ingredients are arranged in the order of cooking. So place them near the stove. If more than one stir-fried dish is to be cooked, place the ingredients of each dish on a separate tray, but arrange them *clockwise* in the order of cooking.

Since stir-frying requires quick cooking over high heat, it is better to limit the amount of meat (chicken and seafood) to one pound for each batch. Your kitchen range is usually not strong enough to supply and maintain the high heat required for larger quantities, and you could easily end up with a stew. Plus, stir-frying is so fast, if you want to double the recipe, just cook it twice. On the other hand, half of a recipe cooks very well, and the smaller the quantity the better, because it is easier to stir-fry thoroughly. Stir-fry dishes are therefore great for single people, since one need not have leftovers.

One should always first heat the wok to the smoking point; then add the oil and heat to the desired degree. (For an average stove, use high for meat, chicken, seafood, and medium-high for vegetables. Although every stove is different, after a few trials, you'll find what are the best settings on yours.) Add the ingredients and stir-fry quickly until cooked. Watch the color of the meat, for when it almost loses all of the raw meat color (depending on the particular recipe), you can either quickly remove it from the wok or finish cooking with the sauce mixture and other ingredients in the recipe. This will insure tender and flavorful meat, since the secret is to have it just cooked but *not overcooked*. The same principle applies to poultry and sea-food. For vegetables, one should cook them just to remove the raw taste, but still retain the crisp texture. Again, do not overcook. As soon as all the ingredients are cooked, one should remove the wok from the heat and transfer the food for immediate serving.

Normally, once cooking has started, one does not stop until the dish is finished. So read the cooking steps thoroughly before starting to cook. In case you forget a step and want to check the recipe, remove the wok from the heat until you catch your breath—then continue the cooking. Experience will help, and after a few times, you will find it quite easy to do.

In the restaurants, the chefs usually cook the marinated meat, poultry, or seafood in three or more cups of oil at a low temperature (like poaching them in the oil). This is to separate and to achieve maximum tenderness and smoothness of the marinated food. They are then stir-fried with vegetables and seasoning mixtures. I find this too oily and impractical for family cooking or everyday food. You have to strain the oil for each dish, and always have the used oil left around the kitchen.

I have simplified these steps in the recipes included from classical dishes and cut down the oil without sacrificing the quality. If you read the paragraphs on the principles of stir-frying thoroughly, follow the recipes carefully, and measure the ingredients accurately, you can achieve excellent results.

STEAMING

It is a major and very common method of cooking in China. Vegetables, meat, poultry, and seafood can all be steamed. It is a very healthy cooking method, for vitamins and minerals are preserved rather than boiled away in water. Because oil is not necessary for cooking in this method, it is excellent for people on diets, or for those who cannot consume oil.

Unlike baking, food cooked by this method never dries out, since it is surrounded by the hot circulating steam.

If a traditional steamer is used, several dishes can be steamed at once on the same burner. Some foods can be steamed by placing them directly on the steamer or on the streaming tray. Others have to be placed in a dish and then steamed. The dish used should be at least 1 inch/2½ cm smaller than the diameter of the steamer. You usually serve the cooked food right from that dish.

To steam, let the water come to boiling before placing the food in the steamer, then check occasionally, since you may need to replenish the water during steaming. Keep a kettle of boiling water on another burner, so when the water gets low in the steamer, you can add more from the kettle. Cold water requires heating the water to steaming temperature all over again.

DEEP-FRYING

Use 2 to 4 cups/½ to 1 L of oil and heat to the required temperature. If you have an electric wok, it is quite handy for deep-frying, since it has a temperature control. However, the teflon lining does not conduct heat very fast, so once food has been immersed in the oil, raise the temperature on the control. A regular wok with a ring underneath can be used effectively on gas burners, but not so well on electric burners, where it is more practical to use a saucepan. There should be enough oil so that food can float easily. Temperature is important, for if the oil is not hot enough, food will absorb more oil and become greasy. If it is too hot, the food will brown too quickly outside but still be raw inside.

Test the oil by dropping a small piece of bread into it. If it turns golden brown in 1 minute, the oil temperature is about 350°F/180°C. If it browns in 40 seconds, the temperature is about 375°F/190°C. If you don't have a piece of bread, dip a dry bamboo chopstick into the oil; if lots of bubbles gather around the chopstick, the oil is ready for frying. Do not overcrowd the deep fryer, for it will take too long for the oil to reach the required temperature again, and the food will get soggy and greasy. Do food in several batches, keeping cooked portions in a warm oven, or refrying them for a few seconds.

BLANCHING

Immerse vegetables and, sometimes, meat in boiling water for one or two minutes. Then quickly rinse with cold water and drain.

BRAISING

Sear food in oil and then simmer with liquid in a covered pot or wok.

SIMMERING

Bring liquid first to boiling, then quickly reduce to very low heat and cook slowly.

Meal Planning

Though traditional menu planning for family meals and entertaining is discussed here, the emphasis of this book is on simple and no-fuss cooking for American life styles. This chapter is filled with ideas and tips for simple everyday dishes that can be ready for short-notice serving. You will also find plan- and cook-ahead techniques and menu suggestions for parties and buffets—ideas to make your party special but also fun and easy for you, so you can spend as much time as possible with your guests.

TRADITIONAL

Traditionally, a Chinese family meal consists of several dishes (meat dishes, plain vegetable dishes, and cold salads—each one of them is considered a dish) and a soup all served at the same time for everyone to share, so no one dish belongs to any one person. The Chinese usually have large families, so dishes range from four to eight at each meal, depending on the size and economic standard of the family.

For the daily meal, there is no great difference between the dishes served at lunch and at dinner. In Shanghai, we used to have the same dishes at lunch and at dinner. Many of the family dishes are made-ahead dishes, to save the cook time by cooking the dish once, then serving half of it at noon, and warming up the other half in the evening.

Rice is eaten throughout the meal to absorb the savoury dishes as well as to provide bulk. The dishes are to accompany the rice, contrary to the Western habit where Americans eat just a little bit of rice to accompany the dishes. Perhaps that is why many complain about being hungry two hours after they've finished a Chinese meal.

The dishes are planned so that there is always a variety of food—meat, poultry, fish, or other seafood, and vegetables; a variety of seasonings—spicy or bland, light or dark; and a variety of cooking methods—stir-frying, steaming, deep-frying, or slow-cooking. A spicy dish is accompanied by a mild one; if one dish is deep-fried, then the other should have some sauce. A dark-colored dish is balanced by a light-colored one.

The dishes are usually served with plain boiled rice, except in the North—the wheat growing region—where people eat pancakes and different kinds of bread to go with the dishes. Since my husband was born and raised in Peking and Tientsin (the Northern region), and I was born and raised in Shanghai (the Eastern region), we integrated the wheat and rice cultures of our backgrounds into one cooking long ago. We serve meals alternating from rice to bread and pancakes. And I do confess that I enjoy breaking the monotony of eating rice every day.

Since the Chinese serve the meal communal style, there is no main dish, and all the dishes are equally important. If we are expecting more people for dinner, rather than cooking more of the same dish, we simply add more new dishes. A good rule of thumb is to add one dish for each additional two persons.

Traditionally, at the family meal, each member has his or her own individualized place setting which consists of a rice bowl, a small plate, a porcelain soup spoon, and a pair of chopsticks.

You just help yourself to a chopstickful of the dish, and eat a bit of the rice from your rice bowl (or if eaten in the Northern style, you take a bite from the plain steamed bun or bread. See pages 241 and 255), then a chopstickful of the next dish, and some more rice (or some plain steamed bun or bread). In a large family, the dishes and soup are placed on a Lazy Susan in the middle of a big round table, so the dishes never need to be passed around. You can just spin the desired dish to your front. Sometimes the diner puts food on top of the rice.

It is a general practice, although strange to Westerners, that Chinese will put the bowl over the lower lip, in a drinking position, and then shovel the rice in with the aid of the chopsticks. In this way, one can eat rice very fast and down to the last grain. The same bowl is used for both rice and soup. You drink the soup from the porcelain spoon or by bringing the bowl to the lip and sipping. Soup can be drunk at anytime during the meal, for it acts as the beverage. Tea is normally not served during the family meal, contrary to what Chinese restaurants do.

The meal usually ends with seasonal fruits and tea. The Chinese do not normally eat dessert; whatever sweets they have are usually served as snacks.

THE ONE-DISH MEAL

In this servantless society where most are also busy with jobs, volunteer work, hobbies, or other activities, few have the time to fuss through several dishes for everyday eating. But there is no reason for us not to enjoy Chinese food by just cooking fewer dishes and larger quantities. American families are usually smaller than Chinese families. There are also many people living alone and many couples who no longer live with their children. For the beginner, it is really better to attempt only one new dish for each meal. Hence, one-dish Chinese cooking. If there are more people in the family, double the recipe or make enough for the total number of people you're serving.

The number of servings given in these recipes are based on serving just this single dish with plain boiled rice, or bread (when eaten in the Northern style) for an average appetitite. The same dish can be served to more people when more than one dish is used.

The recipes with ‡ symbols indicate they can be easily made in large quantities. If you are doing a stir-fried dish—and since most family stoves do not have very strong heat—do not stir-fry more than one pound of meat in a batch. It cooks so fast, if you just double the recipe, you can cook the dish twice. You'll find too, in your pre-cooking food preparation with the food processor, that the more quantity of the same food you process at one time, the more time you will have saved.

The Cantonese teahouses and the rice and noodle shops have many of these one-dish meals on their menus. They are delicious and economical for single diners. They consist of a platter of plain boiled rice topped with a cook-ahead dish, usually with a sauce, or a stir-fried dish. There are also numerous noodle dishes—thin or wide, rice or wheat noodles, cooked in various ways with various toppings served as one-dish meals. If you ever eat in some of these restaurants in Chinatown, you will see many single Chinese dining on one-dish meals for lunch or dinner, or requesting them as take-out orders. They are very popular with students, office workers, and shopkeepers. Often a group at the same table will order such single servings, and eat from their own individual bowls or platters. I remember some of my best lunches were at these tiny, unpretentious restaurants in Shanghai and Hong Kong. I can still remember smelling the delicious aroma from those kitchens!

You'll find yourself much less harassed by not attempting to do too much all at once, and you can pay full attention to one dish. My advice to my students is that it is better to do one dish of top quality than to do a few dishes of mediocre standard. When you are inexperienced, trying to do too many dishes just creates confusion and tension, and you can no longer enjoy doing it. A single dish can be a very tasty dish; a dish well-prepared will give a very satisfying and rewarding feeling to the cook. Many Western people think if they cook Chinese food, they have to cook several dishes or it won't be authentic. I feel it is more important that the dish itself be authentically prepared and properly cooked. And, as to the manner of serving, it should suit each family's life style.

Social structure and life styles are very different in Chinese society. People there don't keep themselves so busy with scheduled activities, and they do not have a long commute to work. Mothers don't have to drive children to different after-school activities. The pace is much more leisurely.

In the old days in China, even the middle-class had servants. They could enjoy eating many dishes at each meal even on ordinary days, for they never had to cook and clean up the mess in the kitchen. Our family chef in Shanghai would shop for food in the morning, then just cook lunch and dinner; the other servants did the cleaning and dish washing for him.

Here in the United States, we have to be a jack-of-all-trades: the cook, the maid, the chauffeur, the gardener, the errand-boy, and often, the repairman, as well. So we have to be practical with our daily cooking. If we plan carefully, and plan our cooking according to the time we have, we don't have to rely on frozen or precooked commercial food. We can cook wholesome and delicious food at home, for many Chinese meals can be prepared in no more than 30 minutes.

When you become more experienced with Chinese dishes, on a not-so-busy day, you could have fun trying to cook a few of your familiar dishes for one meal.

Any main dish in this book can be served as a one-dish meal. If you like soup, you can serve it with the meal. Or you can add a vegetable salad or a quick stir-fried vegetable for extra fibre and nutrients. Many recipes in this book include suggestions on serving the dish as a one-dish meal.

Rice and noodle dishes suitable for one-dish meals:

[§ indicates that the dish can be cooked ahead.]

> Fried Rice §
> Chopped Beef and Egg Fried Rice §
> Soft-fried Noodles with Beef
> Soft-fried Noodles with Chicken

Noodles with Mandarin Meat Sauce §
Noodles in Sesame Sauce, Szechuan-style §
Other dishes suitable for one-dish meals:
Boiled Wonton
Pan-fried Wonton
Wonton in Soup as a Meal
Pan-fried Dumplings Mandarin Style

The advantage of these wontons and dumplings is that they can be made ahead, frozen individually, and then wrapped in a well-sealed plastic bag. They can be cooked without defrosting, so in about 15 minutes, from freezer to table, you've got your meal!

When you have a not-so-busy day, stock up on them, as they are especially handy for short-notice cooking. (I have used them for many emergencies.) They do take time to make for beginners, but once you are experienced, they won't take as long.

MEALS ON SHORT NOTICE

Did you ever have the experience after a hectic day—with dinner time approaching—that you had no meat in the refrigerator? And a trip to the nearest supermarket would take about 20 minutes!

Or have you ever invited friends to stay for lunch, on the spur of the moment, and then realized there was nothing to eat? I'm sure we all have faced those situations when we had to improvise something quickly. Unexpected situations always produce a crisis. But with a well-planned kitchen you can save many unnecessary trips to the food store, and you'll never have to panic again at the last moment. If you keep certain basic foodstuffs on hand, with the help of the food processor and a little imagination (since stir-fry cooking takes only a few minutes), you can create instant haute cuisine.

If you have read the chapter on using the food processor, then you know frozen chicken breasts and 1-inch thick meat can be sliced by the processor in *5 to 10 minutes* after removal from the freezer with the help of a 250°F/120°C oven, or in *25 to 55 seconds* with a microwave oven. Most meat defrosts very quickly after processing and can be used almost immediately. To speed up defrosting, however, you can spread the meat slices or shreds on a platter. In about 5 minutes, they will be ready to use. By the time you mix them with the marinade, they'll be totally defrosted. Or you may defrost the partially frozen slices in a microwave oven in about 10 seconds. (Timing is very important here, for you do not want the meat to be cooked by the microwave oven.)

One-inch frozen meat cubes can be chopped in *10 minutes* after removal from the freezer, or in *1½ minutes* with a microwave oven. Usually, by the time they are chopped, the meat is also thawed. You can cook it right away, and the stir-frying only takes 5 minutes.

Most of the recipes in this book take *no more than 20 or 30 minutes* from preparation to cooking. Cook the rice first before you begin the preparations for the dish. If you want a vegetable dish or a soup, check the list of Super-quick Dishes, as they take less time, or only 12 minutes. *You can have your dinner ready from freezer to table, in less than or about half an hour,* just about the time needed to finish cooking the rice.

If you want to shorten the time for cooking rice, cook an extra amount several days ahead. It only takes *10 minutes* to resteam the cooked rice. Two cups/½ L of rice can be rewarmed in *2 minutes* by microwave oven. Cooked rice freezes very well. Two cups/½ L frozen rice can be rewarmed in *4 minutes* by microwave oven.

Or you may save time by serving the dish Northern-style with Pita bread (pocket bread) or Mandarin pancakes (see recipe, page 115, or substitute Shanghai spring roll wrappers or flour tortillas).

Pita bread, which is sold in the supermarkets, resembles a Northern Chinese bread. If you cut it into halves, you'll get two pockets. Then fill the pocket with the dish and eat. I always have them in my freezer, for they are most handy when there is no time to cook rice.

To heat frozen Pita bread: Wrap the breads in aluminum foil and heat in a 350°F/180°C oven for *10 to 15 minutes.* If you have a microwave oven, you can heat up 3 of them in about *2 minutes.*

To serve the dish with Mandarin pancakes (see illustration on page 245), you place a heaping tablespoon or more of the cooked food in the center of a warm pancake, then fold the pancake into a package and eat with the fingers.

Heating frozen pancakes or substitutes: There's no need to defrost them. Set them (8 to 10 pancakes) on a plate at least 1 inch/2½ cm smaller than the steamer, and put them in the steamer. Bring the water in the steamer to a boil and let them steam on medium heat for *5 minutes.* At the end of this time, they should be warmed through and can be separated for serving.

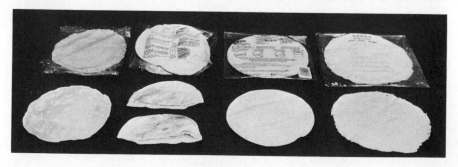

Mandarin pancakes, Pita bread, flour tortillas, Shanghai spring roll wrappers.

Super-quick Dishes

Main Dish	Preparation and Cooking Time:	Page
Stir-fried Chopped Beef With Oyster Sauce	10 minutes	97
Chinese Pepper Steak	15	87
Sliced Beef With Onion (Snow Peas, or Fresh Asparagus)	15	89
Sliced Chicken With Celery (Snow Peas, Fresh Asparagus, or Green Pepper)	15	139
Chopped Pork With Stir-fried Eggs	10	157
Sliced Beef With Stir-fried Eggs	12	156

One-dish Meal

Fried Rice	11	220
Chopped Beef and Egg Fried Rice	15	222

Vegetables and Salads

Fresh Bean Sprout Salad (with or without meat)	12	184
Broccoli Salad	12	185
Stir-fried Broccoli	8	179
Celery Salad	10	186
Stir-fried Celery	12	182
Cucumber and Scallion Salad (thinly sliced)	5	187
Sweet and Sour Cucumber Salad (thinly sliced)	4	188
Spinach Salad	12	189
Watercress Salad	8	193
Stir-fried Zucchini	6	183

Soup

Egg Drop Soup	6	198
Chopped Watercress and Egg Drop Soup	6	199
Chicken Velvet Corn Soup	11	200
Cream of Corn Soup	5	201
Sliced Chicken and Watercress Soup	9	202

In China, people have learned to improvise, economize, and make the best use of what is available. Perhaps, because of limitations in recreation and other entertainment, eating is a preoccupation—and a major pastime. Even the poor people have learned to truly enjoy eating on a small budget. Many of the peasants' economical foods are most delicious and often enjoyed by the wealthy as well.

Traditionally, the Chinese have learned to cook by watching and imitating, and then improvising on their own with whatever ingredients are on hand. They are most creative cooks, for to them cooking is more a matter of approach and method than just following recipes.

It is fairly common in China to have unexpected guests visit before mealtime and then stay for lunch or dinner. It is not considered rude, partly because the Chinese communal style of eating is stretchable and easier to accommodate one or two extra diners. The hostess just cooks more rice, adds more chicken broth or water to the soup. If there is not enough fresh meat and vegetables to go around, dishes can be stretched or new dishes can be created by using eggs and dried and preserved foods. Nowadays stretching a meal is even more easily done with the help of frozen and canned foods.

The advantage of Chinese cooking is its flexibility. This is a very helpful point for the short-notice cook. If the recipe calls for something you don't have, improvise with something else. For instance, in the Minced Beef Szechuan-style dish (page 99), the recipe calls for carrots and celery. But, if you don't have celery, you can still make this dish, by substituting either green peas or chopped snow peas or just omitting celery and using a little more chopped carrots. It is good for the beginning cook to know that most Chinese don't follow cookbooks and no two cooks use the exact same ingredients in a dish. For the first few times, a beginner should follow the recipe carefully so that you know how a properly cooked dish should look and taste. Once you have mastered the dish, then you can improvise on your own.

Food to Keep on Hand for Impromptu Meals

Not all of these are a must, but to keep some in all categories on hand certainly is good insurance.

Canned Food

Water chestnuts
Bamboo shoots
Mushrooms
Chicken broth
Lychee
Loquats

Dried Food

Chinese mushrooms
Tree ears (cloud ear or black fungus)
Tiger lily buds (or golden needles)
Cellophane noodles
Rice
Cornstarch
Thin or extra thin spaghetti
Flour

Seasonings

Soy sauce
Dry sherry
Wine vinegar or Chinese rice vinegar
Sesame oil
Dry hot pepper or crushed red pepper
Oyster-flavored sauce
Brown bean sauce
Hoisin sauce

In the Refrigerator

Fresh eggs
Fresh ginger in a bottle covered with dry sherry (refer to ginger on page 271)
Scallions
Vegetables that won't perish easily, like carrots, celery, onions, bell peppers, radishes, etc.

In the Freezer

Pork, beef, and chicken breasts for slicing and shredding
Pork and beef (1-inch/2½-cm cubes for chopping)
Frozen packaged snow peas
Frozen green peas
Pita bread
Mandarin pancakes (or Shanghai spring roll wrappers or *flour* tortillas)

Prepared Foods

Curry beef turnovers
Cooked meat, shrimp, and fish balls
Shrimp Toast
Fried wontons
Steamed dumplings Cantonese-style
Uncooked dumplings Mandarin-style
Uncooked shaped wontons

The frozen, prepared-ahead foods above will come in very handy for short-notice cooking.

1. Some of them can be used as *appetizers:*
   a. Those can be rewarmed in the oven directly from the freezer: Shrimp balls, shrimp toast, fried wontons, and curry beef turnovers.
   b. Steamed dumplings Cantonese-style can be resteamed directly from the freezer.
2. Cooked frozen pork, beef, and shrimp or fish balls can be directly defrosted and cooked in chicken broth as *soup.*
3. Frozen curry beef turnovers can be rewarmed directly in the oven for about 15 minutes. Served with a soup, they can be used for *lunch* or a *light supper.*
4. Uncooked frozen shaped wontons can be cooked directly in boiling water, cooking slightly longer to make sure that the pork is cooked. For a good *lunch,* serve 12 to 16 of them in soup (page 239) or as boiled wontons (page 238).
5. Uncooked frozen dumplings Mandarin-style can be pan-fried directly in about 15 minutes (page 246) to make quite a filling *lunch* or *dinner.* They are also good served with a soup.

PARTY SUGGESTIONS

TRADITIONAL CHINESE-STYLE

Party dinners and banquets are frequent social events among the affluent Chinese. There are two forms of entertaining: informal family dinners or formal banquets.

Informal entertaining: Informal dinner entertaining is very similar to family-style eating, except that the host and hostess may include one or several expensive or special dishes. They may be the specialties of the house or something just in season. Usually all the dishes and the soup are on the table before the people are seated. This is a much easier and more practical form of entertaining for busy American families.

Many dishes can be cooked ahead. Plan to do no more than two stir-fried dishes at the last minute. In this way, you can sit down and enjoy the meal with the guests. Use the principle on menu planning given at the beginning of this chapter. The guiding principle is variety—variety in types of food, in color, texture and flavor, and in cooking methods. Bear in mind, of course, the individual taste of your guests.

Formal entertaining: There are many occasions that call for dinner banquets. It can be a birthday, a wedding, a welcoming party for out-of-town visitors, or just a group of people honoring mutual friends. A formal dinner banquet has to be planned and ordered ahead. A much-talked-about banquet often has unusual or surprise dishes created by the skilled chef, or perhaps something which has just come on to the market after many months of being out of season. Sometimes it can be a hard-to-obtain food from a faraway region. You eat one course at a time, and rice is usually not served until the end. By then, most people have no room for it. Wine is served throughout the meal.

A typical banquet will start with assorted cold meats, seafood, and pickled vegetables usually presented in an attractive and artistic arrangement. This is followed by four stir-fried dishes presented one at a time. Sometimes one of the stir-fried dishes may be substituted by a deep-fried food like crab claws, shrimp balls, or shrimp toast, etc. They are followed by a soup as a breather in the long procession of dishes. One of the favorites among Americans is the Chicken Velvet Corn Soup (see recipe, page 200). Next come four heavier dishes like Peking Duck, a whole fish, or exotic dishes like shark's fins or sea cucumber. Nowadays even the Chinese are getting more practical in showing their hospitality; less food is planned and wasted. Often a sweet dish or a sweet soup, or both, will conclude the banquet. In former days, the sweet dish provided a second breather for the procession of dishes and was followed by four rice-accompanied dishes and a few small salty dishes, if rice porridge was also served. These dishes are for settling the stomach from the preceding rich dishes. I remember most diners didn't have any more room by then, so many of the dishes were returned to the kitchen untouched.

A banquet can only be handled by experienced chefs, for ordinary cooks who have not gone through professional training do not know how to prepare such extravagant dinners. The wealthy families in Hong Kong, Taiwan, and old China usually have their own chefs who can prepare such parties for them at home. Sometimes a restaurant known for their special dishes would be asked to arrange for catering services. The restaurant then would send one of their trained chefs and his assistants along with all the cooking equipment and a portable restaurant stove to do the banquet at the people's home. For many others, because of lack of space at home, such formal entertaining is done at restaurants.

Such course-after-course formal entertaining is really not practical attempted at home in a servantless society. The host and hostess would have to spend days preparing ahead, and cook all night on the day of the party. They would have no chance to enjoy their guests. Keep in mind, however, that the traditional Chinese host and hostess, after inviting the guests and planning the menu with the chef, do not have to do a stitch of work after that. Even the house is cleaned by the servants. All they have to do on the day of the party is to enjoy their guests and the good food. So, if you are thinking of entertaining with a Chinese dinner banquet, find a good Chinese restaurant within your area, and have them do it for you. They are still less expensive than the Western ones of comparable standards.

One thing you have to know before launching such an adventure is that the dinner banquet is rather rigid as to the number of people. The optimum number per table is 10; if you have less people, you still pay the same price for each table. Twelve is usually the most a table can hold and if you have more than that, you have to either drop someone from the guest list, or order another table of food.

If the idea of doing your own banquet still appeals strongly to you, you can try what some of my students have done. They got together with several of their friends from the cooking class and prepared the course-after-course Chinese dinners. This is fun and a practical venture, for each takes a turn in cooking. In this way, you can still enjoy your company—and the evening!

MODERN STYLE TO SUIT BUSY WESTERN LIFE

Entertaining at home has always been an important social aspect of American life. With the increasing cost of restaurant foods and the great surge of interest in gourmet and ethnic cooking in the last decade, home entertaining has become even more popular with American families. There is something about entertaining friends at home, for it is so much more hospitable and intimate.

What with more women joining the working force, and more men finding cooking a creative and relaxing outlet, this area is no longer the women's domain.

Entertaining in America has been greatly revolutionized, now that people are so much freer in expressing themselves in every aspect of life. A new feeling of relaxed informality that suits one's own life style has made entertaining easy and more fun. Something exciting has happened, for we have become a nation of liberated hosts and hostesses. You no longer have to follow the traditional rules of having everything matching for table settings. Tablecloths, place mats, and napkins come in all colors and designs, and china patterns can be mixed. Nowadays, a creative host or hostess can easily find something to harmonize with a certain mood or style.

Interestingly, Americans have never before been so preoccupied with gourmet cooking and ethnic cuisines, especially Chinese cooking. On the other hand, there have never before been so many Americans who are so weight conscious and concerned about their calories and cholesterol. This accounts for one of the reasons that Chinese cooking has become so popular, for its stir-frying and steaming methods of cooking lend themselves very well to our calorie- and cholesterol-conscious society. The new trend in entertaining is marked by quality and simplicity. Elaborate dinner parties are out, for it is no longer necessary to have a parade of dishes to show hospitality. Often, all that's needed is an unusual simple menu in an interesting setting to achieve the ambiance and the mood of a successful party.

But when it comes to menu-planning of Chinese food, perhaps because it is still rather unfamiliar and foreign to Americans, many are afraid of bending from traditional Chinese serving style, nor would they dare to apply their creative instincts here, as they do with Western cooking! As a result, they have never attempted a Chinese dinner party, for the thought of cooking so many dishes can be overwhelming.

One of the purposes of this book, and the essence of this chapter, is that I hope to show Americans how Chinese cooking can easily be adapted to busy modern living, for family and informal entertaining.

One often tends to forget that other parts of the world have also undergone a cultural revolution. Modern Chinese families in Hong Kong and Taiwan are getting smaller; the number of extended families is decreasing. Help is becoming increasingly expensive and hard to find. Many middle-income families now have to do their own cooking.

When I was learning cooking in Hong Kong, a Chinese cookbook was a rare species. It no longer is so. Television programs on both Chinese and Western cooking have become very popular in recent years. And of course, there is the Chinese counterpart of Julia Child.

There are also many Chinese families like my own living in America and other parts of the Western world. We have kept and preserved our centuries-old cuisine by adapting it to our new servantless households.

The following are my suggestions, drawn from personal experiences, on how to entertain with ease and fun when cooking the Chinese-modern style. They may give your future party a new dimension and change of pace. But most of all, as I stress in all my cooking classes, I will show you the basis of modern and traditional Chinese entertaining, but please feel free to use your own imagination and creativeness to create your own party. Cooking and entertaining should be fun, but no one can enjoy the fun when overworked and tired!!

The success of any party is to have a gracious, relaxed host and hostess. And the secret to this is in planning an interesting and practical menu that you can handle with ease. Be as original as you like, but *organize* and *plan* ahead. Decide on what you can handle gracefully in your kitchen with the equipment and experience you have. Plan your menu with your guests' tastes in mind and look for dishes that can be cooked ahead or partially cooked ahead. Don't attempt more than two stir-fried dishes that have to be cooked at the last minute. Write out your menu and check each recipe to make sure you have all the ingredients. Never experiment on a new dish for your party. Rather, try it out on the family first. Do as many tasks as you can before the party. If, for instance, you are cooking stir-fried dishes, all the preparations of cutting and making sauces should be done before the guests arrive. In this way, you can be sure to enjoy your own party and your guests.

INFORMAL SIT-DOWN DINNER

For the informal sit-down dinner, I like to combine the processional banquet and communal family styles. It is ideal for servantless entertaining. I do as much cooking and preparation as I can in advance and as little as I can once the guests have arrived. No one likes to see food getting cold while sitting on the table—and you know how long it takes for everyone to get seated at a party—so I don't bring out the food all at once as we do in family-style dining.

I would start with something that can be left out like a soup or a cook-ahead appetizer, or sometimes some cold dishes. When the guests have been seated and after they've finished the first part of the meal, I go to the kitchen and finish cooking the one or two stir-fried dishes which only take a few minutes, for all the preparations were done before the party began. If I have more than one cook-ahead dish, then they are kept warm in the oven, on a hottray, or sometimes in a steamer. I often serve one of them while I am cooking in the kitchen. Then I serve the other cook-ahead dishes and boiled rice with the just finished stir-fried dish. I can now enjoy the meal with my guests. In doing so, the food does not get cold just sitting around and the guests can taste the stir-fried dishes at their best, immediately after they are cooked.

Menu Suggestions

If you like to serve an appetizer with cocktails before the meal (this is not a Chinese habit), see the chapter on "Hot Appetizers." The menus given below are for the main meal. For drinks during the meal, see the chapter on "Tea and Wine."

Note: § indicates that the dish can be cooked ahead.

MENU I

A. FOR 6 PERSONS

1. § Lion's Head (use 1½ recipes)—these giant size meat balls can be cooked *3 to 4 days ahead* and reheated before serving.

2. § Hacked Chicken in Spicy Sauce (use double the recipe)—can be cooked *1 to 2 days ahead* and refrigerated. Serve at room temperature, and toss with sauce just before serving.

3. Chinese Pepper Steak—all the preparations can be done *half a day ahead.* This is the only dish that has to be cooked at last minute.

4. § Boiled Rice (use 1½ cups/3½ dL uncooked rice)—you can cook it *1 hour* before serving time, for it will stay warm in the pot for a good 30 minutes. If it is cooked *1½ to 2 hours ahead,* transfer it to a serv-

ing bowl. Cover and keep it warm in a very low oven (200°F/95°C) or on a hot tray until serving time.

5. § Fresh Fruits and/or Almond Cookies—the cookies can be baked *2 weeks ahead* and kept in an air-tight container.

15 Minutes Before Dinner

a. Heat up the Lion's Head, and keep it warm with a cover, on a hot-tray, or in a very low oven.
b. Mix together the Hacked Chicken in Spicy Sauce.

To serve: Start with Hacked Chicken in Spicy Sauce. Later on, excuse yourself, go to the kitchen to cook the Pepper Steak, then bring the steak, Lion's Head, and boiled rice to the dinner table. When the dinner is finished, serve fruit and/or cookies.

B. FOR 8 PERSONS (use 2 cups/½ dL of uncooked rice for boiled rice)

1. Use all the dishes for serving 6 persons.
2. Add § Shrimp Toast—can be made *few weeks ahead* and frozen, or *2 to 3 days ahead* and refrigerated.

20 Minutes Before Dinner

Reheat the Shrimp Toast in a 350°F/180°C oven.

15 Minutes Before Dinner

See 15 minutes before dinner for 6 persons.

To serve: Start the dinner with Shrimp Toast. Later on, excuse yourself, go to the kitchen to cook the Pepper Steak, then bring the steak, Hacked Chicken in Spicy Sauce, Lion's Head, and boiled rice to the dinner table.

When dinner is finished, serve fruit and/or cookies.

C. FOR 10 PERSONS (use 2½ cups/6 dL uncooked rice for boiled rice)

1. Use all the dishes for serving 8 persons.
2. Add another stir-fried dish—Sliced Chicken with Snow Peas— preparations can be done *half a day ahead.* Last minute cooking takes only a few minutes. (Double the recipe, and they can be cooked in one batch.)

20 Minutes Before Dinner

Reheat the Shrimp Toast in a 350°F/180°C oven.

15 Minutes Before Dinner

See 15 minutes before dinner for 6 persons.

To serve: Start the dinner with Shrimp Toast. Then serve the Hacked Chicken in Spicy Sauce while you are in the kitchen cooking the Pepper Steak. Keep the steak warm on a hot tray or in a very low oven, and cook the Chicken With Snow Peas. Bring the steak, chicken, Lion's Head, and boiled rice to the dinner table.

Serve fruit and/or cookies when dinner is finished.

MENU II

A. FOR 6 PERSONS

1. § Fried Crab Patty—can be cooked *few weeks ahead* and frozen, *or 2 to 3 days ahead* and refrigerated.

2. § Sweet and Sour Meat Balls (use 1½ recipes)—the meat balls can be cooked a *few weeks ahead* and frozen, *or 4 to 5 days ahead* and refrigerated. The sauce and pepper can be cooked *half a day ahead*.

3. Beef With Broccoli or Beef in Oyster Sauce—preparations can be done *half a day ahead*. Last minute cooking only takes a few minutes.

4. § Boiled Rice (use 1½ cups/3½ dL uncooked rice)—you can cook it *1 hour* before serving time, for it will stay warm in the pot for a good 30 minutes. If it is cooked *1½ to 2 hours ahead*, transfer it to a serving bowl. Cover and keep it warm in a very low oven (200°F/95°C) or on a hottray until serving time.

5. § Fresh Fruits and/or Steamed Cake—the cake can be made *several weeks ahead* and frozen, *or 4 to 5 days ahead* and refrigerated. Serve it at room temperature, or it can be reheated by steaming.

20 Minutes Before Dinner

a. Reheat the Fried Crab Patty in a 350°F/180°C oven.
b. Reheat the meat balls in a 350°F/180°C oven.

5 Minutes Before Dinner

Reheat the sweet and sour sauce, then add the pepper, hot meat balls, and pineapples to the sauce. Keep the dish warm on a hottray or in a chafing dish.

To serve: Start the dinner with Fried Crab Patty. Later on, excuse yourself to the kitchen to cook the beef dish, then bring the beef, Sweet and Sour Meat Balls, and boiled rice to the dinner table.

When the dinner is finished, serve fruit and/or cake.

B. FOR 8 PERSONS (use 2 cups/½ L of uncooked rice for boiled rice)

1. Use all the dishes for serving 6 persons, and increase Fried Crab Patty to 1½ times the recipe.
2. Add § Chicken Velvet Corn Soup (double the recipe)—can be cooked ½ *to 1 day ahead.*

20 Minutes Before Dinner

Reheat the meat balls in a 350°F/180°C oven.

10 Minutes Before Dinner

a. Reheat the soup, and sprinkle the minced ham on the top just before serving.
b. Reheat Fried Crab Patty in a 350°F/180°C oven. (Total heating time is about 20 minutes. It will still be heating in the oven while the soup is served.)

5 Minutes Before Dinner

Reheat the sweet and sour sauce, then add the pepper, hot meat balls, and pineapples to the sauce. Keep the dish warm on a hottray or in a chafing dish.

To serve: Start with the soup. When the soup is finished, cook the beef dish, then bring the beef, Fried Crab Patty, Sweet and Sour Pork Balls, and boiled rice to the dinner table.

When the dinner is finished, serve fruit and/or cake.

C. FOR 10 PERSONS (use 2½ cups/6 dL uncooked rice for boiled rice)

1. Use all the dishes for serving 8 persons, but increase the Fried Crab Patty and Sweet and Sour Pork Balls from 1½ to double the recipes. Double the beef recipe, and cook in two batches.
2. Add § Cucumber and Scallion Salad (use 3 times the recipe)—can be prepared *half a day ahead,* and serve with the other dishes.

Follow the same time tables and serving suggestions as for 8 persons.

A Special Dinner

A. FOR 6 PERSONS

1. Chicken in Bird's Nest—the bird's nest can be made *few weeks ahead* and frozen, or *a week ahead* and refrigerated. Preparations of the chicken can be done *half a day ahead.*

2. § Fried Wonton and Shrimp in Sweet and Sour Sauce—wontons can be made *few weeks ahead* and frozen, or *3 to 4 days* ahead and refrigerated. The shrimp and sauce can be made *half a day ahead.*

3. § Stir-fried Chopped Beef With Oyster Sauce served with lettuce leaves (double the recipe)—can be cooked *3 to 4 days* ahead and refrigerated.

4. § Shrimp Ball Soup (use Variation 2, and double the recipe)—can be cooked 2 to 3 days ahead.

5. § Boiled Rice (use 1½ cups/3½ dL uncooked rice)—you can cook it *1 hour* before serving time, for it will stay warm in the pot for a good 30 minutes. If it is cooked *1½ to 2 hours ahead,* transfer it to a serving bowl. Cover and keep it warm in a very low oven (200°F/95°C) or on a hottray until serving time.

6. § Fresh Fruit

5 Minutes Before Dinner

a. Heat fried-wontons in a 350°F/180°C oven.
b. Heat the soup.
c. Reheat the beef dish, add green peas, then keep the dish warm on a hot tray or in a low oven.

Serve the soup first, and later on excuse yourself to the kitchen.

During the Meal

a. Turn oven down to 300°F/150°C, and reheat the bird's nest with the wontons.
b. Heat the sweet and sour sauce; when it comes to a boil, add the cooked shrimp and peas, and keep warm.
c. In the meantime, cook Chicken in Spicy Garlic Sauce. Fill the bird's nest and bring to the table.
d. Pour the sweet and sour sauce over the hot wontons. Bring the wontons, chopped beef, lettuce leaves, and boiled rice to the dinner table.

Serve fresh fruit when the dinner is finished.

B. FOR 8 PERSONS (use 2 cups/½ L of uncooked rice for boiled rice)

1. Use 4 times the Chopped Beef recipe.
2. Use 1½ times the Wonton in Sweet and Sour Sauce recipe.

Simple Cook-ahead Dinner

(Can serve any number of people)
All the dishes below can be cooked in large quantities.

MENU I

1. § Steamed Dumplings Cantonese-style—can be made *several weeks ahead* and frozen, *or 3 to 4 days ahead* and refrigerated.

2. § Minced Beef Szechuan-style—can be cooked *3 to 4 days ahead* and refrigerated. Serve with Pita bread.

3. § Vegetable Soup—can be made *1 or 2 days ahead* and refrigerated.

4. § Almond Cookies—can be baked *2 weeks ahead,* and kept in an airtight container.

15 Minutes Before Serving

a. Reheat the dumplings by steaming.
b. Reheat the soup.
c. Wrap the Pita bread in aluminum foil, and warm in a 300°F/ 150°C oven.
d. Reheat the minced beef on the stove top or in a microwave oven. Then keep it warm on a hottray or in a low oven.

To serve: Serve the dumplings first, then serve the soup with the minced beef and bread. Let guests stuff the beef themselves in the pockets of halves of Pita bread.

When dinner is finished, serve almond cookies with tea.

MENU II

1. § Fried Crab Patty—can be made *few weeks ahead* and frozen, *or 2 to 3 days ahead* and refrigerated.

2. § Noodles With Fried Onions—can be made *2 to 3 days ahead,* and refrigerated. Serve at room temperature.

3. § Chicken Velvet Corn Soup—can be made ½ *to 1 day* ahead.

4. § Broccoli Salad—can be made ½ *to 1 day ahead.*

5. § Canned Lychee and Loquat, or fresh fruits.

10 Minutes Before Dinner

a. Heat the Fried Crab Patty in a 350°F/180°C oven. (Total heating time is about 20 minutes. It will still be heating in the oven while the soup is served.)

b. Heat the soup.

To serve: Serve the soup first, then serve the Fried Crab Patty, noodles, and broccoli salad together.

When dinner is finished, serve fruits with tea.

Variations

1. You can use Fried Crab Claws (more elegant) in place of Fried Crab Patties.

2. Fried Rice can be served in place of Noodles With Fried Onions. To cook it ahead, see TIPS in the Fried Rice recipe.

BUFFET PARTY

Many Chinese families in America are fond of entertaining buffet-style. It certainly solves the dilemma of entertaining when you can't seat all the guests at one dinner table. Here's where Chinese cooking is most adaptable to this form of entertaining, for all the food is cut into bite-sized pieces before cooking. It's perfect for buffet-style since you only need a large plate and a pair of chopsticks (you can substitute forks for those who haven't yet mastered that art), but you never need a knife. Everything can be eaten from a plate balanced on the lap.

Buffet entertaining is less formal. To be able to choose what you like and to help yourself to a variety of colorful foods or to try a little bit of every-thing is something everyone enjoys.

The great advantage of a buffet party is that you can invite any number of guests, and the food can be kept warm on hottrays and in chafing dishes throughout the meal. Stir-fried dishes hold up well on hot trays, but if you so choose, you can also cook them while the guests are helping themselves at the buffet table. Again, limit yourself to no more than two stir-fried dishes. Your absence won't be noticeable, since in a few minutes the dishes are done, and ready to pass around to the guests. You can then help your-self to the food and join the company.

Plan a menu with variety, just as you would for an informal sit-down dinner. Here, especially, the contrast of color is important. Look for cook-ahead dishes and if you have a crowd, look for dishes that can be done in large quantities.

Menu Suggestions for Buffet Dinner

If you have less people than the suggested number, eliminate a dish, or cut down on the quantity of the dishes. When you have more, increase the quantity of any of the dishes that can be prepared ahead.

MENU I (12 to 14 people)

1. § Curry Beef Turnovers (double the recipe)—can be cooked *few weeks ahead* and frozen, *or 5 to 6 days ahead* and refrigerated.

2. § Sweet and Sour Pork Balls (double the recipe)—the meat balls can be cooked a *few weeks ahead* and frozen, *or 4 to 5 days ahead* and refrigerated. The sauce and pepper can be cooked *half a day ahead*.

3. § Hacked Chicken in Spicy Sauce (4 times the recipe)—can be cooked *1 to 2 days ahead* and refrigerated. Serve at room temperature, and toss with sauce just before serving.

4. § Broccoli Salad (3 times the recipe)—can be prepared *½ to 1 day ahead* and served cold.

5. Beef in Oyster Sauce or Chinese Pepper Steak (double the recipes)— all the preparations can be done *half a day ahead*. This is the only dish that has to be cooked at last minute. For best results, cook one recipe portion at a time.

6. § Boiled rice (use 4 cups/1L uncooked rice)—you can cook it *1 hour* before dinner, for it will stay warm in the pot for a good 30 minutes. If it is cooked *1½ to 2 hours ahead,* transfer it to a serving bowl. Cover and keep it warm in a very low oven (200°F/95°C) or on a hot-tray until serving time.

7. § Fresh Fruit
   § Almond Cookies—can be baked *2 weeks ahead* and kept in an air-tight container.

30 Minutes Before Dinner

a. Reheat Curry Beef Turnovers in 350°F/180°C oven, then they can be kept warm in a low oven or on a hot tray.
b. Reheat meat balls in a 350°F/180°C oven or in a microwave oven.

15 Minutes Before Dinner

a. Mix together the Hacked Chicken in Spicy Sauce.
b. Reheat the sweet and sour sauce, then add the pepper, hot meat balls, and pineapples to the sauce. Keep the dish warm on a hottray or in a chafing dish.

10 Minutes Before Dinner

Cook the beef dish, and you can keep it warm on the hot tray during the meal on the buffet table.

To serve: Place all the food on the buffet table; the hot food can be kept warm on hot trays or in chafing dishes throughout the meal.

When the dinner is finished, serve fresh fruit and cookies.

MENU II (12 to 14 people)

1. § Fried Crab Patty (double the recipe)—can be prepared *few weeks ahead* and frozen, *or 2 to 3 days* ahead and refrigerated.

2. § Pork Shreds in Hoisin Sauce (double the recipe)—can be cooked *3 to 4 days ahead* and refrigerated.

3. § Minced Beef Szechuan-style (double the recipe)—can be cooked *3 to 4 days ahead* and refrigerated.

4. § Sweet and Sour Cucumber Salad (3 times the recipe)—can be prepared *half a day ahead* and served cold.

5. Chicken With Mushrooms (double the recipe)—all the preparations can be done *half a day ahead*.

6. § Fried Rice (use 3 times the recipe)—can be cooked *half a day ahead.* Leave the peas out, and add just before serving.

7. § Egg Tarts (double the recipe)—can be baked *few weeks ahead* and frozen, *or 2 to 3 days ahead* and refrigerated. Serve at room temperature. If served warm, reheat in 300°F/150°C for 20 minutes.

45 Minutes Before Dinner

Reheat rice (with cover) in a 350°F/180°C oven, stirring a few times during heating.

30 Minutes Before Dinner

Reheat Fried Crab Patty in a 350°F/180°C oven.

15 Minutes Before Dinner

a. Reheat Pork Shreds in Hoisin Sauce on the stove top or in a microwave oven, then keep warm on a hot tray or in a low oven.
b. Reheat Minced Beef Szechuan-style on the stove top or in a microwave oven, then keep warm on a hot tray or in a low oven.

10 Minutes Before Dinner

a. Add peas to the reheated fried-rice, and keep warm in the oven.
b. Cook Chicken With Mushrooms.
To Serve: Place all the food on the buffet table; the hot food can be kept warm on hot trays throughout the meal.

When the dinner is finished, serve Egg Tarts. (To serve them warm, heat them in 300°F/150°C oven *during the meal*.)

ONE MAIN DISH MEAL ENTERTAINING (AND DESSERT SUGGESTIONS)

The international one-dish meal has become a popular form of American entertaining, for it frees the host or hostess from constant pot-watching, and most of the preparation can be done ahead. For one-dish entertaining, you should select dishes that will please everyone's taste.

Spaghetti, a popular food of Americans, is also an important Chinese staple. And just about every nationality has its own version. The Chinese have recorded the cooking of such dough, much like the present-day spaghetti, as far back as 3000 B.C. Spaghetti is inexpensive and filling, but above all, it is so tasty and versatile, that by the mere change of a sauce, one can transform it to a completely new dish. The Chinese alone have a variety of ways of preparing it.

If you are looking for a change of pace from popular Western one-dish meals—such as Paella, Boeuf Bourguignon, and pasta dishes, here are two delicious Chinese noodle dishes. The real advantage of them is that you can be free as a breeze when the guests arrive. When served cold—which is great for summertime entertaining—both dishes can be done completely ahead. You can have everything organized and the table set in advance. Both dishes can be cooked in large quantities and served as a sit-down buffet. They are also good as an after-theatre supper.

You spread the noodles, chicken, meat, sauces, and cold vegetables on the table, then let everyone mix one's own meal. There is this certain joy one gets from participating in such a meal. The idea is much like the popular salad bar common to many American restaurants. The Chinese mix the noodles, meat, and vegetables all in one bowl and eat, much like a salad buffet. This can be a marvelous idea for home entertaining.

Curiously, the salad bar idea is rarely used in American homes. These two Chinese noodle dishes are always self-service in Chinese homes, yet in Chinese restaurants they are served already portioned out in individual bowls. The reason for this is that they always charged per serving. I have heard many Americans rave about this refreshingly delicious sesame sauce noodle dish served in Chinese restaurants, but few of them realize it is so easy to make.

Simple dishes as such can often be presented with a flair when the foods are arranged artistically and served in interesting utensils. It can be a simple thing such as an unusual tureen or a beautiful platter. Here is a good opportunity to show off your finest china. Look into your collections and let your imagination work for you.

The noodles are quite filling, so beautiful fresh seasonal fruits will make a nice ending. If you want to add a special touch to your party, watermelon is a favorite Chinese summer fruit. Buy a whole melon, and carve it with a

sharp knife into a broad-handled basket. It can be done one day in advance and kept in the refrigerator. Some gourmet shops sell a fruit notcher which makes V-shaped cuts on the fruit, although you can also use a knife to achieve the same effect. Hollow the melon out and fill with assorted melon balls or other seasonal fruits or any variations you might create.

Noodles have a very special significance in Chinese life. Because they are usually very long, they symbolize as long life. The traditional thinking was "to live long is to be blessed." So noodles are always served on birthdays, and they are not supposed to be cut short on such occasions. Though modern Chinese families, through Western influence, now also have birthday cakes, it is not unusual nowadays to have both cake and noodles for such celebrations.

Noodles in Sesame Sauce, Szechuan-style (page 228)

This dish is usually served at room temperature. If it is done the day before and kept refrigerated, bring it back to room temperature before serving. For company, try to arrange the shredded chicken neatly or artistically in a serving bowl or on a platter. To add color, you can add a thin garnish/topping of very finely shredded scallions. (If you have a Fine Slicing Disk for your food processor, they can be shredded easily by the machine; otherwise, they are best done by hand.) If you are using additional variations such as shredded ham and shredded egg sheets (page 231) together with the chicken shreds, you can make up a colorful arrangement—with the red, yellow, and white colors.

Fresh bean sprouts are available in most supermarkets now, but be sure they are fresh. They should be white and juicy looking; if they are turning brown, don't buy them. Canned bean sprouts should not be used here, for they do not give the same flavor and crunchy texture. It would be better if you used shredded fresh cucumbers instead. Or, you could use both cucumber and fresh bean sprouts. Shredded iceberg lettuce, although not traditional, is a good substitution or variation.

Noodles with Mandarin Meat Sauce (page 224)

This dish can be served warm or cold. When served warm, the sauce and noodles can be kept warm on hottrays or in chafing dishes during the meal.

Across the country, wherever there are Chinese families in the suburb of every large American city, you will find their own Chinese social clubs, and this dish has often been served at these clubs' family picnics. It is an ideal dish since everything can be done ahead and in large quantities, then served cold.

MANDARIN PANCAKE PARTY

One of the most popular Northern Chinese dishes in America is Moo-shu Pork served with Mandarin pancakes. However, in the Northern region these pancakes are commonly served with many other dishes. My husband has fond memories of eating them as a meal with a variety of fillings. Not only are they delicious, but it's fun to stuff your pancake, then roll it to eat with your fingers. (See Moo-shu Pork, page 113, for illustration on wrapping.) We enjoy them as an everyday meal as well as for informal entertaining.

The pancakes (see recipe, page 244) can be made ahead and frozen; just resteam them before serving. Some Chinatown food stores now sell the ready-made Mandarin pancakes, but I find them rather thick and heavy. However, I am sure they will improve upon them in the future. Whenever I don't make my own, I substitute the ready-made Shanghai-style spring roll wrappers. (They are thinner than the homemade pancakes.) Another substitute you can use that is readily available in American supermarkets is wheat flour tortillas.

You can serve the pancakes with one main dish accompanied by several side dishes, or serve several main dishes with or without the side dishes. With a little planning, you'll find most of the preparation and cooking can be done ahead.

The following are a few of the suggested dishes. Traditionally the food for pancake wrappings is cut into shreds or minced.

Main Dishes

§ Moo-shu Pork—can be completely or partially cooked ahead, re-warmed in the wok on the stove top, or in a serving platter in a microwave oven.

Stir-fried Beef Shreds With Onion and Pepper (or Beef Shreds With Onion, or Beef Shreds With Pepper)—they are best tasting when cooked at the last minute, though you could rewarm them in a microwave oven.

§ Minced Beef Szechuan-style—can be cooked ahead, and reheated on the stove top, or in a serving platter in a microwave oven.

§ Ground Beef With Cellophane Noodles—can be cooked half a day ahead, reheated on the stove top, or covered and reheated in a 300°/ 150°C oven. Reheat very well in a microwave oven.

§ Pork (Beef or Lamb) Shreds in Hoisin Sauce—can be cooked ahead and reheated on the stove top, or covered and reheated in a 300°/150°C oven. Reheat very well in a microwave oven.

Stir-fried Chicken Shreds With Green Pepper.

§ Fresh Bean Sprout Salad, or its variations—served cold.

Chopped Pork With Stir-fried eggs, or plain scrambled eggs.

Side Dishes and Sauces

§ Coarsely chopped roasted peanuts.

§ Finely shredded scallions—can be shredded by fine slicing disk.

§ Fried finely shredded potatoes—shredded by julienne disk or fine slicing disk. Rinse with cold water, and blot dry, then deep-fry in 400°/205°C oil until crisp and golden brown. They can be kept crisp in an air-tight container for over a week. If necessary, they can be recrisped in a 350°F/180°C oven.

§ Shredded egg sheets (see page 231)

Brown bean sauce

Hoisin sauce

Hot chili oil

Plan on serving 4 to 5 pancakes per person for an average appetite. You can wrap one or several kinds of food in one pancake, and add sauce or seasoning if you like the food more spicy. Place all the food on the table, and try to keep the Mandarin pancakes or their substitutes warm in a steamer or other warming devices during the meal and within easy reach. All the cooked dishes suggested above will hold very well on hottrays for a long period. You can also serve a soup with the meal.

Menu Suggestions

MENU I

A. FOR 6 PERSONS

1. Moo-shu Pork
2. Minced Beef With Cellophane Noodles (double the recipe)
3. Pork Shreds in Hoisin Sauce (double the recipe)
4. Fresh Bean Sprout Salad

Preparation and Cooking

1. *A few weeks or few days ahead,* make Mandarin pancakes, or buy the ready-made ones. Keep them in tightly-sealed plastic bags in the freezer. Defrost them on the day of serving.

2. *1 or 2 days ahead,* cook Pork Shreds in Hoisin Sauce. Keep in the refrigerator.

3. *Half a day ahead,* cook Minced Beef With Cellophane Noodles, no need to refrigerate. Cook Moo-shu Pork partially, leaving the eggs to be cooked at the last minute. Set up steamer for steaming the pancakes. Prepare Bean Sprout Salad, and toss later.

4. *Half an hour ahead,* rewarm Pork Shreds in Hoisin Sauce and Minced Beef With Cellophane Noodles in their serving platters in a 300°F/150°C oven. Both dishes should be covered during warming, and stir to mix just before serving. You can garnish the cellophane noodles with finely minced scallions. Both dishes can also be rewarmed on the burner or by the microwave oven just a few minutes before serving.

5. *10 minutes before serving,* steam the pancakes over boiling water, and keep them warm over low simmering water during the meal. Toss the Bean Sprout Salad. Reheat and finish cooking the Moo-shu Pork. Place all the dishes on the table and serve. If desired, you can offer brown bean or hoisin sauce and hot oil for additional spice.

Serve fresh fruit or your favorite dessert after the meal.

B. FOR MORE PEOPLE, any of the dishes can be doubled.

MENU II

A. FOR 6 PERSONS

1. Minced Beef Szechuan-style (3 times the recipe)
2. 5 shredded egg sheets
3. 6 cups fried finely shredded potatoes
4. Fresh Bean Sprout Salad (2 times the recipe)
5. 1 cup coarsely chopped peanuts
6. Brown bean sauce and hot oil

Preparation and Cooking

1. *A few weeks or few days ahead,* make Mandarin pancakes, or buy the ready-made pancakes or their substitutes. Keep them in tightly-sealed plastic bags in the freezer.

2. *3 to 4 days ahead,* cook Minced Beef Szechuan-style. It is better to cook it in two batches and then combine them together, and keep in the refrigerator.

Prepare shredded egg sheets, and keep in the refrigerator.

Fry potato shreds, and keep them in an air-tight container at room temperature.

3. *Half a day ahead,* defrost Mandarin pancakes, and set up the steamer for later use.

Prepare bean sprout salad, and keep in the refrigerator. Toss the salad last minute.

Coarsely chop the peanuts.

4. *15 minutes before serving,* steam the pancakes over boiling water, and keep them warm over low simmering water during the meal.

Toss the Bean Sprout Salad, and set on the table with shredded egg sheets, chopped peanuts, brown bean sauce, and hot oil.

Rewarm the Minced Beef Szechuan-style in a wok on the burner, or rewarm uncovered in a microwave oven (stir one or two times during heating). Bring the beef dish and the potato shreds to the table and serve.

Serve fresh fruit or your favorite dessert after the meal.

Tips

1. You could cook the beef dish at the last minute, since this is the only main dish. Have the preparation done in the morning, and cook the dish in 2 batches just before serving.

2. For *more people,* just add one or more dishes.

WRAPPING DUMPLING (MANDARIN-STYLE) PARTY
(page 246)

Dumplings are often served as the main dish for a meal in the Northern provinces of China. Sometimes relatives and intimate friends are invited to come and help in wrapping the dumplings—and then to enjoy them together. Time goes very quickly with everyone helping, and the dish requires very little preparation beforehand. This social function is popular with Chinese families in America when they have their get-togethers, for everyone shares the work, conversations come spontaneously, and somehow it generates an intimate, relaxed atmosphere.

Mandarin-style dumplings can be steamed, boiled, or pan-fried; the pan-fried ones are most popular. They are quite filling. A soup, which serves as a beverage, will go well with them. Our favorite is Hot and Sour Soup. The two together make a delicious meal.

The Mandarin-style dumplings mentioned here are different from the Cantonese steamed dumplings which have stuffings exposed on the tops. They are only steamed, never boiled or pan-fried.

A word of warning: If you are planning to launch such a dumpling party, be sure that you have mastered the art, for your guests may be there to learn from you. It can be a disaster when the blind lead the blind.

This can also be a spontaneous dinner for unexpected company. Most likely you'll have flour on hand, then all you need is pork cubes in the freezer. If you don't have cabbage, just use more pork for the stuffing and adjust the seasoning to taste. (Cook a little bit of the raw stuffing and taste first before wrapping the dumplings.) The processor will chop the meat and knead the dough, then you can get everyone into action.

MONGOLIAN FIRE POT PARTY (page 211)

This is the Chinese version of fondue cooking. It is a fun event where guests do their own cooking, and especially good on cold winter nights. It adapts so well in our servantless society, and is an easy way to entertain. The great advantage is that all the food can be prepared and assembled in advance, including the table settings. The number of people to be served at this kind of meal will depend on the capacity of the cooking pot and the size of the table. When there are more people, just use two or more cooking pots and bring out more tables.

Total preparations require a minimum of time. And just before serving, all you need to do is bring the stock to boiling, set out the plates of uncooked meat, sauces, and condiments and arrange them around the cooking pot. Seat the guests around the table, and have each cook his own meal. Or set the cooking pot on a large coffee table—better still in front of a cozy fire—and have the diners seated around it on comfortable cushions. You will be the most relaxed host and hostess!

PARTIES BASED ON CHINESE PASTRIES AND SNACKS

One of the Cantonese specialties very popular with the Chinese is the Dim Sum. This is a phonetic translation of the Cantonese words "dot-the-heart"—a sort of snack. These meat-filled or sweet pastries are served by Cantonese teahouse restaurants from early morning to mid-afternoon. The Chinese go there for breakfast, snacks, or lunch; and drink tea along with the savoury pastries. Many leisure-class Chinese in Hong Kong go there to meet friends or for a break during a long shopping day.

There is usually no menu provided, for the waitresses come around with large trays or pushcarts filled with little plates or steamers, each containing three or four dainty little pastries. They are usually steamed, but some are baked or fried. You point to the ones you want, and the waitress will place them on your table. You pick one or two kinds at a time, since there will be other varieties coming out later on. The waitresses come intermittently with hot pastries fresh from the kitchen. And you pay according to the number of plates you have on your table!

As more and more Chinese have immigrated to the United States, Cantonese teahouses have mushroomed all over the Chinatowns of American big cities. I am amazed at the number of new ones that have opened in New York's Chinatown within the last three years, and the blooming business they all have.

Some regular Cantonese restaurants have now changed their lunch to the teahouse-style, and serve regular meals at dinner only. On weekends, it is a very popular family outing for suburban Chinese to come into the city to have lunch at these teahouses, and then do their food shopping in Chinatown before going home. It's often a mob scene in these places—very noisy and hectic, but lots of fun for a very reasonable price. With the increased interest in Chinese foods, many Americans have become hooked on such a casual and unique way of eating once they've been to a Cantonese teahouse.

Because all these pastries can be made ahead of time, and many are good finger foods, they're great for casual American entertaining.

DIM SUM PARTY (Dot-the-Heart Party)

This can be a brunch or a lunch. If you don't have the time to make these pastries, and you live near a big city Chinatown, you can purchase these snacks from the teahouses or specialty pastry shops. Then all you need to do is to rewarm them just before serving time. You can bring them out, one variety at a time, teahouse-style, or have them all warmed just before serving time. Keep them warm on steamers or hottrays set on a buffet table. Then let the guests help themselves, so that will free you from running back and forth to the kitchen. In Chinatown, you can find inexpensive shallow bamboo steamers made explicitly for Dim Sum. Buy 4 or 5 tiers (12 to 13 inches/30 to 32½ cm in diameter) fitting one over another, and then set them inside an electric wok. Not only they are very functional (for they can heat and warm 4 to 5 tiers of food), they also make a good-looking serving piece for your buffet table. You may find steamers that will fit your round electric frying pan which can be used in place of the electric wok.

I usually make these snack foods ahead of time on a not-so-busy day for stocking in the freezer. (Luckily, the food processor has shortened the preperation time.) They are ideal for people with busy schedules or unexpected guests. With these pastries on hand, all you do is set out the necessary utensils for rewarming before the guests arrive. Tea is usually all you need for a beverage to complete this menu. (For this is what people drink at the teahouses; many teahouses let you select the flavor of the tea.)

When you use two or more varieties of pastries, plan the menu with variety in mind—using different stuffings and cooking methods. If you have a recipe that is to be steamed, then plan a rewarmed one next in the oven, so both can be heated at the same time. Also in this way, you have more variety in texture and taste.

The Dim Sum also make an easy-to-serve and interesting brunch for overnight guests. And it's such a nice change from omelets or other Western foods! Most snacks can be kept warm in the steamer or on the hottray, so even the late risers can help themselves anytime they choose.

Food to Be Fried or Refried   *Pieces*

Spring Rolls
{ ½ pound/225 g
    pork   12
  ¼ pound/115 g
    shrimp

Food to Be Reheated in the Steamer
[Pieces are walnut size unless otherwise indicated.]

Steamed Dumplings
  Cantonese-style
	½ pound/225 g
	  pork
		16

Steamed Shrimp Balls*	1 pound/450 g shrimp	20
Steamed Pork Balls*	½ pound/225 g pork	12
Pearl Balls	1 pound/450 g pork	24

Minced Meat and Vegetable
  Steamed Buns
	½ pound/225 g
	  pork
		16
		(3 inches/8 cm)

Beef Balls With Szechuan
  Preserved Vegetables*
	1 pound/450 g
	  beef
		20

Food to Be Reheated in 350°/180°C Oven
[Pieces are finger size unless otherwise indicated.]

Shrimp Toast	1 pound/450 g shrimp	48
Fried Shrimp Balls*	1 pound/450 g shrimp	20

Fried Wontons	{ ½ pound/225 g
	    pork
	  ¼ pound/115 g
	    shrimp
		45

Fried Crab Patties	{ 1 pound/450 g
	    shrimp
	  ½ pound/225 g
	    crab
		(1½ × 2 inches/
		  4 × 5 cm)
		
		15

Fried Pork Balls*	½ pound/225 g pork	12

Fried Beef Balls With
  Szechuan Preserved
  Vegetables*
	1 pound/450 g
	  beef
		20

Curry Beef Turnovers	1 pound/450 g beef	35 (4 inches/10 cm)

*Indicates that they can also be heated in the microwave oven.

Chinese Sweets

    Almond Cookies
    Sesame Cookies
    Steamed Cake
      (can be served cold or
      warm)
    Egg Tarts
      (can be served cold or
      warm)

EVENING SNACK PARTY

Did you ever have friends you've wanted to invite for a get-together, but never got around to it? The very idea of having friends for a dinner party often hinders us from getting together with the people we like. The stumbling block, of course, is that so often we do not have the time for such preparations.

But some of our best evenings can often be spent with a few friends over an after-dinner drink, or perhaps with some snack foods. After all, if the host and hostess are relaxed, that's what creates the most congenial atmosphere.

The Chinese people are great snack lovers. They have snacks in the morning, in the afternoon, and sometimes, in the evening. Some of the most traditional evening snacks are a bowl of seasoned congee (soupy rice) or noodles in soup, for which Americans may have to acquire a taste. Although Dim Sum are traditionally daytime snacks, because they can be made ahead and frozen, they are very adaptable for such evening entertaining. If you have some of these cook-ahead snacks in the freezer, you can even have a spur-of-the-moment get-together with friends. And sometimes these spontaneous parties work out best. All you need are one or two kinds of snack foods for a nice change from the usual dips, crackers and cheese.

COCKTAIL PARTY

Cocktail party is a Western idea, but these delicate and delicious Dim Sum adapt well as finger foods for such occasions. They can be made ahead and frozen, so they're perfect for cocktail party entertaining. You can set an Oriental theme by serving all Oriental hors d'oeuvres, or you can use one or two kinds of Chinese pastries to accent the other appetizers. Either way, they will make a welcome change.

For Cocktail and Snack Parties

Food to Be Fried or Refried		*Pieces*
Spring Rolls (to serve, cut in halves after cooked)	½ pound/225 g pork ¼ pound/115 g shrimp	12 (24 halves)

Food to Be Rewarmed in the Steamer		Walnut size
Steamed Dumplings Cantonese-style	1 pound/450 g pork	32
Steamed Shrimp Balls*	1 pound/450 g shrimp	20
Steamed Pork Balls*	1 pound/450 g pork	24
Steamed Beef Balls With Szechuan Preserved Vegetables*	1 pound/450 g beef	20

Food to Be Rewarmed in 350°/180°C Degree Oven		Finger size
Shrimp Toast	1 pound/450 g shrimp	48
Fried Shrimp Balls*	1 pound/450 g shrimp	20
Fried Wonton	½ pound/225 g pork ¼ pound/115 g shrimp	45
Fried Pork Balls*	1 pound/450 g pork	24
Fried Beef Balls With Szechuan Preserved Vegetables	1 pound/450 g beef	20
Curry Beef Turnovers	1 pound/450 g beef	65
Deep Fried Peanut Chicken (or Almond)	½ pound/225 g chicken 2 cups/½ L nuts	24

*Indicates that they can also be reheated in the microwave oven.

Chinese Sweets (serve at room temperature)

Sesame Cookies
Almond Cookies
Steamed Cake (can be served
   warm)
Egg Tarts (can be served warm)

Chinese Regional Cooking

Culinary art is a reflection of the country's culture, and as you know, China has one of the longest continuous civilizations in the world. The Chinese civilization goes back some 4000 years, and classic Chinese cooking goes back to this, and has been perfected through many centuries.

Because of the great difference in the geography and climates of the many areas of China, and the difficulty in transportation and lack of means to preserve food in the old days, each region and its subregion developed a characteristic cookery of its own using whatever was locally available.

In general, Chinese cuisine can be divided into four major regions: Northern, Eastern, Western, and Southern. However, as transportation and communication improved over the years, special dishes of one region have intermingled and been adapted by other areas. The origins of some food have been forgotten, so that regional cooking can only be spoken of on a general basis. There are many dishes which are popular throughout the country, and therefore cannot be classified as "regional" dishes. Whenever possible, the origin of the dish will be identified in the recipes.

NORTHERN

Northern cooking is also associated with *Mandarin* cooking. Mandarin, which means high officials, has been associated with Peking, which has been the capital of China for centuries. For this reason, the best cooking was supposed to have been done in the Imperial Palace in the capital city.

Wheat is the main staple of this area, for its cold weather is unsuitable to cultivating rice. Breads, pancakes, and noodles are served in place of rice, and the Northern cooking is known for its generous and frequent use of garlic and scallions. The popular Moo-shu Pork dish served with Mandarin pancakes and the Hot and Sour Soup are both from this region.

Northern cooking is also influenced by the Mongols, who ruled China in the thirteenth century. They introduced the use of lamb, which has remained a popular meat in the North, and often not used in other regions. The best known culinary contribution of the Mongols is the Monoglian Fire Pot, which has been adapted throughout the country, and is a very popular winter meal.

63

EASTERN

Shanghai is the best known city in China. Fish and seafood are abundant in this region, so local dishes specialize in seafood as well as braised and gravy-laden dishes using soy sauce and sugar. One of the best known dishes of this region is Lion's Head. The best rice wine, green tea, and vinegar of China come from this region.

WESTERN

This type of cooking is also known as *Szechuan* or *Hunan* cooking, taking the name from the two neighboring provinces. The liberal use of hot peppers, which is distinctive of this mountainous, hot, and humid area, along with other seasonings, such as oil, ginger, and garlic, not only stimulates the palate in sub-tropical weather, but also retards food spoilage. A dish often has a spectrum of flavors—hot, sour, salty, sweet, and fragrant—to be tasted all at once. But I must mention that not all Szechuan and Hunan dishes are hot and spicy.

SOUTHERN

The cuisine here is known as Cantonese. In this area the weather is mild and the soil is rich. Since fresh foods are available all year round, few seasonings are needed to enhance their natural flavor. Less soy sauce is used here, and many dishes are stir-fried or steamed. Seafood is abundant, and superbly prepared. Cantonese roast pork and roast poultry are unsurpassed and known throughout China.

The Cantonese were the first Chinese to emigrate to the United States and other parts of the world, so for many decades this was the only Chinese food known to the Western world. They were also the first to adapt Western vegetables like corn and tomatoes to their cooking along with Western spices and pastries.

Helpful Hints on Preparation and Cooking

1. Read the chapter on The Food Processor before attempting any recipe in this book. Food for the recipes can be prepared without the food processor. Use a sharp knife or cleaver to mince, chop, slice, and shred the food. (See page 14 for details.)

2. Before you prepare a dish, read through that recipe completely. (*Note:* Alternate ingredients for the recipes are enclosed in parentheses.)

3. If you are cooking a stir-fried dish, arrange ingredients within easy reach of the burner just before cooking, and follow the order in the Have Ready Before Cooking column. Then read through the cooking steps, so you'll have a mental picture of the procedures before you start. This will make stir-fried cooking much easier, and avoid last minute confusion.

4. To get good results with the recipes, accurate measurement of ingredients is important. Always make each measurement level; using a kitchen scale can be most helpful. A few ounces more or less of an ingredient can make the dish either too bland or too salty.

5. The time given in each recipe is a guideline for you. Thawing time varies with different ovens and with different room temperatures and with different sizes of meat.

Preparation time is actually based on using the food processor and does not include the time spent for washing utensils. Everyone works at a different tempo, so the time may vary.

Cooking time depends largely on the intensity of the heat produced by your burners.

6. When a recipe indicates Ahead of Time, Steaming, or Baking, this free time will let you gauge whether you can start preparing rice or cooking a soup or a vegetable dish.

7. Unless indicated, it is not necessary to wash the food processor beaker when progressing from one ingredient to the next in *the same recipe.*

8. It is not necessary to cook with Chinese utensils. The recipes use the

65

word "wok" in general terms. A heavy skillet can be used instead. (*Note:* You may need more cooking oil in a flat-bottomed pan.) To use a wok on an electric burner, see the section on the wok in the chapter on Chinese cooking utensils.

9. In stir-fry cooking, always heat the wok to very hot before adding the cooking oil. If your meat sticks to the wok, either the wok is not well-seasoned, or not hot enough, or you may need more oil.

In case bits of meat stick to the wok, rinse and dry it before proceeding to the next step.

10. Soy sauce varies in color and taste from brand to brand. (See the chapter on Chinese Ingredients for more information.) For uniform results, all recipes were tested with Kikkoman soy sauce, unless otherwise specified. Since Kikkoman is a good all-purpose soy sauce, available in almost every American supermarket, there is no need to hunt for imported Oriental brands.

11. Chicken broth is an ingredient of many of the recipes. Canned broth varies in saltiness and color from brand to brand. All of the recipes were tested with College Inn brand, which is light-colored and closely resembles homemade chicken broth.

12. Cooking oil includes peanut oil, corn oil, and any vegetable oil except olive oil. Oil used for deep-frying can be reused; just strain it and keep in a covered bottle in the refrigerator. Oil used for seafood should be reused only with seafood, because other food cooked in it will take on the seafood flavor. To refresh the used oil, fry two slices of fresh ginger or two quarters of a potato when heating the oil, and discard them when golden brown. When the oil becomes heavy and dark, it should be thrown out.

13. Variation at the end of a recipe gives possible substitutes for ingredients you may not have on hand.

14. Tips at the end of a recipe gives information on how to keep and reheat the cook-ahead dish.

15. When using sauce ingredients or any cornstarch mixture, always give a good stir to recombine it with the liquid before adding to the hot wok. Then keep on stirring rapidly until the sauce thickens. All this will prevent the lumping of the sauce.

16. Do not stir-fry more than 1 pound of meat in one batch. The heat of average burners is not strong enough to cook an excess amount quickly. Cook the dish two times—one batch at a time—when using 2 pounds of meat.

17. Number of servings for an average appetite is based on just this dish served with rice, or bread if eaten in the Northern style. Each dish can serve more people if other dishes are added.

18. Your cooked dish will stay warm longer on the dining table if you preheat your serving platter. The Have Ready Before Cooking column lists serving platter as the last item, so you can heat it in a warm oven (250°F/120°C) just before you start cooking.

19. If you do not want to wash so many bowls and containers for the ingredients in stir-fried dishes, especially when you are doing more than one last-minute dish, use disposables like paper cups, paper plates, plastic wrap, or aluminum foil.

20. When cooking several dishes, try to wash and put away utensils and bowls as you go along. Some can be reused without washing, so you won't end up with a kitchen full of dirty bowls and dishes.

21. If you pound the garlic clove with the flat side of a knife, its skin can be easily removed.

22. Unless indicated in the recipe, both the green and the white parts of the scallion are used.

23. You'll find it very handy to have two or more sets of measuring spoons—one set for dry ingredients, one set for wet ingredients, and an extra tablespoon for measuring oil.

SYMBOLS

§   When appearing after a step, it indicates that the recipe can be prepared or cooked in advance through that particular step. So when § appears after the last cooking step in a recipe, it means that the dish can be completely cooked in advance.

★   When appearing after the name of a dish, it indicates that the dish can be frozen.

‡   When appearing after the number of servings, it indicates that the dish can be cooked in large quantities.

Hot Appetizers

The Western manner of serving appetizers before a principal meal is not a Chinese habit. It is only found at a formal dinner banquet, where assorted cold meat, seafoods, and pickled vegetables are cut thinly and neatly to be served on one big platter or several small dishes as a first course. However, they are not finger foods like the hot appetizers so popular with Westerners that Chinese restaurants here generally serve.

In China, these foods are either served as Dim Sum—meaning "dot the heart"—and are taken as snacks or lunch, or as a main course in a Chinese meal. They can usually be cooked ahead and rewarmed, therefore, they are wonderful used as Western hors d'oeuvres. You'll find a variety of them in this book, and they'll go well even with your Western meals.

STEAMED DUMPLINGS CANTONESE-STYLE ★

烧賣   Shao-mai

Makes 32 dumplings using 3-inch/8-cm round wrappers ‡
or 20 dumplings using 4-inch/10-cm round wrappers
Serves 3 as a meal ‡

This is a specialty of the Cantonese teahouses, which are blooming all over
American Chinatowns in the recent years. These dumplings are easy to
make, and can be made ahead, frozen, and resteamed, or reheated in a
microwave oven.

The smaller ones are good as appetizers. To serve the dumplings as a
meal, accompany with a soup such as Chopped Watercress and Egg Drop
Soup.

Sometimes you can find ready-made round wrappers in the Oriental food
stores. If they are not available, buy the thin wonton wrappers, or the Cantonese egg roll wrappers, and cut them into 3-inch/8-cm or 4-inch/10-cm
circles with cookie cutters. Although the teahouses use the round wrappers,
I find it easiest to just leave the wonton wrappers in squares, or cut the egg
roll wrappers into 4 equal 3½-inch/9-cm squares, which saves time and
leaves no wasted dough.

If none of these wrappers is available to you, make your own (see page
234).

The Filling:

Fresh Ginger	2 ½-inch/1½-cm cubes
Scallion	1, cut into 1-inch/2½-cm sections
Dry Chinese Mushrooms	4 large
Water Chestnuts	6
Boneless Pork	1 pound/450 grams, in 1-inch/2½-cm cubes
Cornstarch	1 teaspoon
Sugar	½ teaspoon
Salt	1 teaspoon or to taste
Soy Sauce	4 teaspoons

Wrappers for the Dumplings
32 3-inch/8-cm rounds; 20 4-
inch/10-cm rounds; or
square wrappers

AHEAD OF TIME:

1. If *frozen pork cubes* are used, thaw partially or completely, following these directions:

20 minutes or more to partially thaw meat at room temperature

10 minutes or more to partially thaw meat in a 250°F/120°C oven

1½ minutes or more to completely thaw meat in a microwave oven

2. Snap the stems off the Chinese mushrooms. Soak the mushrooms in boiling water to cover for 20 minutes, or until soft.

PREPARATION: 15 to 20 minutes

STEAMING: 20 minutes

Preparation:

1. With *Steel Blade* in place, start the machine, and drop ginger through the feed tube. Process until finely minced. Add scallion and chop coarsely. (To chop by hand see page 14.)

2. Drain mushrooms and cut into halves. Add mushrooms, water chestnuts, and pork cubes to the beaker. Process with 4 quick on/off turns. Then add the remaining 4 ingredients, and process with quick on/off turns, checking every few seconds until meat is evenly chopped. (To prepare by hand see page 14.) §

3. For 4-inch/10-cm circles or 3½-inch/9-cm squares, place 1 tablespoon of the filling in the center of each wrapper. Use less if 3-inch/8-cm circles are used.

4. Gather the sides of wrapper around the filling, letting them pleat naturally. Squeeze the neck of the dumpling to make sure the wrapper sticks to the filling. Then flatten its bottom on the table and make it stand upright. It has an open top that shows the filling. §

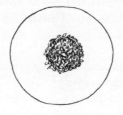

Steaming:

Place the dumplings on a greased heatproof plate at least ½ inch/1½ cm smaller in diameter than the pot in which you plan to steam them. If a bamboo steamer is used, either grease the rack or line the rack with lettuce leaves, then place dumplings on the top.

Bring the water in pot or steamer to a rolling boil; cover the pot or steamer, and steam the dumplings over medium-high heat for 20 minutes. Serve directly from the plate or the bamboo steamer. The cooked dumplings can be kept warm in the steamer over slow simmering water until serving time. Serve with soy sauce or Chinese rice vinegar, or a mixture of the two. (Chinese rice vinegar is milder than American vinegar. It is delicious as a dip. So many of my students, once they've tasted it, have fallen in love with it. If you use American vinegar, use less or dilute it with a little water.) §

Tips:

Uncooked dumplings can be kept in the refrigerator for half a day. Cooked ones can be kept for several days, and rewarmed in the steamer before serving. Both cooked and uncooked dumplings can be frozen.

Variations:

1. Beef may be used instead of pork, but it doesn't have the same delicate flavor.

2. You can substitute fresh mushrooms for dry Chinese mushrooms and bamboo shoots for water chestnuts.

SHRIMP TOAST★

蝦仁吐司   Xia-ren-tu-si

48 pieces ‡

This is a very popular appetizer, which the Chinese also use as a main course. Like all deep-fried foods, shrimp toast is at its best when served immediately. However, it can be made ahead, refried or reheated in the oven, and still be a delicious treat to serve.

Raw Shrimp with Shells	1 pound/450 g
Water Chestnuts	8
Scallions	2, white tops only in 1½-inch/4-cm sections
Egg	1
Dry Sherry	2 teaspoons
Cornstarch	2 tablespoons
Salt	1½ teaspoons or to taste
Sugar	2 teaspoons
Bread	12 slices
Fresh Parsley	few sprigs
Cooking Oil	3 cups/¾ L

AHEAD OF TIME:

Prepare the bread at least 2 days before using. With a knife, trim the crust off the bread, and cut each slice into four triangles. Spread the triangles out on a cookie sheet and let them dry in air for at least 2 days. They should be dry and hard, so they will be nice and crisp without absorbing too much oil when deep-fried. The dry bread can be stored in an air-tight container for many weeks. For same-day preparation, see Tips.

PREPARATION: 45 minutes; deduct 15 minutes if shelled and deveined shrimp are used

COOKING: 15 minutes

Preparation:

1. Shell and devein the shrimp. Wash them in cold water and pat dry. Cut into 1-inch/2½-cm pieces.

2. With *Steel Blade* in place, add water chestnuts and scallion tops; chop with 2 quick on/off turns. Add shrimp, egg, dry sherry, cornstarch, salt, and sugar. Turn machine on and off rapidly, checking every few seconds, until the mixture is coarsely chopped. (To chop by hand see page 14.)

3. Spread each triangle with about 1 teaspoon of the shrimp mixture. Garnish each with a small leaf of parsley pressed into the center of the shrimp mixture.

You can prepare the uncooked toast half a day ahead, and keep it in the refrigerator. §

Cooking:

Heat the oil for deep-frying to 350°F/180°C. Gently lower the bread, shrimp side down, into oil. After 1 minute, turn over and fry for another minute until the bread is golden brown. Drain on paper towels and serve hot. §

Tips:

If you want to make the shrimp toast on the same day, dry the fresh bread in a 200°F/95°C oven for 1 hour or until the bread is dry and hard. (The triangles will dry faster if you bake them on a rack over the cookie sheet.)

You can dry the bread in less than 10 minutes in a microwave oven. Just line the inside of the microwave oven with double layers of paper towels. Arrange 24 fresh-bread triangles on top of the towels. Heat on "Bake" for 3 minutes (or on a low setting—lower heat gives better results). Turn the triangles upside down and bake for another 3 minutes. Your microwave oven may be different, so time may vary somewhat.

To save time, frozen, deveined, and shelled shrimp can be substituted for the fresh. (Raw shrimp with shells are usually fresher than the frozen, deveined, and shelled shrimp in the freezer section of the supermarket.) Defrost and pat dry before using.

Cooked shrimp toast can be kept in the refrigerator for 2 to 3 days, or in the freezer for 1 to 2 months. To serve, reheat in a 350°F/180°C oven for 20 minutes or until heated through. (Heat them with shrimp side down on a rack over a baking pan.) Frozen ones will take longer to heat, but be careful not to overheat as shrimp will get dry and tough when overcooked.

SHRIMP BALLS★ (Steamed or Fried)

娛球   Xia-qiu (Zeng or Zha)

Makes 20 1¼-inch/3¹/₅-cm balls ‡

Both steamed and fried shrimp balls can be served as appetizers or as a main course. They can be cooked with vegetables and other ingredients to create a variety of new dishes, depending on the chef's imagination. Shrimp balls are very delicate, and are often served as banquet dishes. Traditionally, the shrimp was chopped by hand, hence, a time-consuming dish. I like their texture better when the mixture is finely minced. Steamed shrimp balls are delicious low-calorie food, and they make a delicate soup.

Fresh Ginger	½-inch/1½-cm cube
White Scallion Tops	2, cut into 2-inch/5-cm sections
Water Chestnuts	6
Shrimp in Shell	¾ pound/340 g (for 20 to 30 shrimp per
(Fresh shrimp would be	pound) *or* 1 pound/450 g (for 40 to
best; the fresher the better.)	50 shrimp per pound), shelled and
	deveined
Cornstarch	1½ teaspoons
Salt	1 teaspoon or to taste
Sesame Oil	2 teaspoons
Egg White	1
Dry Sherry	1 tablespoon
Sugar	½ teaspoon

PREPARATION: 12 minutes if shrimp are already shelled, otherwise, add 15 more minutes

STEAMING: 10 minutes *or*

FRYING: 10 minutes

Preparation:

1. With *Steel Blade* in place, mince ginger and scallions. Add water chestnuts, and give 2 quick on/off turns. Cut the shelled and deveined shrimp into 1-inch/2½-cm pieces, then place them in the beaker along with the remaining ingredients. Process until they are finely minced. (To prepare by hand see page 14.) §

2. Shape the mixture into 1¼-inch/3¹/₅-cm balls with wet hands. Balls are easier to shape if you let the mixture set in the refrigerator for 2 hours. §

Cooking (by one method or the other):

Steaming:

Place shrimp balls on a plate or a shallow dish at least 1 inch/2½ cm smaller in diameter than the steamer. Bring water in the steamer to a rolling boil, then place shrimp dish on the steamer rack. Steam for 10 minutes or until done. They can be kept warm in the steamer over very low simmering water. §

Frying:

Heat 2 cups of oil in a wok or saucepan to about 325°F/165°C. Test by dropping a small piece of bread in the oil; if it browns in 1 minute, the oil is ready. Fry 2 to 3 minutes or until shrimp balls are light golden on both sides. (Turn the balls over once during frying.) Do not overcook. Drain on paper towels. Serve them with soy sauce, Worcestershire sauce, or Roasted Salt with Szechuan Peppercorn mixture. §

Tips:

Both steamed and fried shrimp balls can be kept in the refrigerator for several days, and can be frozen. Steamed balls can be resteamed. Fried shrimp balls can be rewarmed in a 350°F/180°C oven for about 15 minutes or until heated through. Do not overcook, as shrimp will get tough and dry.

They can both be reheated by the microwave oven.

Variation:

Coating the uncooked shrimp balls with very coarse fresh bread crumbs makes a delicious variation. Use 6 slices of fresh white bread with the crust trimmed off. Process 2 slices at a time, each cut into quarters. With the *Steel Blade* in place, coarsely crumble the bread. Do not over process! Repeat with the other 4 slices. Roll 1 tablespoon shrimp mixture in the crumbs, and form it into a ball. Makes about 24. Deep-fry in 2 cups/½ L oil at 325°F/165°C until the crust is golden. They are crunchy outside and tender inside. Cooked ones can be refrigerated for several days and can be frozen. Rewarm in a 350°F/180°C oven for 15 to 20 minutes on a rack over a baking pan, turning over once. Frozen ones will take longer to heat, but be careful not to overheat as shrimp will get dry and tough when overcooked.

FRIED WONTONS★

炸餛飩   Zha-hun-tun

Makes 45 ‡

Fried wontons make excellent appetizers and finger food. They can be fried ahead, frozen, and then rewarmed in the oven. They are delicious with sweet and sour sauce, or serve them with soy sauce and Chinese vinegar.

Filling Mixture

Boneless Pork	½ pound/225 g, in 1-inch/2½-cm cubes
Shrimp in Shell	¼ pound/115 g, shelled, deveined, cleaned, dried, and cut into 1-inch/2½-cm pieces
Dry Sherry	1 tablespoon
Soy Sauce	1 tablespoon
Salt	½ teaspoon or to taste
Sugar	½ teaspoon
Cooking Oil	1 tablespoon
Cornstarch	2 teaspoons in 1 tablespoon water
Thin Wonton Wrappers	45
Cooking Oil	3 cups/¾ L

PREPARATION OF THE FILLING: 12 minutes. Allow 20 minutes to cool the filling before shaping.

SHAPING: 30 to 60 minutes

FRYING: 12 minutes

Preparation of the Filling:

1. With *Steel Blade* in place, add pork cubes, and process with 3 quick on/off turns. Then add the remaining 5 ingredients of the filling mixture to the beaker. Use quick on/off turns, checking carefully, until they reach the texture of ground meat. Do not over process. (To prepare by hand see page 14.)

2. Heat 1 tablespoon oil in the wok. Cook the meat mixture until the pork loses its pink color. Add the cornstarch mixture, and cook until there is no liquid left in the cooked mixture. The filling should not have any liquid, or it will make the wrapper soggy. If your pork is fatty, you may find a layer of oil separating from the cooked mixture. Drain the oil away after cooking.

3. Cool the filling before wrapping the wontons. The filling can be refrigerated for 1 to 2 days before assembling. §

Shaping: See Wontons, page 237.

Frying:

Heat 3 cups/¾ L of oil in a wok or saucepan to 350°F/180°C, and deep-fry the wontons 10 to 12 at a time for about 2 minutes, or until they are crisp and golden, turning at least once. Drain on paper towels. They can be kept warm in a 250°F/120°C oven, or on a hottray. §

Tips:

Fried wontons can be kept in the refrigerator for 3 to 4 days, or in the freezer for 1 to 2 months. Reheat in a 350°F/180°C oven for 20 minutes or until crisp. It is better to raise them on a rack over a bake pan and turn over once during heating.

Variations:

1. Use all pork without the shrimp, add 2 more ounces/60 g of pork, or substitute beef for pork.

2. Substitute 2 chopped scallions and 6 chopped waterchestnuts for the shrimp.

3. Substitute 3 ounces/85 g crab meat for shrimp.

SWEET AND SOUR SAUCE (5 minutes):
Tian-suan-zhi

Combine 4 tablespoons sugar, 1 tablespoon wine vinegar, 2 tablespoons ketchup, 1 tablespoon soy sauce, and ½ cup/1 dL water in a saucepan. Stir and bring the mixture to a boil. Mix 1 tablespoon cornstarch with 2 tablespoons water, and slowly add the mixture to the hot sauce. Cook, stirring, until the sauce is thickened. Serve as a dip.

PORK BALLS★ (Steamed or Fried)

豬肉丸子   Zhu-rou-wan-zi (Zheng or Zha)

Makes 12 walnut-size meat balls ‡

Pork balls are very versatile, for they can be served as a main course for a
Chinese meal or as an appetizer, Western style. They can be cooked with
vegetables and other ingredients to create new dishes. Steamed pork balls
are often used in soups.

By chopping your own meat, you can control the fat content. Very lean
pork has no more calories and cholesterol than very lean beef. Steaming
does not introduce any cooking oil, so steamed meat balls are good for people who are calorie- and cholesterol-conscious.

If you want to make more meat balls, just repeat the process, using
½ pound/225 g of meat in each batch.

Fresh Ginger	½-inch/1½-cm cube
Scallion	1, cut into 1-inch/2½-cm sections
Boneless Pork	½ pound, /225 grams in 1-inch/2½-cm cubes
Water Chestnuts	4
Cornstarch	1½ teaspoons
Salt	½ teaspoon or to taste
Soy Sauce	1 teaspoon
Egg White	1

AHEAD OF TIME:

If *frozen pork cubes* are used, thaw partially or completely, following these
directions:

20 minutes or more to partially thaw meat at room temperature
10 minutes or more to partially thaw meat in a 250°F/120°C oven
55 seconds or more to completely thaw meat in a microwave oven

PREPARATION: 8 minutes

STEAMING: 15 minutes *or*

FRYING: 8 minutes

Preparation:

With *Steel Blade* in the dry beaker, turn machine on, and drop ginger
through the feed tube. Process until finely minced. Add scallion, and process until coarsely chopped. Add pork cubes and water chestnuts, and process with 3 quick on/off turns. Then add the remaining 4 ingredients to
the beaker, and process with quick on/off turns, checking every few sec-

onds until the mixture is the texture of regular ground meat. (To prepare by hand see page 14.)

Shaping with wet hands, make the mixture into 12 meat balls. §

Cooking (by one method or the other):
Steaming:
Place meat balls on a plate or a shallow dish at least 1 inch/2½ cm smaller than the steamer. Bring the water in the steamer to a rolling boil. Place pork dish in the steamer rack, and steam for 15 minutes on medium-high heat or until pork is cooked. §

Frying:
Heat ½ cup/1 dL oil in a wok to 375°F/190°C (or fill a skillet with ½ inch/1½ cm oil). Fry the meat balls until they are brown on both sides about 4 minutes. Fry in 2 batches. You can fry them in one batch if you use more oil. §

Tips:
Both steamed and fried pork balls can be made ahead, and kept in the refrigerator for several days, or frozen for several months. It takes about 10 minutes to resteam the balls. Fried pork balls can be reheated in a 350°F/180°C oven for 15 minutes or until heated through. Both can be reheated by the microwave oven.

Variations:
1. Process the pork until it reaches the puree stage, then form into balls, cook by either steaming or frying. This makes a very tender and delectable meat ball, a different texture from the meat balls above. Again, it is easier to shape the balls with wet hands. This texture is not found in traditional pork balls, for ordinarily it would take too long to achieve this puree by hand chopping.

2. Beef can be used instead of pork in the above recipe, but the pork balls are more delicate in flavor.

CURRY BEEF TURNOVERS★

咖喱餃   Ga-li-jiao

Serves 4 to 5‡

Makes 35 4-inch/10-cm *or* 65 3-inch/8-cm turnovers ‡
They are sold at the Chinese bakeries and some teahouse restaurants. Good
snacks, they can be made in different sizes. The smaller ones are better for
cocktail appetizers. The larger ones, served with a soup (such as Vegetable
Soup) make a nice lunch or supper.

Curry Beef Filling:

Medium Onion	1
Boneless Beef	1 pound/450 grams, in 1-inch/2½-cm cubes
Mashed Potato	¾ cup/1¾ dL (or use instant mashed potato)
Curry Powder	5 teaspoons or to taste
Soy Sauce	2 teaspoons
Salt	1½ teaspoons or to taste
Sugar	1 teaspoon
Cooking Oil	3 tablespoons

AHEAD OF TIME:
   If *frozen beef cubes* are used, thaw partially or completely following these
directions:
      20 minutes or more to partially thaw meat at room temperature
      10 minutes or more to partially thaw meat in a 250°F/120°C oven
      1½ minutes or more to completely thaw meat in a microwave oven

PREPARATION AND COOKING FOR THE FILLING: 20 minutes

PREPARATION FOR THE PASTRY: 4 to 6 minutes

SHAPING THE TURNOVERS: 30 minutes for 35 4-inch/10-cm turnovers *and*
55 minutes for 65 3-inch/8-cm turnovers

BAKING: 15 minutes

Preparation and Cooking:
   1. Peel and quarter the onion. With *Steel Blade* in place, chop the onion
with quick on/off turns. Remove the onion and set aside. (To mince by
hand see page 14.)
   2. Divide the beef into two equal portions, about 1 cup each. With *Steel
Blace* in place, chop beef one portion at a time with quick on/off turns. It
should be the texture of ground beef. (To chop by hand see page 14.)

3. Heat 1 tablespoon oil in the wok, and cook chopped onion until transparent but not wilted. Remove from the wok. Add the remaining 2 tablespoons oil to the wok, and turn heat to high. Cook beef until it loses the pinkish color. Return onion to the wok, and add mashed potato, curry powder, soy sauce, salt, and sugar. Blend thoroughly and let *cool* before using the filling. §

Pastry:

Each batch makes 17 4-inch/10-cm *or* 24 3-inch/8-cm circles. It only takes 2 minutes to make one batch of dough. For best results, do not use more than 1½ cups/3½ dL of flour at one time. It is better to repeat the process 2 or 3 times as needed for the above filling mixture.

All-purpose Flour	1⅓ cups/3¼ dL
Salt	½ teaspoon
Vegetable Shortening	½ cup/1 dL plus 2 tablespoons
Cold Water	¼ cup/½ dL

Preparation:

With *Steel Blade* in place, put flour, salt, and shortening in the beaker. Process until the mixture has the consistency of coarse meal, about 10 to 15 seconds.

With the machine running, pour in water in a steady stream through the feed tube; a ball of dough will form above the rotary blade in 20 to 40 seconds. Remove. Do not overprocess. (To prepare without the food processor, cut the shortening into the flour and salt with a pastry blender until the mixture resembles small peas. Then sprinkle 1 tablespoon of water at a time over the mixture. Gently mix with a fork. Add just enough water to moisten the dough. Gather up and form into a ball.) The dough may be used immediately. §

Shaping:

1. On a lightly floured surface or a pastry cloth, flatten dough slightly, and roll into a square about ¹/₁₆ inch/¼ cm thick. Using cookie cutters or glasses for appropriate sizes, cut pastry into desired circles. Combine the scraps and roll out to make more circles.

2. Use about 2 level teaspoons of filling for a 4-inch/10-cm circle, and 1 teaspoon of filling for a 3-inch/8-cm circle. Place the filling in the center of each circle, and moisten the edge with a little water, then fold the dough into a semicircle. Pinch the edges together firmly to seal, and press with the tines of a fork around the edges to give a decorated look.

3. This step is not necessary, but you'll get richer looking turnovers if you brush the tops with a beaten egg. Prick the tops with a fork. §

Baking:

Place the turnovers on an ungreased baking sheet, and bake in a preheated 450°F/230°C oven for 15 to 20 minutes. §

Tips:

1. The cooked turnovers can be kept in the refrigerator for over a week, or can be frozen, then reheat them in 350°F/180°C oven for 15 to 20 minutes.

2. The uncooked turnovers can be kept in the refrigerator for several hours, or can be frozen. Bake the frozen ones without defrosting.

3. Pastry dough can be kept in the refrigerator for one day, or can be frozen. Bring it to room temperature before using.

4. Curry beef filling can be kept in the refrigerator for 3 to 4 days, or can be frozen.

Other Suggestions for Hot Appetizers

BEEF BALLS WITH SZECHUAN PRESERVED VEGETABLE (page 103)

榨菜牛肉丸子   Zha-cai-niu-rou-wan-zi

DEEP-FRIED PEANUT CHICKEN
(or ALMOND CHICKEN) (page 149)

花生雞(杏仁雞)   Hua-sheng-ji (or Xing-ren-ji)

FRIED CRAB PATTY (page 164)

炸蟹餅   Zha-xie-bing

FRIED CRAB CLAWS (page 163)

炸蟹鉗   Zha-xie-qian

SPRING ROLLS (page 249)

春捲   Chun-juan

PEARL BALLS (page 120)

珍珠丸子   Zhen-zhu-wan-zi

Beef and Lamb

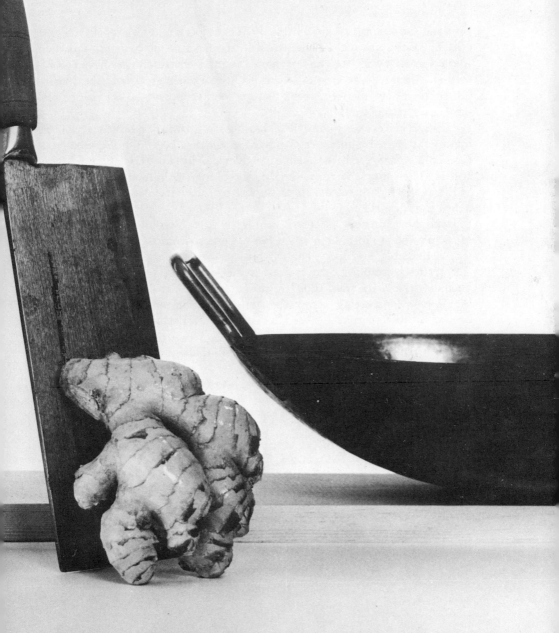

Beef and lamb are used much less often than pork and chicken in Chinese cooking. Cows are mainly used to help the farmers in the field, and their meat is usually very tough. For many centuries the Buddhists have considered it religiously cruel to eat them because of their great contributions to humanity. I have many relatives like my mother, a devoted Buddhist, who have never tasted beef.

However, over the years, there has been a growing acceptance of beef, mainly through the influence of the West. Quality beef from the other continents is more easily accessible, and especially for the Chinese living abroad. The Chinese have adapted their cooking methods and seasonings to beef and created many delicious dishes, so today the use of beef has widened significantly.

Lamb and mutton are used mainly by the Northerners and Chinese Moslems who are forbidden to eat pork. Chinese from the other regions use very little lamb, and many shun it because of its strong flavor.

For stir-fry cooking, flank steak is the beef most often used. It has a good flavor, and its grain runs lengthwise over the slab-like structure, making it easy for cutting across the grain. Any cut of beef which can be broiled or roasted may be used for stir-frying. Do not use cuts that are meant for stewing or braising.

Leg of lamb is best for the stir-fried lamb dishes.

CHINESE PEPPER STEAK

青椒牛肉片   Qing-jiao-niu-rou-pian

Serves 2 to 3

This is a simple and very basic stir-fried dish. It is a good dish for the beginner, and for the people who want a quick meal. Once you know how to cook the pepper steak, you can vary the fresh vegetables and use whatever you may have on hand to create other dishes.

Flank Steak	¾ pound/340 grams, precut to fit feed tube and frozen

Marinade:

Cornstarch	2 teaspoons
Dry Sherry	1 tablespoon
Soy Sauce	1 tablespoon

Bell Peppers	2 medium (2 green, or 1 red and 1 green)

Sauce Ingredients:

Salt	¼ teaspoon or to taste
Sugar	½ teaspoon
Cornstarch	1½ teaspoons
Soy Sauce	1½ tablespoons
Dry Sherry	1 tablespoon
Wine Vinegar	1 teaspoon (optional)

Fresh Ginger	2 thin slices (optional)
Cooking Oil	4 tablespoons

AHEAD OF TIME:
Partially defrost *frozen beef* just long enough to slice following these directions:

20 minutes or more to partially thaw meat at room temperature
10 minutes or more to partially thaw meat in a 250°F/120°C oven
55 seconds or more to partially thaw meat in a microwave oven

PREPARATION: 10 minutes

COOKING: 5 minutes

Preparation:

1. With *Medium Slicing Disk* in place, slice beef. (To slice by hand see page 14.) In a bowl, mix the marinade until smooth. Using your hand, mix the beef thoroughly with the marinade.

2. Seed the peppers, and cut by hand into 1½ × ½-inch/4-cm × 1½-cm strips. Place them in a bowl.

3. Mix the sauce ingredients in a bowl. §

Have Ready Before Cooking:

1. Bottle of cooking oil
2. Bowl with vegetables
3. Bowl with beef mixture, place ginger slices on top
4. Bowl with sauce ingredients
5. Serving platter

Cooking:

1. Heat wok over medium heat, then add and heat 1 tablespoon oil. Add peppers to the wok, and stir-fry for about 2 minutes. They should still be crisp. Remove from the wok.

2. Heat the wok over high heat, then add 3 tablespoons oil. When the oil is hot, fry ginger slices until golden, then discard. Add beef and stir-fry over high heat until beef just loses the red color, about 2 minutes. Return vegetables to the wok, and stir to mix.

3. Give the sauce ingredients a good stir, and add to the beef, stirring and mixing thoroughly until the sauce coats the meat with a translucent glaze. Transfer to a serving platter and serve immediately.

Note:

In this recipe, cutting the peppers by hand into 1½ × ½-inch/4-cm × 1½-cm strips is for the aesthetic appearance of the Chinese dish. When the meat is in slices, then the vegetables are cut into similar shape and size. This is characteristic in Chinese cooking. If you slice the peppers with the medium slicing disk of the processor, you'll get pepper shreds. Vegetable shreds are used when the meat in the dish is in shreds. Recipes in this book will follow this principle.

Variations:

1. Add 5 sliced fresh mushrooms or water chestnuts.

2. Add dried Chinese mushrooms (soak in boiling water for 20 minutes before using).

3. If you do not have fresh ginger, just leave it out. You can still cook the dish, but don't use ginger powder as a substitute.

SLICED BEEF WITH ONION
洋蔥牛肉片 Yang-cong-niu-rou-pian

Substitute 2 medium onions for bell peppers in the Chinese Pepper Steak. Peel and cut onions into ½-inch/1½-cm wedges, then separate them into individual petals.

SLICED BEEF WITH SNOW PEAS
雪豆牛肉片 Xue-dou-niu-rou-pian

Substitute 4 ounces/115 g of fresh snow peas (washed and stringed) or 1 package of frozen snow peas for bell peppers in Chinese Pepper Steak.

SLICED BEEF WITH FRESH ASPARAGUS
蘆筍牛肉片 Lu-sun-niu-rou-pian

Substitute ¾ pound/340 g of fresh asparagus for bell peppers in Chinese Pepper Steak. Rinse and wash asparagus, and break off and discard tough ends. Cut diagonally into 1½-inch/4-cm lengths.

BEEF WITH BROCCOLI

芥蘭牛肉片   Gai-lan-niu-rou-pian

Serves 2 to 3

Many of the Chinese stir-fried dishes do not have a gravy; the sauce is supposed to just coat the meat and the vegetables, as it is in the Chinese Pepper Steak. But many Americans like to have the gravy for that was what they were accustomed to in some Chinese restaurants.

This is a variation of the Pepper Steak with a gravy. Again, you can vary the vegetables to create other dishes.

Flank Steak   ¾ pound/340 g, precut to fit feed tube and frozen

Marinade:

Cornstarch   1 tablespoon
Dry Sherry   1 tablespoon
Soy Sauce   4 teaspoons

Sauce Ingredients:

Chicken Broth   ½ cup/1 dL
Soy Sauce   1 tablespoon
Sugar   ½ teaspoon
Salt   ¼ teaspoon or to taste
Cornstarch   2 teaspoons

Fresh Broccoli   1 pound/450 g (about half bunch)
Cooking Oil   5 tablespoons

AHEAD OF TIME:

Partially defrost *frozen beef* just long enough to slice following these directions:

20 minutes or more to partially thaw meat at room temperature
10 minutes or more to partially thaw meat in a 250°F/120°C oven
55 seconds or more to partially thaw meat in a microwave oven

PREPARATION: 15 minutes

COOKING: 7 minutes

Preparation:
1. With *Medium Slicing Disk* in place, slice beef across the grain. Mix it thoroughly with the marinade. (To slice by hand see page 14.)
2. Combine the sauce ingredients in a bowl.
3. Wash broccoli under cold running water. Cut off flowerets from large stems about 1½ inch/4 cm long. Cut the large flowerets smaller to ½ × ½ inch/1½ × 1½ cm on the top. Cut off the tough bottoms of the large stems, scraping and peeling off the hard skin.

Slice the stems by hand or with the *Medium Slicing Disk,* and combine them with the flowerets in a bowl. §

Have Ready Before Cooking:
1. Bottle of cooking oil
2. Bowl with vegetable
3. Bowl with beef mixture
4. Bowl with sauce ingredients
5. Serving platter

Cooking:
1. Heat wok over medium heat, then add 1 tablespoon oil. When oil is hot, add broccoli, stir-frying for few seconds. Cover the wok and cook for 2 minutes, stirring occasionally. (If the broccoli looks too dry, and shows signs of burning, add 1 tablespoon water.) The broccoli should be tender but still crisp to the taste. Transfer broccoli back to the same bowl.
2. Heat the wok over high heat until very hot. Add 4 tablespoons oil and heat almost to the smoking point. Add beef and stir-fry over high heat until beef just loses red color, about 2 minutes. Remove beef from the wok.
3. Give the sauce mixture a quick stir to recombine it, and add to the wok. Cook, stirring constantly, until the sauce thickens and turns translucent. Return the broccoli (not the liquid, if there is any in the bowl) and the beef, stirring to mix until the ingredients are coated with a light clear glaze. Transfer to the serving platter and serve immediately.

Variations:
1. Dried Chinese mushrooms add nice color and flavor to the dish. Soak with boiling water for 20 minutes before cooking.
2. Add 5 sliced fresh mushrooms or water chestnuts.

BEEF IN OYSTER SAUCE

蠔油牛肉片   Hao-you-niu-rou-pian

Serves 2 to 3

Oyster sauce adds a rich flavor and glaze to this attractive-looking beef dish. Serve with boiled rice and a vegetable salad.

Flank Steak	¾ pound/340 g precut to fit feed tube and frozen

Marinade:

Cornstarch	2 teaspoons
Soy Sauce	4 teaspoons
Dry Sherry	1 tablespoon

Fresh Snow Peas	4 ounces/115 g
(*or* Frozen Snow Peas)	(6-ounce/180-g package, thawed)

Sauce Mixture:

Oyster Flavored Sauce	3 tablespoons or to taste
Dry Sherry	1 tablespoon
Sugar	2 teaspoons
Cornstarch	½ teaspoon
Water	1 tablespoon

Cooking Oil	5 tablespoons
Salt	¼ teaspoon
Fresh Ginger	2 slices

AHEAD OF TIME:
·Partially defrost *frozen beef* just long enough to slice following these directions:

20 minutes or more to partially thaw meat at room temperature
10 minutes or more to partially thaw meat in a 250°F/120°C oven
55 seconds or more to partially thaw meat in a microwave oven

PREPARATION: 12 minutes

COOKING: 6 minutes

Preparation:
1. With *Medium Slicing Disk* in place, slice beef across the grain. (To slice by hand see page 14.) Then mix with marinade in a bowl.
2. Wash and string the fresh snow peas. (It is not necessary to string the frozen snow peas.)
3. Mix the sauce mixture in a small bowl. §

Have Ready Before Cooking:
1. Bottle of cooking oil
2. Bowl with snow peas
3. Salt, ¼ teaspoon
4. Bowl with beef; place 2 slices ginger on the top
5. Bowl with sauce mixture
6. Serving platter

Cooking:
1. Keep the serving platter warm in the oven.
2. Heat the wok, then heat 2 tablespoons oil over medium-high heat. Add the snow peas and ¼ teaspoon salt, and stir-fry for 1 to 2 minutes. Remove from the wok, and arrange them around the warmed serving platter, leaving the middle empty for the beef. Keep the snow peas warm in a low oven.
3. Heat the wok over high heat. Add and heat 3 tablespoons oil. When oil is very hot, fry ginger for 30 seconds and remove. Add beef to the hot oil; stir quickly over high heat for about 2 minutes or until beef just loses red color. Give the sauce mixture a good stir, and add to the beef. Stir and mix thoroughly until sauce coats the meat. Arrange the beef in the middle of the platter with snow peas surrounding it. Serve immediately.

Variations:
1. Substitute half can of baby sweet corn for half of the fresh snow peas.
2. Substitute ¾ pound/340 g fresh broccoli for the snow peas. (For cutting, see Stir-fried Broccoli page 179.)
3. Substitute ¾ pound/340 g fresh asparagus for snow peas. Cut them into 1½-inch/4-cm diagonal pieces.
4. Add 4 dry Chinese mushrooms presoaked in boiling water (snap the stems off before soaking). Cut them into smaller pieces, and cook them with the snow peas.

STIR-FRIED BEEF SHREDS WITH ONION AND PEPPER

葱椒牛肉絲   Cong-jiao-niu-rou-si

Serves 2 to 3

The crisp onions add a delightful flavor to the beef. If sweet red pepper is in season, use half red and half green pepper; they'll make a very colorful dish. Served with boiled rice or Mandarin pancakes (or its substitutes), it makes a nice family meal. For company, you can dress the dish up with deep-fried cellophane noodles (see variations).

Boneless Beef (*or* Flank Steak)	¾ pound/340 g precut to fit feed tube and frozen

Marinade:

Salt	½ teaspoon
Ground Pepper	¼ teaspoon
Dry Sherry	1 tablespoon
Cornstarch	2 teaspoons

Green Bell Pepper	1
Medium Onion	1

Sauce Ingredients:

Soy Sauce	2 tablespoons or to taste
Dry Sherry	1 tablespoon
Sugar	1 teaspoon
Cornstarch	1 teaspoon

Cooking Oil	3 tablespoons

AHEAD OF TIME:
   Partially defrost *frozen beef* just long enough to slice following these directions:

   20 minutes or more to partially thaw meat at room temperature
   10 minutes or more to partially thaw meat in a 250°F/120°C oven
   55 seconds or more to partially thaw meat in a microwave oven

PREPARATION: 12 minutes

COOKING: 7 minutes

Preparation:

1. With *Medium Slicing Disk* in place, slice the beef, then quickly remove the still partially frozen slices from the beaker. Reprocess the slices for julienne strips. (To slice by hand see page 14.) Mix the marinade in a bowl, then mix it thoroughly with the beef.

2. Cut ends from the green pepper, remove seeds and membranes. Cut lengthwise into quarters or into 2-inch/5-cm sections. Wedge them vertically in the feed tube and slice with *Medium Slicing Disk.* (To slice by hand see page 14.) Remove pepper and place in a small bowl.

3. Cut ends off the onion and peel, then cut lengthwise into halves. Place onion vertically in the feed tube and slice with *Medium Slicing Disk.* (To slice by hand see page 14.) Remove and put in a small bowl.

4. Mix sauce ingredients in a bowl. §

Have Ready Before Cooking:

1. Bottle of cooking oil
2. Bowl with onion shreds
3. Bowl with pepper shreds
4. Bowl with beef shreds
5. Bowl with sauce ingredients
6. Serving platter

Cooking:

1. Heat wok over medium-high heat, then add and heat 1 tablespoon oil. Add onion and stir-fry for 1 minute. Then add green pepper and fry for 1 or 2 minutes more. Remove vegetables from the wok.

2. Heat the wok over high heat, then add 2 tablespoons oil. When oil is hot, add beef shreds and stir-fry quickly, separating the beef shreds until the color of beef changes (about 2 minutes). Return vegetables to the wok. Give the sauce mixture a good stir, add to the wok and stir to mix until sauce turns to a translucent glaze. Remove from wok and serve immediately.

Variations:

For a festive dish, serve the beef on a bed of deep-fried cellophane noodles. Fry the noodles before you cook the beef dish. Cut or break loose ½ ounce/15 g noodles into two portions. Heat 3 cups/¾ L oil to 425°F/220°C. (Test oil by dropping in a small piece of noodle; if it pops up right away, the oil is ready.) Fry the noodles one portion at a time and on both sides. Remove with a strainer or slotted spoon, and drain on paper towels. §

Make a ring of fried noodles around the edge of the serving platter (save a few pieces to decorate the top), and keep them warm in the oven while you are cooking the beef. Pour the finished dish in the middle of the ring, and sprinkle a few of the white fluffy noodles on the top. Serve immediately.

The noodles can be fried several days ahead, and kept in an air-tight container. They can be rewarmed in a 300°F/150°C oven on the serving platter.

STIR-FRIED BEEF SHREDS WITH ONION
洋蔥牛肉絲   Yang-Cong-niu-rou-si

Serves 2 to 3

Substitute green pepper with a medium onion in the above recipe. Cook the two onions for 2 to 3 minutes, and remove from the wok. Then follow and finish step 2.

STIR-FRIED BEEF SHREDS WITH PEPPER
青椒牛肉絲   Quíng-jiao-niu-rou-si

Serves 2 to 3

Substitute 1 green pepper for the onion in Stir-fried Beef Shreds With Onion and Pepper recipe. Cook the 2 green peppers (or use 1 red and 1 green pepper) for about 2 minutes, and remove from the wok. Then follow and finish step 2.

HUNAN BEEF (see page 105)
湖南牛肉   Hunan-niu-rou

Substitute beef for lamb in the recipe.

SLICED BEEF IN BLACK BEAN SAUCE (see page 111)
豆豉牛肉片   Dou-chi-niu-rou-pian

Substitute beef for pork in the recipe.

BEEF SHREDS IN HOISIN SAUCE (see page 116)
京醬牛肉絲   Jing-jiang-niu-rou-si

Substitute beef for pork in the recipe.

SLICED BEEF IN SPICY GARLIC SAUCE (see page 144)
魚香牛肉片   Yu-xiang-niu-rou-pian

Substitute beef for chicken in the recipe.

STIR-FRIED CHOPPED BEEF WITH OYSTER SAUCE ★

燒油牛肉鬆   Hao-you-niu-rou-song

Serves 2 ‡

This dish can be served with plain boiled rice, or served with lettuce leaves. Just put a spoonful of meat in the center of the leaf, wrap and eat. Another fun way to serve this dish is to fill the pocket of a half of Pita bread with or without shredded lettuce. This bread tastes best when it is warm, so wrap it in aluminum foil and heat in a 350°F/180°C oven for 10 minutes. (Unwrapped Pita bread can also be warmed by microwave oven in less than a minute.)

Pita bread is quite similar to a Northern Chinese bread, and when I serve this dish with Pita bread, it brings back old memories for my husband. In Peking, there was a little restaurant where he and his family used to go, and they served a dish very similar to this. This restaurant was in North Lake Park, formerly part of the Imperial Garden in Peking.

Beef Mixture:

Boneless Beef	½ pound/225 g, in 1-inch/2½-cm cubes
Dry Sherry	1 tablespoon
Soy Sauce	1 tablespoon
Cornstarch	2 teaspoons
Scallions	2, in 1½-inch/4-cm sections
Frozen Green Peas	½ cup/1 dL, defrosted (see Tips) (optional)
Fresh Mushrooms	4 (or use canned sliced mushrooms)
Cooking Oil	1 tablespoon
Fresh Ginger	1 slice (optional)
Oyster-Flavored Sauce	1½ tablespoons or to taste
(or Soy Sauce)	(to taste)

AHEAD OF TIME:

1. If *frozen beef cubes* are used, thaw partially or completely following these directions:

      20 minutes or more to partially thaw meat at room temperature

      10 minutes or more to partially thaw meat in a 250°F/120°C oven

      55 seconds or more to completely thaw meat in a microwave oven

2. Thaw the green peas.

PREPARATION: 5 minutes

COOKING: 5 minutes

Preparation:

1. With *Steel Blade* in place, coarsely chop the mushrooms, then remove them from the beaker. (To chop by hand see page 14.)

2. Replace the *Steel Blade,* chop beef cubes with 3 quick on/off turns. Then add the remaining ingredients for the beef mixture. Process until beef is chopped to a coarse texture—coarser than ground beef. (To chop by hand see page 14.) §

Cooking:

1. Heat wok over high heat first, then heat the oil. Saute ginger for 1 minute. Add the beef mixture, and stir-fry for another minute or until beef loses its red color.

2. Add mushrooms and peas, stirring for another minute. Stir in oyster sauce and mix thoroughly. Discard ginger and serve. Can be cooked ahead and refrigerated, then reheated before serving. §

Tip:

To use frozen peas without thawing, add 1½ tablespoons oil to the wok. Heat the oil and cook the peas first with the ginger before adding the beef mixture.

Variation:

Pork can be used instead of beef.

MINCED BEEF SZECHUAN-STYLE

四川牛肉鬆   Sichuan-niu-rou-song

Serves 3

Delicious and fast to make, this dish was served at a dinner banquet for one of my cooking classes in a New York restaurant. It was most enthusiastically received by my students. As a single main dish, it can be served with boiled rice, or wrapped in lettuce leaves and eaten as lettuce packages. It is wonderful and fun served with warm Mandarin pancakes (see recipe, page 244). You spoon the minced beef in the center of the pancake or the lettuce leaf, and fold into a package. Then hold in your hand and eat. It is equally good when served with Pita bread.

Fresh Ginger	2 ½-inch/1½-cm cubes
Garlic	2 large cloves, peeled
Carrot	1 medium, peeled and cut into 1-inch/2½-cm sections
Water Chestnuts	½ 8-ounce/225-g can
Celery	1 large stalk, stringed and cut into 1-inch/2½-cm sections

Beef Mixture:

Boneless Beef	1 pound/450 g in 1-inch/2½-cm cubes
Dry Sherry	1 tablespoon
Soy Sauce	2 tablespoons
Cornstarch	1 tablespoon

Sauce Mixture:

Soy Sauce	1½ tablespoons or to taste
Sugar	½ teaspoon
Vinegar	1 teaspoon
Dry Sherry	1 tablespoon
Cornstarch	1 teaspoon

Dry Hot Pepper (*or* Crushed Red Pepper Flakes)	2 or to taste, cut in halves and seeded (½ teaspoon or to taste)
Cooking Oil	3 tablespoons
Sesame Oil	1 tablespoon (optional)

AHEAD OF TIME:

If *frozen beef cubes* are used, thaw partially or completely, following these directions.

> 20 minutes or more to partially thaw meat at room temperature
> 10 minutes or more to partially thaw meat in a 250°F/120°C oven
> 1½ minutes or more to completely thaw meat in a microwave oven

PREPARATION: 15 minutes

COOKING: 7 minutes

Preparation:

1. With *Steel Blade* in place, process ginger and garlic until finely minced. Transfer to a small bowl. (To mince by hand see page 14.)

2. Replace the *Steel Blade,* and with quick on/off turns, chop carrots very coarsely. Without removing carrots, add water chestnuts and celery to the beaker, and chop with quick on/off turns until vegetables are about the size of small peas. (To chop by hand see page 14.) Transfer to a bowl.

3. Replace the *Steel Blade,* and add half of the beef cubes. Chop with 3 quick on/off turns, then add half of the remaining three ingredients for the beef mixture to the beaker. Coarsely chop the beef. (Its texture should be coarser than that of the hamburger meat.) Remove the chopped beef, and repeat the process with the other half of the beef mixture. (To chop by hand see page 14.)

4. Mix the sauce ingredients in a bowl. §

Have Ready Before Cooking:

1. Bottle of cooking oil
2. Bowl with chopped vegetables
3. Dry hot pepper
4. Bowl with minced ginger and garlic
5. Bowl with coarsely chopped beef
6. Bowl with sauce mixture
7. Sesame oil, 1 tablespoon (optional)
8. Serving platter

Cooking:

1. Heat the wok, and then heat 1 tablespoon cooking oil. Stir-fry vegetables for 1 to 2 minutes, and remove from the wok.

2. Heat the wok, then heat 2 tablespoons oil. Fry the hot peppers for 30 seconds or until brown (the longer you cook, the hotter the dish gets). Add minced ginger and garlic to the oil, and cook for 20 seconds. Then add chopped beef mixture to the wok, stirring until beef loses its red color.

3. Return vegetables to the wok. Give the sauce mixture a good stir, and pour into the wok, stirring until sauce thickens and coats the meat. Add sesame oil (optional). Mix and serve hot. §

Tips:

This dish can be cooked ahead, and recooked just until it is heated through. Or it can be rewarmed by microwave oven. Heat it in an uncovered serving platter for 4 minutes, stirring once after the first 2 minutes.

Variations:

1. This dish is very good topped with coarsely chopped roasted peanuts. (Chop peanuts with *Steel Blade* before processing the ingredients in the dish. Wipe the beaker clean with a paper towel, then chop the ginger and garlic.)

2. Sprinkle crushed potato chips on top of the dish.

3. Serve on a bed of deep-fried cellophane noodles. See Variation of Stir-fried Beef Shreds With Onion and Pepper.

4. Green peas, chopped fresh snow peas, and chopped broccoli stems can be substituted for chopped celery.

5. Chopped bamboo shoots can be substituted for water chestnuts.

MINCED BEEF WITH CELLOPHANE NOODLES

粉絲牛肉末   Fen-si-niu-rou-mo

Serves 2 ‡

Cellophane noodles are made from mung beans. Once soaked, they become translucent, hence they are also known as "transparent noodles." Chinese consider them as more of a vegetable, so they are often stir-fried with meat and served with rice, or with Mandarin pancakes.

Dry Cellophane Noodles	4 ounces/115 g

Meat Mixture:

Boneless Beef or Pork	½ pound/225 g, in 1-inch/2½-cm cubes
Soy Sauce	2 teaspoons
Dry Sherry	2 teaspoons
Cornstarch	2 teaspoons
Cooking Oil	3 tablespoons
Soy Sauce	4 tablespoons or to taste
Sesame Oil	4 teaspoons (optional)

AHEAD OF TIME:

1. Pour 2 quarts of boiling water over cellophane noodles and let stand for 15 minutes or until soft.

2. If *frozen meat cubes* are used, thaw partially or completely following these directions:

20 minutes to partially thaw the meat at room temperature

10 minutes to partially thaw the meat in a 250°F/120°C oven

55 seconds to thaw meat completely in a microwave oven

PREPARATION: 4 minutes

COOKING: 5 minutes

Preparation:

1. Drain the cellophane noodles in a colander. Use kitchen shear or knife to cut them into 3-inch/8-cm lengths.

2. With *Steel Blade* in place, put meat cubes in the beaker, and chop with 3 quick on/off turns. Add the remaining ingredients for the meat mixture. Chop with quick on/off turns until meat is coarsely chopped. (To chop by hand see page 14.) §

Cooking:

Heat wok over high heat, then add 3 tablespoons oil. When oil is hot, stir-fry the meat mixture until it loses its reddish color. Add the drained cellophane noodles and soy sauce. Stir to mix, and cook until liquid is all absorbed. Add sesame oil for flavoring. §

Variation:

If you like the dish with a spicy taste, add 3 ounces/85 g Szechuan preserved vegetable. Chop with the *Steel Blade* and remove from the beaker before mincing the beef. Cook the preserved vegetable with the beef mixture, using half the amount of the soy sauce or to taste.

Tips:

The dish can be reheated on the stove top, or covered and reheated in a 300°F/150°C oven. It can also be reheated in a microwave oven.

BEEF BALLS WITH SZECHUAN PRESERVED VEGETABLE*

榨菜牛肉丸子   Zha-cai-niu-rou-wan-zi

Makes 20 walnut-size balls ‡

The flavor of the beef balls is enhanced by the Szechuan preserved vegetable, which is both spicy and salty. They can be served as appetizers Western style. For a single main dish, serve with Ginger and Scallion Lo-mein and a vegetable salad.

Szechuan Preserved Vegetable	2½ ounces/70 g (2 × 2 × 1-inch/ 5 × 5 × 2½-cm piece or 6 tablespoons chopped) or to taste.
Scallions	2, in 2-inch/5-cm sections
Boneless Beef	1 pound/450 g, in 1-inch/2½-cm cubes
Dry Sherry	2 tablespoons
Cornstarch	2 tablespoons
Sesame Oil	2 tablespoons (optional)
Salt	¼ teaspoon or to taste
Ground Pepper	½ teaspoon or to taste

AHEAD OF TIME:

If *frozen beef cubes* are used, thaw partially or completely following these directions:

20 minutes or more to partially thaw meat at room temperature
10 minutes or more to partially thaw meat in a 250°F/120°C oven
1½ minutes or more to completely thaw meat in a microwave oven

PREPARATION: 12 minutes

COOKING: 10 minutes by steaming or frying

Preparation:

1. Cut Szechuan preserved vegetable into 1-inch/2½-cm cubes. With *Steel Blade* in place, process the vegetable until finely minced. Remove from the beaker. (To mince by hand see page 14.)

2. Replace the *Steel Blade,* coarsely chop the scallion sections, then add beef cubes. Chop with 3 quick on/off turns. Add the remaining 5 ingredients, and process until beef is evenly chopped to about the texture of ground beef. (To chop by hand see page 14.)

3. Return the chopped preserved vegetable to the beaker, process with quick on/off turns only until the vegetables are well mixed with the beef mixture, or mix by hand. Do not over process.

4. With wet hands, shape into 20 walnut-size balls. §

Cooking (by one method or the other):
  Steaming:
To save time, set up the steamer, and heat the water while you are doing the preparation. Place beef balls on a plate or a shallow dish at least 1 inch/2½ cm smaller than the diameter of the steamer. Steam the beef balls over the boiling water on medium-high heat for 8 minutes or until cooked. The cooked balls can be kept warm in the steamer over very low simmering water. §
  Frying:
Heat 1 cup/¼L of oil in a wok or saucepan to 375°F/190°C. Fry the balls until they are brown on both sides, about 3 minutes. Do in 2 to 3 batches. §

Variation:
Use pork instead of beef.

Tips:
Fried and steamed beef balls can be refrigerated for 3 to 4 days, or frozen for 1 to 2 months. Both can be rewarmed in a 350°F/180°C oven, or in a microwave oven.

BEEF BALLS WITH TURNIPS IN BLACK BEAN SAUCE

蘿蔔牛肉丸子   Luo-bo-niu-rou-wan-zi

Serves 2 ‡

This aromatic and hearty family dish from the South can be cooked ahead and in large quantities. As a single main dish, serve with boiled rice and a green vegetable.

Cooked Beef Balls with Szechuan Preserved Vegetable	10 to 12 (or ½ recipe)
Chinese Large White Turnips (*or* Western turnips)	¾ pound/340 g
Fresh Ginger	¼-inch/¾-cm cube
Garlic	2 cloves, peeled
Salted Black Beans	1 tablespoon
Cooking Oil	1 tablespoon
Chicken Broth	1¼ cups/3 dL
Salt	½ teaspoon or to taste
Cornstarch	2 teaspoons in 4 teaspoons water

PREPARATION: 6 minutes

COOKING: 15 minutes

Preparation:

1. Peel turnips and cut into 1-inch/2½-cm cubes.
2. With *Steel Blade* in place, chop ginger and garlic. Then add the black beans, chop with 3 quick on/off turns. (To chop by hand see page 14.)

Cooking:

1. Heat 1 tablespoon oil in the wok over medium heat, and cook chopped ginger, garlic, and black beans for 30 seconds. Do not burn garlic, or it will taste bitter. Add 1¼ cups/3 dL of chicken broth and turnips, and bring to a boil. Let them simmer for 7 minutes.
2. Add beef balls, and simmer for 5 minutes. Add salt to taste. Give the cornstarch mixture a good stir, and slowly add to the wok, stirring until sauce becomes translucent. §

Variation:

If you don't like turnips, use potatoes instead. Fry the potato cubes in 2 tablespoons oil first before adding to the water and seasoning. Cook the dish until the potatoes are soft.

HUNAN LAMB

湖南羊肉   Hunan-yang-rou

Serves 2 to 3

This popular lamb dish served by the Hunan and Szechuan restaurants is spicy and garlicky, and complemented by the mild flavor of the leeks. Delicious with boiled rice, you can serve it with a vegetable salad such as Sweet and Sour Cucumber Salad.

Dry Chinese Mushrooms	5 (optional)
Boneless Leg of Lamb	¾ pound/340 g, precut to fit feed tube and frozen
Fresh Ginger	2 ½-inch/1½-cm cubes
Garlic	3 large cloves, peeled

Marinade for Lamb:

Dark Soy Sauce	1 tablespoon (see Variations)
Dry Sherry	1 tablespoon
Cornstarch	2 teaspoons

Sauce Ingredients:

Dark Soy Sauce	1 tablespoon (see Variations)
Light Soy Sauce	1½ teaspoons (see Variations)
Salt	¼ teaspoon or to taste
Sugar	½ teaspoon
Wine Vinegar	1½ teaspoons
Dry Sherry	1 tablespoon
Juice from Mushrooms (*or* Water)	4 tablespoons
Cornstarch	2 teaspoons
Large Leeks (*or* Scallions)	2 (about 3½ cups/⁴/₅L after cutting up) (8)
Dry Hot Peppers (*or* Crushed Red Pepper Flakes)	2, cut into halves with seeds removed (½ teaspoon or to taste)
Cooking Oil	5 tablespoons
Sesame Oil	2 teaspoons (optional)

AHEAD OF TIME:

1. Partially defrost *frozen lamb* just long enough to slice following these directions:

   20 minutes or more to partially thaw meat at room temperature

   10 minutes or more to partially thaw meat in a 250°F/120°C oven

   55 seconds or more to partially thaw meat in a microwave oven

2. Snap the stems off the Chinese mushrooms. Soak the mushrooms in boiling water to cover for 20 minutes, or until soft.

PREPARATION: 16 minutes

COOKING: 8 minutes

Preparation:

1. With *Steel Blade* in place, finely chop ginger and garlic, then transfer to a small bowl. (To chop by hand see page 14.)

2. With *Medium Slicing Disk* in place, slice lamb and transfer to a bowl. (To slice by hand see page 14.) Mix thoroughly with the marinade.

3. Mix the sauce ingredients in a bowl.

4. If leeks are used, wash and remove all the sandy particles. Cut them crosswise into 1½-inch/4-cm slant sections. Then cut the thick sections

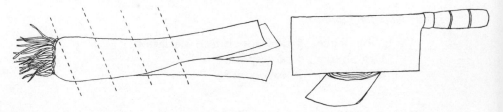

lengthwise from the top, so you can separate the layers into individual pieces. Discard the roots and the tough leaves.

If scallions are used, just cut off the roots, then cut into 1½-inch/4-cm lengths.

5. Drain the softened mushrooms and cut into smaller pieces. Put in the same bowl with lamb. §

Have Ready Before Cooking:
1. Bottle of cooking oil
2. Bowl with leeks
3. Dry hot peppers
4. Bowl with chopped ginger and garlic
5. Bowl with lamb and mushrooms
6. Bowl with sauce mixture
7. Sesame oil, 2 teaspoons (optional)
8. Serving platter

Cooking:
1. Heat the wok, then heat 1 tablespoon oil. Stir-fry leeks or scallions over medium-high heat for 1 to 2 minutes. Remove from the wok.
2. Heat wok over medium-high heat, then heat 4 tablespoons oil. Fry hot peppers until brown, about 30 seconds. Add garlic and ginger, and cook for 20 seconds.
3. Quickly add lamb to the wok, stir-fry over high heat until lamb is no longer red, about 1 to 2 minutes.
4. Return the leeks to the wok. Give the sauce mixture a good stir, and pour into the wok, stirring until it thickens and coats the meat. Remove from heat, add sesame oil (optional), and serve immediately.

Variations:
1. You can use all-purpose soy sauce in place of the dark and light soy sauce, however, the dish will not have the rich brown color it should.
2. Substitute boneless veal or beef for lamb.

LAMB SHREDS IN HOISIN SAUCE (see page 116)
京醬羊肉絲   Jing-jiang-yang-rou-si

Substitute lamb for pork in the recipe.

SLICED LAMB IN SPICY GARLIC SAUCE (see page 144)
魚香羊肉片   Yu-xiang-yang-rou-pian

Substitute lamb for chicken in the recipe.

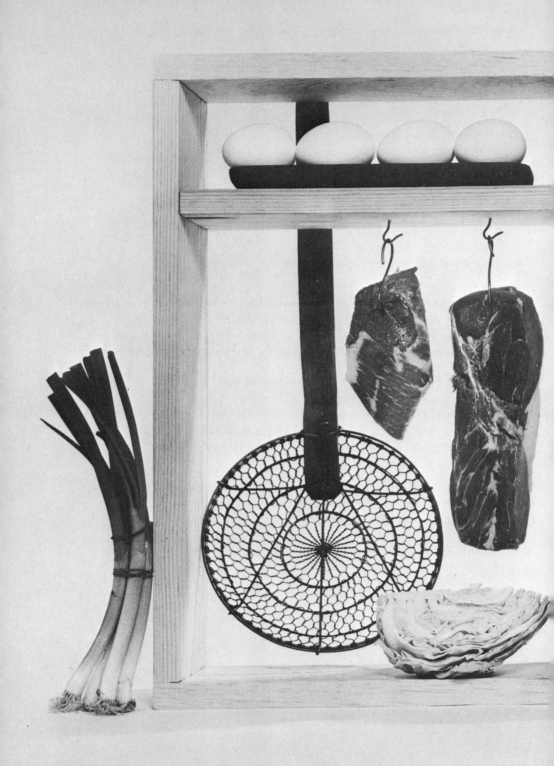

Pork

Pork is the most common and popular meat in Chinese cooking. The words "meat" and "pork" are often interchangeably used.

Pigs are one of the easiest animals to raise, for they do not need the vast grazing land required for raising cattle and can be fed almost anything. They are especially suitable to countries like China, which abound with small farms.

Pork is uniformly tender (unlike beef), so you can use any part of lean pork for Chinese stir-fry cooking. It is richer in B vitamins than any other meat. Unfortunately, many Americans are so afraid of trichinosis from uncooked pork that they either avoid using it, or cook it till it's so well done that it becomes dry and tough, so that it's almost tasteless. Unnecessary overcooking of pork also destroys a considerable amount of many of these vitamins.

Pork changes from pink to light gray color at a temperature of 150°F/66°C. (Trichinae are destroyed when pork is cooked a few minutes at 131°F/55°C.) So use the absence of pink as your guide for cooking pork. It should be cooked, but still tender and succulent.

One of the great assets of the food processor is to mix and chop the meat mixture all in one step. Meat balls from such a mixture have a lighter texture than the ones mixed by hand. Such a light texture is much valued by Chinese food connoisseurs, and traditionally it is only achieved by adding pork fat. Now you can obtain a tender texture by using lean meat, truly a delight to those who want to reduce their intake of animal fat.

The Chinese have an infinite way of using chopped pork. Since pork has a more delicate flavor than beef, it is often used in small amounts to enhance the flavor of seafood, egg, and vegetable dishes. I have included a variety of such dishes in the book, since the processor can chop even the smallest amount of meat easily and efficiently.

SLICED PORK IN BLACK BEAN SAUCE

豆豉肉片   Dou-chi-rou-pian

Serves 2 to 3

Black beans and garlic give this dish a rich and hearty flavor.

Dry Chinese Mushrooms	4 (optional)
Boneless Pork	¾ pound/340 g, precut to fit feed tube and frozen
Fresh Ginger	½-inch/1½-cm cube
Garlic	1 large clove, peeled
Scallion	1, in 2-inch/5-cm sections
Salted Black Beans	2 tablespoons, rinsed and drained

Marinade for Pork:

Cornstarch	1 tablespoon
Dry Sherry	1 tablespoon
Soy Sauce	1 tablespoon

Sauce Ingredients:

Brown Bean Sauce	1 level tablespoon
Soy Sauce	1½ tablespoons or to taste
Sugar	2 teaspoons or to taste
Dry Sherry	1 tablespoon
Liquid from Dry Mushrooms (*or* Water)	4 tablespoons, discard sandy residue
Cornstarch	2 teaspoons

Broccoli Flowerets	1 cup/¼ L, in 1¼-inch/3¹/₅-cm lengths
Red Bell Pepper	1, seeded
Water Chestnuts	5
Cooking Oil	5½ tablespoons

AHEAD OF TIME:

1. Partially defrost *frozen pork* just long enough to slice following these directions:

> 20 minutes or more to partially thaw meat at room temperature
> 10 minutes or more to partially thaw meat in a 250°F/120°C oven
> 55 seconds or more to partially thaw meat in a microwave oven

2. Snap stems off the Chinese mushrooms. Soak the mushrooms in boiling water to cover for 20 minutes, or until soft.

PREPARATION: 16 minutes

COOKING: 7 minutes

Preparation:

1. With *Steel Blade* in place, chop ginger and garlic, then chop scallion with them. Add black beans to the beaker, and chop with 4 quick on/off turns. (To chop by hand see page 14.) Transfer the chopped ginger, garlic, scallions, and black beans to a small bowl.

2. With the *Medium Slicing Disk* in place, slice the pork. (To slice by hand see page 14.) Transfer to a bowl, and mix with the marinade.

3. Mix the sauce ingredients in a bowl.

4. Cut broccoli flowerets smaller to ½ × ½-inch/1½ × 1½-cm on the top. Cut red pepper into ¾-inch/2-cm squares. Slice water chestnuts by hand or with *Medium Slicing Disk*. Cut drained mushrooms to smaller pieces. Place all the vegetables in a bowl. §

Have Ready Before Cooking:
1. Bottle of cooking oil
2. Bowl with pork
3. Bowl with vegetables
4. Bowl with ginger, garlic, scallion, and black beans
5. Bowl with sauce ingredients
6. Serving platter

Cooking:

1. Heat the wok over high heat. Add 3 tablespoons oil, and heat until very hot. Add pork, and stir-fry until pork just loses its pink color. Remove from the wok.

2. Heat the wok and 1 tablespoon oil on medium-high heat. Add the vegetables. Stir to coat them with oil. Cover the wok, and cook for 1 minute, stirring once. Remove from the wok.

3. Heat the wok with 1½ tablespoons oil, fry the ginger and black bean mixture for 30 seconds over medium heat.

4. Return the vegetables and pork to the wok. Mix and rewarm over high heat. Add the sauce mixture, stirring until the sauce thickens. Serve immediately.

Variations:

1. If you don't have brown bean sauce, substitute soy sauce, and adjust the sauce to taste.

2. Fresh mushrooms may be used in place of dry mushrooms.

3. Substitute 1 green bell pepper for the broccoli flowerets.

4. Substitute ½ of a 15-ounce/425-g can of baby sweet corn for the red bell pepper.

SLICED PORK IN SPICY GARLIC SAUCE (see page 144)

魚香肉片 Yu-xiang-rou-pian

Substitute pork for chicken in the recipe.

MOO-SHU PORK

木樨肉   Mu-xu-rou

Serves 3

This Northern dish has become a most popular dish with Americans. The name comes from the pieces of scrambled eggs which symbolize the yellow cassia blossoms, called Moo-shu in Chinese.

Traditionally, it is served with Mandarin pancakes—a fun way to eat—and is a very common lunch for the Northern people.

Mandarin Pancakes	12 (see recipe, p. 244)
Dried Tiger Lilies	½ cup/ 1dL
Dried Tree Ears	¼ cup/½ dL
Boneless Pork	½ pound/225 g, precut to fit feed tube and frozen

Marinade:

Cornstarch	1 teaspoon
Soy Sauce	1 tablespoon
Dry Sherry	2 teaspoons

Scallions	4
Eggs	4, beaten with 2 teaspoons soy sauce
Cooking Oil	7 tablespoons
Sesame Oil	1 tablespoon (optional)

Sauce Mixture:

Soy Sauce	1 tablespoon
Dry Sherry	1 tablespoon
Sugar	1 teaspoon
Salt	½ teaspoon or to taste
Cornstarch	½ teaspoon

AHEAD OF TIME:

1. Pour 1 cup of boiling water in each separate bowl containing tiger lilies and tree ears. Let them soak for 15 minutes before draining.

2. Partially defrost *frozen pork* just long enough to slice following these directions:

> 20 minutes or more to partially thaw meat at room temperature
> 10 minutes or more to partially thaw meat in a 250°F/120°C oven
> 35 seconds or more to partially thaw meat in a microwave oven

PREPARATION: 15 minutes

COOKING: 8 minutes

Preparation:

1. With *Medium Slicing Disk* in place, slice pork first, then reprocess to cut into shreds. (To slice and shred by hand see page 14.) Mix with the marinade.

2. Cut scallions into 2-inch/5-cm sections. You can shred them with *Fine Slicing Disk* (lay scallions horizontally in the feed tube), or shred by hand.

3. Cut the drained tiger lilies into 2 sections, and cut off any hard stems. Cut the drained tree ears into smaller pieces by hand or very coarsely chop with *Steel Blade.* Put tiger lilies, tree ears, and scallions in one bowl.

4. Beat eggs with 2 teaspoons soy sauce.

5. Mix sauce mixture in a bowl. §

Have Ready Before Cooking:

1. Bottle of cooking oil
2. Bowl with beaten eggs
3. Bowl with pork mixture
4. Bowl with tiger lilies, tree ears, and scallions
5. Bowl with sauce mixture
6. Sesame oil, 1 tablespoon (optional)
7. Serving platter

Cooking:

1. Heat the wok over medium-high heat, then heat 2 tablespoons oil, and swirl around. Add the beaten eggs, and stir-fry until eggs are set. Remove from the wok.

2. Heat the wok over high heat, then heat 5 tablespoons oil. When oil is hot, add pork, and stir-fry until meat is no longer pink. Add tree ears, tiger lilies, and scallions, stirring to mix and to heat through, about 1 to 2 minutes.

3. Give the sauce mixture a good stir, and pour into the wok, stirring to mix. Return the cooked eggs, and break them into small pieces while mixing.

4. If desired, add 1 tablespoon sesame oil for extra flavor. Transfer to the platter and serve. §

To Serve:

Before cooking the pork dish, set up a steamer, and steam the Mandarin pancakes for 6 minutes or until hot. They can be kept warm in the steamer over low simmering water.

Place 1 warm Mandarin pancake on your plate and spoon about 2 tablespoons Moo-shu Pork along the center of the pancake. Roll the pancake to enclose the filling. Then fold one side of the roll over to prevent the stuffing from dripping out, as you pick up the roll to eat from the open side.

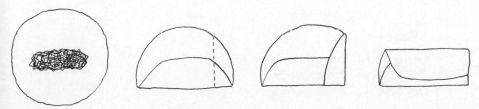

Tips:

This dish can be completely or partially cooked ahead, and rewarmed over the burner, or in a microwave oven. Eggs taste best when freshly cooked, so you can cook the pork and vegetables with the sauce mixture ahead. And cook the eggs just before serving.

Variations:

1. Authentically, the dish does not contain bamboo shoots or cabbage as many of the restaurants do to stretch the dish. Cabbage, if not over used, adds a good flavor. You can use 5 large leaves from the round cabbage. Shred with *Medium Slicing Disk,* then blanch them in boiling water for 1 minute. Quickly rinse with cold water. Drain and dry very well. Add the cabbage along with the tree ears, tiger lilies, and scallions to the pork mixture in step 2. Add an additional ½ teaspoon salt (or to taste) to the dish.

2. This dish is also delicious to serve with rice.

3. It is not traditional, but you can substitute chicken or beef for the pork, thus creating Moo-shu Chicken or Moo-shu Beef, as you may find on the menus of some Chinese restaurants.

PORK SHREDS IN HOISIN SAUCE

京醬肉絲   Jing-jiang-rou-si

Serves 2

This Northern dish can be served with rice. But it is especially good wrapped in Mandarin pancakes and served with a soup or a vegetable.

This recipe can be doubled and cooked together in one batch.

Boneless Pork   ½ pound/225 g, precut to fit the feed tube and frozen

   Marinade:

   Cornstarch   2 teaspoons
   Soy Sauce   2 teaspoons
   Dry Sherry   2 teaspoons

Bamboo Shoots   1 6-ounce/180 g can
   Scallions   5, in 2-inch/5-cm sections
Hoisin Sauce   2 level tablespoons
   Soy Sauce   1 tablespoon or to taste
Cooking Oil   3 tablespoons

AHEAD OF TIME:

Partially defrost *frozen pork* just long enough to slice following these directions:

   20 minutes or more to partially thaw meat at room temperature
   10 minutes or more to partially thaw meat in a 250°F/120°C oven
   35 seconds or more to partially thaw meat in a microwave oven

PREPARATION: 12 minutes

COOKING: 7 minutes

Preparation:

1. With *Medium Slicing Disk* in place, first slice the pork, then reprocess quickly to get shreds. (To slice and shred by hand see page 14.) Transfer to a bowl, and mix thoroughly with the marinade.

2. Replace the *Medium Slicing Disk,* and fit the bamboo shoots in the feed tube. Slice first, then reprocess to get shreds. (To slice and shred by hand see page 14.) Transfer to a bowl.

3. If you have a *Fine Slicing Disk,* lay the scallion sections horizontally in the feed tube, and process to get fine shreds; or, shred them by hand.

4. Mix hoisin sauce and soy sauce in a bowl. §

Have Ready Before Cooking:
1. Bottle of cooking oil
2. Bowl with pork shreds
3. Bowl with bamboo shoots
4. Bowl with shredded scallions
5. Bowl with hoisin and soy sauce
6. Serving platter

Cooking:

1. Heat wok over high heat, then heat 2 tablespoons oil. Stir-fry pork shreds quickly until meat loses its pink color. Remove from the wok.

2. In the same wok, heat 1 tablespoon oil. Cook and stir the bamboo shoots for 2 minutes or until hot.

3. Return pork to the wok, then add scallion shreds, and hoisin and soy sauce mixture. Stir quickly until everything is evenly mixed. Transfer to the serving platter, and serve. §

Tip:

This dish can be cooked ahead and rewarmed, leaving the scallions out, and adding them while reheating.

Variations:

1. Shredded lamb or beef can be used in place of pork.

2. Fresh green pepper shreds can be used in place of the bamboo shoots. However, pepper will not rewarm well.

SPICY BEAN CURD WITH MINCED PORK

麻婆豆腐   Ma-po-dou-fu

Serves 2 ‡

This well-known and hearty dish is one of our favorite ways of cooking bean curd. The Chinese name literally means "Old Pockmarked Lady's Bean Curd." People say the wife of a restaurant owner in Szechuan created this dish over a century ago.

Bean curd is made from soy beans. It is high in protein, but low in fat, calories, and cholesterol! It is a very important source of protein for Oriental nations. Since it is very inexpensive there, it is known as the poor man's meat. Bean curd is soft and bland in taste, but easily adapts to flavors and seasonings. Old or young, rich or poor, every Chinese likes it.

Fresh Bean Curd	1 pound/450 g (or 4 3 × 3 × ¾-inch/8 × 8 × 2-cm pieces)
Scallion	1
Garlic	2 large cloves
Salted Black Beans	2 tablespoons, rinsed briefly and drained
Boneless Pork	¼ pound/115 g, in 1-inch/2½-cm cubes

Sauce Mixture:

Brown Bean Sauce	1 level tablespoon
(*or* Soy Sauce)	(1 tablespoon or to taste)
Dry Sherry	1 tablespoon
Chicken Broth	½ cup/1 dL
Cornstarch	1 tablespoon in 2 tablespoons water
Hot Dry Red Peppers	1 or 2, broken into half and seeded
(*or* Crushed Red Pepper Flakes)	(¼ to ½ teaspoon)
Cooking Oil	2 tablespoons
Sesame Oil	2 teaspoons (optional)

AHEAD OF TIME:

If *frozen pork cubes* are used, thaw partially or completely following these directions:

20 minutes or more to partially thaw meat at room temperature
10 minutes or more to partially thaw meat in a 250°F/120°C oven
30 seconds or more to completely thaw meat in a microwave oven

PREPARATION: 10 minutes

COOKING: 8 minutes

Preparation:

1. Cut bean curd into 1-inch/2½-cm cubes, and leave them in a colander to drain.

2. Scallion is used here for garnishing. It looks nicer if cut by hand into ¹/₁₆-inch/¼-cm slices. However, you could chop it with the *Steel Blade.* Cut scallion into 1½-inch/4-cm sections, and process. Transfer to a small bowl.

3. With *Steel Blade* in place, start the machine, and drop garlic through the feed tube. Process until finely chopped. Add salted black beans to the beaker, and process with 3 quick on/off turns. (To chop by hand see page 14.) Transfer the black beans and garlic to a small bowl.

4. Replace the *Steel Blade,* and with quick on/off turns, coarsely chop the pork. (To chop by hand see page 14.) Transfer to a bowl.

5. Combine the sauce mixture in a bowl.

6. Combine the cornstarch mixture in a bowl. §

Have Ready Before Cooking:
1. Bottle of cooking oil
2. Hot dry peppers or pepper flakes
3. Bowl with garlic and black beans
4. Bowl with ground pork
5. Bowl with sauce mixture
6. Bean curd
7. Bowl with cornstarch mixture
8. Sesame oil, 2 teaspoons (optional)
9. Bowl with chopped scallions
10. Serving platter

Cooking:

1. Heat 2 tablespoons oil in a wok over medium-high heat. Fry hot dry peppers or pepper flakes for 30 seconds or until brown. Add garlic and black beans, and cook for 30 seconds. Add the chopped pork, stirring until pork loses its pink color.

2. Add sauce mixture to the wok, and bring to a boil. Add bean curd and stir gently, for it will break easily. Simmer with the cover on for 2 to 3 minutes or until the bean curd is piping hot.

3. Give the cornstarch mixture a good stir, and add slowly to the wok, stirring gently until the sauce is thickened.

4. Add sesame oil (optional), stir lightly to mix. Transfer the bean curd to a serving bowl, and garnish with chopped scallion. It is delicious with plain boiled rice. §

Tips:

The dish can be cooked ahead, but add sesame oil and scallions at the last minute, when it is reheated.

Variations:

1. This dish is quite spicy, but if you are afraid of spicy food, you can omit the hot peppers. It is also very tasty without the hot spice.

2. Beef can be used in place of pork.

PEARL BALLS ★

珍珠丸子   Zhen-zhu-wan-zi

Makes 24 ‡

These luscious meat balls are coated with glutinous rice, which turns translucent after cooking, resembling the color of pearls.

They can be served as a main course for the Chinese meal, or as appetizers, Western style. As a single main dish for three persons, serve with a soup and a vegetable salad.

Glutinous Rice	¾ cup/1¾ dL
Fresh Ginger	½-inch/1½-cm cube
Scallion	1, in 1½-inch/4-cm sections
Water Chestnuts	8
Boneless Pork	1 pound, in 1-inch/2½-cm cubes
Soy Sauce	1 tablespoon
Salt	1¼ teaspoons or to taste
Cornstarch	1 tablespoon
Egg	1

AHEAD OF TIME:

1. Soak the rice in cold water for at least 2 hours with about 1½ inches/4 cm of water above the rice.

2. If *frozen pork cubes* are used, thaw partially or completely following these directions:

20 minutes or more to partially thaw meat at room temperature

10 minutes or more to partially thaw meat in a 250°F/120°C oven

1½ minutes or more to completely thaw meat in a microwave oven

PREPARATION: 25 minutes

STEAMING: 20 minutes

Preparation:

1. With *Steel Blade* in place, chop ginger and scallion until finely minced. Add water chestnuts to the beaker, and chop with 2 quick on/off turns.

2. Add pork cubes and chop with 4 quick on/off turns. Add the remaining 4 ingredients, and process until pork is finely chopped. (To prepare by hand see page 14.)

3. Drain the soaked rice through a sieve just before using, and transfer to a bowl.

4. Make pork mixture into walnut-sized balls, then roll one meat ball at a time in the rice. Roll it again between your palms, so the rice will adhere to the meat. Repeat the process with the remaining pork mixture.

5. Arrange the balls on a lightly oiled heat-proof platter at least 1 inch/2½-cm smaller than the steamer. There should be a ½-inch/1½-cm space between the meat balls. Use 2 plates if necessary. Rice will dry out, so *steam* the balls *right after rolling*.

Steaming:

To save time, set up the steamer, and bring the water to boil while you are shaping the balls. Set the plate on the rack, and steam on medium heat for 20 minutes. Serve hot. They can be cooked ahead and resteamed. §

Tip:

The cooked pearl balls can be kept in the refrigerator for several days. For freezing, spread the cooked balls on a lightly oiled tray until they are frozen. Then store them in an air-tight plastic container in the freezer.

Variation:

If you cannot get glutinous rice (available in Oriental food stores), substitute the short or medium grain rice from the supermarkets. Glutinous rice gives a softer and more sticky texture.

SWEET AND SOUR MEAT BALLS

甜酸丸子   Tian-suan-wan-zi

Serves 3 ‡

If you love the well-known Sweet and Sour Pork, then you will also like this Northern dish. The meat balls have an advantage over the Sweet and Sour Pork, for they can be cooked ahead and in large quantities. Hence, they are good for parties, and can be kept warm in a chafing dish or on a hot tray. For a simple family meal, they are delicious with plain boiled rice, and a broccoli or cucumber salad is all you need to complete your meal.

Pork Mixture:

Fresh Ginger	2 ½-inch/1½-cm cubes
Scallions	2, cut into 2-inch/5-cm sections
Water Chestnuts	8
Boneless Pork	1 pound/450 g, in 1-inch/2½-cm cubes
Soy Sauce	1 tablespoon
Dry Sherry	1 tablespoon
Cornstarch	1 tablespoon
Egg	1
Sesame Oil	2 teaspoons (optional)

Sweet Bell Peppers	2 (1 red and 1 green, or 2 green)
Pineapple Chunks	1 cup/¼ L well drained
Garlic	1 clove, crushed
Ginger	1 slice
Cooking Oil	½ cup/1 dL

Sauce Ingredients:

Water	¾ cup/1¾ dL
Sugar	¼ cup/½ dL or to taste
Wine Vinegar	2 tablespoons or to taste
Ketchup	2 tablespoons
Soy Sauce	1 tablespoon
Salt	½ teaspoon or to taste
Cornstarch	4 teaspoons in 2 tablespoons water

AHEAD OF TIME:

If *frozen pork cubes* are used, thaw partially or completely following these directions:

      20 minutes or more to partially thaw meat at room temperature

      10 minutes or more to partially thaw meat in a 250°F/120°C oven

      1½ minutes or more to completely thaw meat in a microwave oven

PREPARATION: 16 minutes

COOKING: 20 minutes

Preparation:

1. With *Steel Blade* in a dry beaker, process ginger until finely minced. Add scallions and process until coarsely chopped. Then add water chestnuts, and give 2 on/off turns. Add pork cubes and process with 3 quick on/off turns. Add the remaining 5 ingredients for the pork mixture; process until the pork is evenly chopped. (To prepare by hand see page 14.) Using wet hands, shape the mixture into 24 walnut-sized balls.

2. Wash and cut bell peppers into ¾-inch/2-cm cubes.

3. Drain the pineapple in a colander.

4. Crush and peel garlic, and place it with ginger.

5. Have the sauce ingredients within reach near the stove. Mix the cornstarch with water in a small bowl. §

Cooking:

1. Heat ½ cup/1 dL oil in a wok (or fill a saucepan with ½-inch/1½-cm oil) to 350°F/180°C. Fry the meat balls in 2 batches, turning once, for about 3 minutes or until they are golden brown. §

2. Remove oil, then clean and dry the wok. Heat 1 tablespoon oil in the wok over medium heat, fry garlic and ginger for 1 minute. Add peppers and stir-fry for 2 minutes. Remove the vegetables and discard garlic and ginger. This can be done half a day ahead. §

3. Add sauce ingredients, except the cornstarch mixture, to the wok. Bring them to a boil. Give the cornstarch mixture a good stir, and slowly pour into the hot sauce, stirring constantly until the sauce is thickened. The sauce can also be made half a day ahead. §

4. Add the meat balls to the hot bubbling sauce; cook with cover on for 1 or 2 minutes or until the meat balls are heated through. Add bell peppers and the well drained pineapples to the wok, and bring the sauce back to a boil. Serve immediately.

Tips:

The fried meat balls can be made ahead, and can be kept in the refrigerator for several days. They can also be frozen for many weeks.

Just before serving, rewarm the meat balls in a 350°F/180°C oven or a microwave oven. The sweet and sour sauce and the peppers can be made a half day ahead, but don't combine them until the last minute. (The vinegar in the sauce will discolor the peppers over a prolonged period.)

When the meat balls are hot, reheat the sweet and sour sauce. Then add the meat balls, peppers, and the drained pineapples to the sauce, and bring them to a boil. Serve immediately.

Or you can combine the cold meat balls, sauce, and vegetables (just before serving) in a microwave-oven-proof dish, and heat the whole dish together in a microwave oven. It only takes a few minutes.

Variation:

You may substitute fresh snow peas for the bell pepper. Or add sliced water chestnuts, and sliced bamboo shoots.

LION'S HEAD ★ (Large Pork Balls With Cabbage in Casserole)

獅子頭   Shi-zi-tou

Serves 3 ‡

Since the lion is the king of the jungle, the Chinese people have named this dish for the giant size of the meat balls, with the cabbage supplying the lion's mane, so to say. It is a famous dish from the Eastern region and a very popular family dish, for it can be prepared several days ahead. (Just reheat to serve.)

Chinese gourmets rate this dish by the lightness of the texture of the meat balls. Traditionally, the light texture is achieved by adding a significant amount of pork fat to the pork mixture. In our cholesterol-conscious society, I have found that by adding some water chestnuts, and chopping them together with the pork and seasonings in a processor, you can achieve a tender texture without using the pork fat.

Meat Ball Mixture:

Fresh Ginger	½-inch/1½-cm cube
Boneless Pork	1 pound/450 g in 1-inch/2½-cm cubes
Scallions	2, cut into 2-inch/5-cm sections
Water Chestnuts	8
Salt	¾ teaspoon or to taste
Cornstarch	1 tablespoon
Water	3 tablespoons
Soy Sauce	4 teaspoons
Dry Sherry	1 tablespoon
Egg	1

<pre>
        Bok Choy   1½ pounds/675 g
(or Celery Cabbage)
        Cooking Oil   3 tablespoons
          Soy Sauce   1 tablespoon or to taste
              Sugar   1 teaspoon
          Dry Sherry   1 tablespoon
</pre>

AHEAD OF TIME:

If *frozen pork cubes* are used, thaw partially or completely following these directions:

20 minutes or more to partially thaw meat at room temperature

10 minutes or more to partially thaw meat in a 250°F/120°C oven

1½ minutes or more to completely thaw meat in a microwave oven

PREPARATION: 15 minutes

COOKING: 45 minutes

Preparation:

1. With *Steel Blade* in place, process ginger in a dry beaker until finely minced. Add pork, scallions, and water chestnuts to the beaker, and chop with 7 quick on/off turns. Then add the remaining 6 ingredients for the meat ball mixture, processing until finely chopped. (To chop by hand see page 14.) Remove beaker from the processor, and shape the mixture into 4 large meat balls with wet hands.

2. Wash and remove all the sandy particles from bok choy or cabbage. Cut crosswise into 2-inch/5-cm sections. §

Cooking:

1. Heat 3 tablespoons oil in a wok. Fry 2 meat balls at a time until both sides are browned (about 3 minutes). Remove and fry the other two meat balls. (Use more oil if frying in a saucepan.)

2. Remove all but 2 tablespoons oil in the wok, stir-frying vegetables for 1 to 2 minutes over medium heat. Remove wok from the heat.

3. Line the stems of the vegetable in the bottom of a casserole. Place the meat balls on top, then cover with the leaves of the vegetable.

4. Add 1 tablespoon soy sauce or to taste, 1 teaspoon sugar, and 1 tablespoon sherry; bring to a boil, then simmer on low heat with cover on for 30 minutes. Serve hot. §

Variation:

½ to 1 cup/1 dL to ¼ L crab meat can be added to the processed pork mixture for more flavor; add salt to taste.

STUFFED GREEN PEPPERS

釀青椒   Rang-qing-jiao

Serves 3 to 4 ‡

The dried mushrooms and shrimp impart a subtle and delicate flavor to the stuffing. Contrasting with the robust and spicy sauce, it is an example of the Chinese genius for seasoning and flavoring dishes to produce a separate, distinct taste in a single dish. A homely stuffed pepper dish is turned into an epicurean delight.

Pork Mixture:

Dried Chinese Mushrooms	3 large
Dried Shrimp	3 tablespoons
Boneless Pork	¾ pound/340 g in 1-inch/2½-cm cubes
Water Chestnuts	6
Egg White	1
Dry Sherry	3 tablespoons
Soy Sauce	1½ tablespoons
Salt	½ teaspoon or to taste
Sugar	1½ teaspoons

Seasoning Mixture:

Fresh Ginger	½-inch/1½-cm cube
Scallion	1
Salted Black Beans	1 tablespoon
Crushed Red Pepper Flakes	¼ teaspoon or to taste
(*or* Hot Dry Red Pepper)	(1)

Sauce Mixture:

Chicken Broth	1 cup/¼ L
Hoisin Sauce	1 tablespoon
Soy Sauce	2 tablespoons or to taste
Dry Sherry	1 tablespoon
Sugar	2 teaspoons
Cornstarch	4 teaspoons in 3 tablespoons water
Green Bell Peppers	4 small, about 2 inches long
Cornstarch	1 tablespoon or more for dusting
Cooking Oil	2 tablespoons
Sesame Oil	1 tablespoon (optional)

AHEAD OF TIME:

1. Snap the stems off the Chinese mushrooms. Put the mushrooms and shrimp into separate bowls and cover with boiling water. Soak for 20 minutes.

2. If *frozen pork cubes* are used, thaw partially or completely following these directions:

> 20 minutes or more to partially thaw meat at room temperature
> 10 minutes or more to partially thaw meat in a 250°F/120°C oven
> 1 minute or more to completely thaw meat in a microwave oven

PREPARATION: 30 minutes

COOKING: 15 minutes

Preparation:

1. Chop the seasoning mixture with *Steel Blade:* Finely mince ginger first, then chop scallion. Briefly rinse the black beans and drain well. Add to the beaker, chop with 3 quick on/off turns. (To chop and mince by hand see page 14.) Transfer the ginger, scallion, and black beans to a bowl, and top them with crushed red pepper flakes.

2. Drain the softened shrimp and mushrooms.

3. With *Steel Blade* in place, process pork mixture by coarsely chopping pork cubes and mushrooms first. Then add the shrimp and remaining ingredients to the beaker. Chop until finely minced. (To chop by hand see page 14.)

4. Mix sauce ingredients in a bowl.

5. Mix 4 teaspoons cornstarch in 3 tablespoons water.

6. Cut the tops off the green peppers, and remove the seeds. Cut each pepper lengthwise into 4 sections about 1½ inches/4 cm wide and 2 inches/5 cm long.

7. Dust the inside of the green peppers with 1 tablespoon or more cornstarch, so the stuffing will adhere.

8. Divide the pork mixture into 16 portions. Spread and mount them on the pepper strips.

9. Lightly oil a heat-proof platter or a 10-inch/25-cm Pyrex pie plate. Place stuffed peppers on the plate with the meat side down. §

Steaming and Cooking:

1. If you are cooking the stuffed peppers right after the preparation, preheat the steamer while you are doing the preparations, for this will save you time.

2. Steam the stuffed peppers over boiling water on medium-high heat for 10 minutes or until the meat is cooked.

3. 4 minutes before the peppers are done, heat 2 tablespoons oil in the wok. Fry the ginger, scallion, black beans, and red pepper for 30 seconds. Add sauce mixture, and bring to a boil. Give the cornstarch mixture a

good stir, gradually add it to the sauce, and stir constantly until the sauce is thickened. Add the sesame oil.

4. Transfer the cooked stuffed peppers to a serving platter (without the liquid), pour the sauce over them, and serve. §

Tips:

The dish can be made ahead. It is best reheated by the microwave oven. Peppers tend to lose their crisp texture when reheated on a stove top, so do not overheat, or cook them less the first time. Cornstarch may lose its thickening power in the sauce from long standing. If this happens, just thicken the sauce with more of the cornstarch mixture.

Variation:

You may omit the hot pepper flakes, if you don't want the dish spicy; the sauce is still delicious.

STUFFED CABBAGE ROLLS ★

菜心包肉   Cai-xin-bao-rou

Serves 3 ‡

Round Cabbage Leaves	8 large or 16 small
Meat Mixture:	
Fresh Ginger	½-inch/1½-cm cube
Scallions	2, in 2-inch/5-cm sections
Water Chestnuts	4 large or 6 small
Boneless Pork	¾ pound/340 g, in 1-inch/2½-cm cubes
Salt	½ teaspoon
Soy Sauce	1 tablespoon
Dry Sherry	1 tablespoon
Cornstarch	1 tablespoon
Sauce Ingredients:	
Broth (from the steamed cabbage rolls) and Chicken Broth	1 cup/¼ L (combine to get 1 cup/¼ L)
Oyster-Flavored Sauce (*or* Soy Sauce)	1 tablespoon (to taste)
Soy Sauce	1½ teaspoons or to taste
Sugar	½ teaspoon
Cornstarch	1 tablespoon in 2 tablespoons water

AHEAD OF TIME:

If *frozen pork cubes* are used, thaw partially or completely following these directions:

>20 minutes or more to partially thaw meat at room temperature
>10 minutes or more to partially thaw meat in a 250°F/120°C oven
>1 minute or more to completely thaw meat in a microwave oven

PREPARATION: 30 minutes

COOKING: 30 minutes

Preparation:

1. Put cabbage leaves in a large pot of boiling water with 1 teaspoon of salt, and simmer for 5 minutes. Immediately drain in a colander.

2. With *Steel Blade* in a dry beaker, process ginger until finely minced. Add scallions, and process until coarsely chopped. Then add water chestnuts and pork cubes, and process with 3 quick on/off turns. Add the remaining 4 ingredients for the meat mixture. Process until meat is finely chopped. (To chop by hand see page 14.)

3. Cut a large cabbage leaf into halves along the stem, and remove the hard stem. Use the small cabbage leaf whole, but cut off the hard base.

4. Divide the meat mixture into 16 portions, or place 1 heaping tablespoon mixture at one end of a cabbage leaf. Roll and wrap the two sides inward into an oblong roll. Repeat with the other leaves.

5. Place the rolls seam side down on a heat-proof dish at least 1 inch/2½ cm smaller than the steamer. §

Cooking:

1. Place the cabbage roll dish on the steamer rack, and bring the water in the steamer to a rolling boil. Steam the cabbage rolls over medium-high heat for 15 minutes. § .

2. Pour out and save all the broth that has collected in the cabbage roll dish. Add enough chicken broth to make 1 cup/¼ L, then mix with oyster sauce, soy, and sugar. Heat to a boil. Give the cornstarch mixture a good stir, pour slowly into the sauce, stirring constantly until the sauce is thickened and turns translucent. Pour over the cabbage rolls and serve. §

Tip:

Cooked cabbage rolls can be refrigerated or frozen, and reheated with the sauce, over the stove top or by the microwave oven. You may have to thicken the sauce again with more of the cornstarch mixture.

STEAMED PORK PATTY ★

清蒸肉餅   Qing-zheng-rou-bing

Serves 3 ‡

This is a typical Chinese family dish. It can be made ahead and reheated, so it is a handy dish to have when you plan to serve several dishes at one meal. As a single main course, serve with boiled rice and stir-fry broccoli or a vegetable salad. You can prepare the vegetables while the meat is being steamed.

There are many varieties produced by using additional ingredients on top of the patty. The texture of the patty is sort of like a Western meat loaf, but the patty is more delicate in flavor.

Fresh Ginger	2 ½-inch/1½-cm cubes
Scallion	1, cut in 1-inch/2½-cm sections
Boneless Pork	1 pound/450 g, in 1-inch/2½-cm cubes
Egg White	1
Cornstarch	2 teaspoons
Dry Sherry	1 tablespoon
Soy Sauce	2 tablespoons
Salt	½ teaspoon or to taste

AHEAD OF TIME:

If *frozen pork cubes* are used, thaw partially or completely following these directions:

20 minutes or more to partially thaw meat at room temperature

10 minutes or more to partially thaw meat in a 250°F/120°C oven

1½ minutes or more to completely thaw meat in a microwave oven

PREPARATION: 6 minutes

STEAMING: 15 minutes

Preparation:

1. With *Steel Blade* in place, process ginger in dry beaker until finely minced. Add scallion and pork cubes, and process with 4 quick on/off turns. Add the remaining 5 ingredients, and process with quick on/off turns until pork is finely chopped. Do not over process. (To chop by hand see page 14.)

2. Transfer the mixture to a serving bowl or 8-inch/20-cm pie plate at least 1 inch/2½ cm smaller in diameter than the steamer.

Flatten and smooth the surface evenly. Uncooked meat patty can be kept in the refrigerator for half a day before steaming. §

Steaming:

To save time, you can set up the steamer and bring the water to boiling while preparing the meat mixture.

Place the pork dish on the steamer rack, then cover and steam over medium-high heat for 15 minutes or until pork is cooked. §

Tips:

The cooked meat patty is best tasting when freshly cooked, but it can be kept in the refrigerator for 3 to 4 days.

The dish will collect excess water from oversteaming, thus diluting the flavor of the meat patty. So it is better not to oversteam when rewarming. Steam the meat patty for 8 to 10 minutes or until heated through. It can also be rewarmed covered in a microwave oven for about 4 minutes.

The cooked meat patty can be kept warm covered on a hot tray or in a warm oven.

STEAMED PORK PATTY WITH CHINESE SAUSAGES

臘腸蒸肉餅   La-chang-zheng-rou-bing

Serves 2 to 3 ‡

The Chinese pork sausage has a delicate sweet flavor. It enhances the flavor of the meat patty. As a single main course, serve with boiled rice and stir-fried zucchini or with a vegetable salad.

Fresh Ginger	½-inch/1½-cm cube
Boneless Pork	¾ pound/340 g, in 1-inch/2½-cm cubes
Egg White	1
Soy Sauce	2½ tablespoons or to taste
Cornstarch	2 teaspoons
Sugar	¼ teaspoon
Dry Sherry	1 tablespoon
Scallions	2, cut into 1-inch/2½-cm sections
Chinese Sausages	1 to 2

AHEAD OF TIME:

If *frozen pork cubes* are used, thaw partially or completely following these directions:

20 minutes or more to partially thaw meat at room temperature
10 minutes or more to partially thaw meat in a 250°F/120°C oven
1 minute or more to completely thaw meat in a microwave oven

PREPARATION: 10 minutes

STEAMING: 15 minutes

Preparation:

1. With *Steel Blade* in place, process ginger in a dry beaker until finely minced. Add pork cubes, and process with 3 quick on/off turns. Then add the remaining ingredients except the Chinese sausages to the beaker, and process with quick on/off turns until pork is finely chopped. (To chop by hand see page 14.)

2. Transfer the mixture to an 8-inch/20-cm pie plate or a shallow serving bowl at least 1 inch/2½-cm smaller in diameter than the steamer. Flatten and smooth out the surface.

3. Chinese sausages look prettier if they are sliced diagonally into ⅛-inch/½-cm slices. (This is best done by hand.) Then arrange the slices on top of the pork mixture. Uncooked meat patty can be kept in the refrigerator for half a day before steaming. §

Steaming:

To save cooking time, you can set up the steamer and bring the water to boiling while preparing the meat mixture.

Place the pork dish on the steamer rack, then cover and steam over boiling water on medium-high heat for 15 minutes or until the pork is cooked. §

Tips:

The cooked meat patty can be kept warm covered on a hottray or in a warm oven.

The dish is best tasting when freshly cooked, but it can be kept in the refrigerator for 3 to 4 days.

Excess water may be collected in the dish from oversteaming, thus diluting the flavor of the meat patty, so it is better not to oversteam when rewarming. Steam the cooked meat patty for 8 to 10 minutes or until heated through. It can also be rewarmed covered in a microwave oven for about 4 minutes.

STEAMED PORK PATTY WITH SALTED DUCK EGG

鹹蛋蒸肉餅   Xian-dan-zheng-rou-bing

Serves 3 to 4 ‡

This is a variation from the plain steamed pork patty. The salted egg is duck egg preserved in brine. In the old days before refrigeration, the Chinese invented this method for preserving eggs, a method which is still very much in use in this modern age. Use the egg sparingly, since it's quite salty. It enhances the flavor of pork and stimulates the appetite.

As a single main course, serve with boiled rice and a vegetable salad (Radish or Sweet and Sour Cucumber Salad).

Fresh Ginger	2 ½-inch/1½-cm cubes
Boneless Pork	1 pound/450 g, in 1-inch/2½-cm cubes
Scallions	2, cut in 1-inch/2½-cm sections
Cornstarch	2 teaspoons
Dry Sherry	2 teaspoons
Soy Sauce	2 tablespoons or to taste
Egg White	1
Salted Duck Eggs	2 (available in Chinese food stores)

AHEAD OF TIME:

If *frozen pork cubes* are used, thaw partially or completely following these directions:

20 minutes or more to partially thaw meat at room temperature

10 minutes or more to partially thaw meat in a 250°F/120°C oven

1½ minutes or more to completely thaw meat in a microwave oven

PREPARATION: 10 minutes

STEAMING: 20 minutes

Preparation:

1. With *Steel Blade* in place, process ginger in a dry beaker until finely minced. Add pork cubes and scallions, and process with 3 quick on/off turns. Then add cornstarch, sherry, soy sauce, and egg whites, and process with quick on/off turns until the pork is finely chopped. (To mince and chop by hand see page 14.)

2. Transfer the mixture to an 8-inch/20-cm pie plate or a shallow serving bowl at least 1 inch/2½-cm smaller in diameter than the steamer. Flatten and smooth out the surface.

3. Rinse out all the black mud-like coating from the salted eggs, and wash until the shell is thoroughly clean. Crack them open and pour the

white and yolk on top of the pork patty. Be sure to have the white of the egg spread all over the patty, and arrange the yolk symmetrically in position. (Salted egg yolk is not soft like fresh egg yolk.) Uncooked meat patty can be kept in the refrigerator for half a day before steaming. §

Steaming:

Place the pork dish on the steamer rack over boiling water, cover and steam on medium-high heat for 20 minutes or until pork is cooked. Can be cooked ahead. §

(To save cooking time, you can set up the steamer and bring the water to boiling while the meat mixture is being prepared.)

Tips:

The cooked meat patty can be kept warm covered on a hot tray or in a warm oven. It can be kept in the refrigerator for 3 to 4 days.

Excess water may be collected in the dish from oversteaming, thus diluting the flavor of the meat patty, so it is better not to oversteam when rewarming. Steam the cooked meat patty for 8 to 10 minutes or until heated through. It can also be rewarmed covered in a microwave oven for about 4 minutes.

Chicken
and Egg Dishes

Chicken is high in protein, but low in cholesterol, and has a delicate flavor. But above all, it is the best buy among meat and poultry in the United States.

It is a common and popular food in China, and many families, especially in rural areas, raise their own chickens. Chicken parts are not sold in the markets. Most people buy a live chicken, and then kill it at home.

No parts of a chicken ever go to waste. The blood is saved and congealed into a smooth custard-like jelly, then cut up into small cubes and used as an ingredient in soup. The liver, giblet, heart, feet, and wings are used in making soup, or braised to serve as another dish—often a delicacy. Bones are saved for making basic stocks.

Chicken can be cooked whole, or in parts with or without the bones by braising, steaming, deep-frying, stir-frying, or roasting. There are infinite ways of cooking chicken with a variety of Chinese seasonings.

This book, of course, only serves dishes that can be used with the food processor. Only chicken breasts are used, as they are easier for processing (the legs and drumsticks have more gristle), and they look much more elegant in the stir-fried dishes in the recipes. Furthermore, chicken breast has less fat than the dark meat—a plus health factor in using them.

SLICED CHICKEN WITH CELERY

芹菜雞片   Qin-cai-ji-pian

Serves 2

This is a simple, basic stir-fried dish, and a good dish for beginners, or for people who just want a quick meal. Once you know how to cook this dish, you can vary the fresh vegetables, or use whatever you may have on hand to create other dishes. Chicken breast is considered a delicate food by the Chinese, therefore, many stir-fried chicken dishes are seasoned with salt rather than soy sauce to bring out their delicate and natural flavor.

By cooking the food quickly, it never overcooks, so the vegetables stay crisp and the chicken stays moist and tender. A delicious dish is created by using the most basic ingredients and only salt for seasoning—demonstrating the merit of stir-fried cooking.

You can double the recipe, and cook in one batch.

Chicken Breast	1 large, whole, boneless, skinless, and frozen (8 ounces/225 g)

Marinade:

Dry Sherry	1 tablespoon
Cornstarch	1 teaspoon
Salt	½ teaspoon or to taste

Hearts of Celery	½ pound/225 g (tender stalks are better)
Salt	¼ teaspoon or to taste
Cooking Oil	4 tablespoons

AHEAD OF TIME:
Partially defrost *frozen chicken* just long enough to slice following these directions:

20 minutes or more to partially thaw meat at room temperature
5 minutes or more to partially thaw meat in a 250°F/120°C oven
35 seconds or more to partially thaw meat in a microwave oven

PREPARATION: 10 minutes

COOKING: 5 minutes

Preparation:

1. Cut chicken breast crosswise into halves. With *Medium Slicing Disk* in place, pack and place the breasts cut side down in the feed tube and slice. (To slice by hand see page 14.) Mix them thoroughly with marinade in a bowl.

2. Wash the celery thoroughly, and peel off outer layer with a potato peeler to remove tough strings.

3. Cut off the root ends, then cut stalks in lengths so that they are shorter than the feed tube. Wedge them tightly and vertically in the feed tube and slice with the *Medium Slicing Disk.* (To slice by hand see page 14.) §

Have Ready Before Cooking:
1. Bottle of cooking oil
2. ¼ teaspoon salt or to taste
3. Celery
4. Bowl with chicken
5. Serving platter

Cooking:

1. Heat the wok, then heat 1 tablespoon oil over medium-high heat. Add salt and celery, and stir-fry for 2 minutes. Remove from the wok.

2. Heat the wok until very hot, and add 3 tablespoons oil. Heat until hot and add the chicken. Stir and separate the chicken until chicken just turns white, 1 to 2 minutes.

3. Return the celery and mix thoroughly with the chicken. Transfer to the serving platter and serve immediately.

Variations:

SLICED CHICKEN WITH SNOW PEAS
雪豆雞片 Xue-dou-ji-pian

Substitute 4 ounces/115 g of fresh snow peas or 1 package frozen snow peas for celery. Wash and remove strings from fresh snow peas before cooking. (This is not necessary if you are using the frozen ones.)

SLICED CHICKEN WITH FRESH ASPARAGUS
蘆筍雞片 Lu-sun-ji-pian

Substitute ½ pound/225 g fresh asparagus for celery. Wash asparagus and break off tough ends. Cut stalks into 1½-inch/4-cm sections. With *Medium Slicing Disk* in place, pack them horizontally in the feed tube and slice. (To slice by hand see page 14.)

SLICED CHICKEN WITH GREEN PEPPER

青椒雞片 Qing-jiao-ji-pian

Substitute 1 large green pepper for celery. Seed the pepper and cut into 1½ × ½-inch/4 × 1½-cm strips.

SLICED CHICKEN IN HOISIN SAUCE

京醬雞片 Jing-jiang-ji-pian

This is a variation in the seasoning, using Hoisin sauce in the Northern style. You can buy any one of the vegetables suggested above. Omit the salt that is used to season and cook with the vegetables. Add 1 tablespoon sugar and 3 level tablespoons Hoisin sauce in cooking step 3. Stir and mix the sauce thoroughly with the chicken and vegetables, then serve immediately.

STIR-FRIED CHICKEN SHREDS WITH GREEN PEPPER

青椒雞絲 Qing-jiao-ji-si

This is a classic dish from the Eastern region. The variation is in the method of cutting. Chicken is shredded instead of sliced, so here the vegetables should be shredded also. You can use any one of the vegetables suggested for the sliced chicken dishes in place of the green pepper.

The processor is marvelous for shredding peppers, since it shreds them so evenly and thinner than you could do by hand, finishing in seconds.

To shred green pepper, cut ends off. Remove seeds and membranes. Cut lengthwise into 1½-inch/4-cm sections. With *Medium Slicing Disk* in place, wedge the pepper vertically in the feed tube and slice. (To shred by hand see page 14.)

To shred chicken, after the partially frozen chicken is sliced, quickly remove the still partially frozen slices from the beaker. Reprocess with the *Medium Slicing Disk* to get julienne strips. (To slice and shred by hand see page 14.)

Mix chicken shreds with the marinade, and follow the cooking procedure for Sliced Chicken With Celery.

For additional color and flavor, you can add ¼ cup/½ dL finely shredded, cooked Smithfield ham near the end of the cooking period.

CHICKEN WITH MUSHROOMS

磨菇雞片   Mo-gu-ji-pian

Serves 2

The Cantonese pronunciation of this dish is Moo Goo Gai Pan. Moo Goo is the phonetic translation of button mushrooms, and Gai Pan is chicken slices.

Chicken Breast	1 boneless, skinless, and frozen (8 ounces/225 g)

Marinade:

Cornstarch	1 teaspoon
Salt	½ teaspoon
Dry Sherry	2 teaspoons
Fresh Mushrooms	¼ pound/115 g
Water Chestnuts	8
Fresh Snow Peas	2 ounces/60 g
(*or* half a package defrosted Frozen Snow Peas)	
Garlic	1 clove, peeled and crushed

Sauce Ingredients:

Chicken Broth	¼ cup/½ dL
Soy Sauce	1 tablespoon
Dry Sherry	1 tablespoon
Sugar	½ teaspoon
Cornstarch	1½ teaspoons
Cooking Oil	4 tablespoons

AHEAD OF TIME:
Partially defrost *frozen chicken* just long enough to slice following these directions:

20 minutes or more to partially thaw meat at room temperature
5 minutes or more to partially thaw meat in a 250°F/120°C oven
35 seconds or more to partially thaw meat in a microwave oven

PREPARATION: 17 minutes

COOKING: 6 minutes

Preparation:

1. Cut partially frozen chicken breast crosswise into halves. Pack the breasts cut side down in the feed tube, and slice with *Medium Slicing Disk.* (To slice by hand see page 14.) Mix chicken with the marinade.

2. Replace the *Medium Slicing Disk.* Slice mushrooms, then water chestnuts. (To slice by hand see page 14.) Remove the ends and strings of fresh snow peas. Place all the vegetables in the same bowl with crushed garlic on top.

3. Combine the sauce ingredients. §

Have Ready Before Cooking:

1. Bottle of cooking oil
2. Bowl with chicken
3. Bowl with vegetables
4. Bowl with sauce ingredients
5. Serving platter

Cooking:

1. Heat the wok on high heat until very hot. Add 3 tablespoons oil, and heat until oil is hot. Add chicken, stirring constantly until chicken just turns white, about 2 minutes. Remove from the wok.

2. Heat 1 tablespoon oil over medium heat. Fry garlic, and discard when it turns golden.

3. Add vegetables to the garlic-flavored oil, stirring over medium-high heat for 2 to 3 minutes. Return chicken to the wok, and turn heat to high, stirring to mix.

4. Give the sauce mixture a good stir and pour into the wok, stirring to mix until the sauce becomes translucent. Transfer to the serving platter, and serve immediately.

Variations:

1. Toast ⅓ cup/¾ dL of slivered almonds in a 325°F/165°C oven for 8 to 10 minutes or until golden. Let them cool to room temperature. Sprinkle on top of the chicken just before serving.

2. Substitute 1 cup/¼ L of cut up broccoli, asparagus, or Bok Choy for snow peas.

SLICED CHICKEN IN SPICY GARLIC SAUCE

魚香雞片   Yu-xiang-ji-pian

Serves 2

This dish has the characteristic flavor of many Szechuan dishes. Chinese call
it "Yu-xiang," and literally it means "fish-flavored." However, it has no
fish whatsoever in the sauce. Originally, the sauce was used in the fish
dishes in Szechuan. Since fish is not abundant in this mountainous region
of China, the sauce has been used with meats, chicken, shrimp, and vegetables, as well. It has a sublime flavor—peppery hot with a subtle sweet and
sour taste, and enhanced by the fragrance of fresh ginger and garlic. Many
restaurants translate this sauce to "Spicy Garlic Sauce."

Chicken Breast	1 skinless, boneless, and frozen (8 oun-ces/225 g)
Dried Tree Ears	2 tablespoons
Fresh Ginger	2 ½-inch/1½-cm cubes
Garlic	3 cloves, peeled
Water Chestnuts	5

Marinade for Chicken:

Soy Sauce	1 tablespoon
Dry Sherry	1 teaspoon
Cornstarch	1½ teaspoons

Broccoli Flowerets	1 cup/¼ L, in 1¼-inch/3¹/₅-cm lengths
Red Bell Pepper	1, seeded

Sauce Ingredients:

Soy Sauce	2 tablespoons or to taste
Dry Sherry	1 tablespoon
Wine Vinegar	2 teaspoons
Cornstarch	2 teaspoons
Sugar	1½ tablespoons
Salt	¼ teaspoon or to taste
Water	1 tablespoon

Dry Hot Pepper (*or* Crushed Red Pepper Flakes)	2, cut in halves and seeded (¼ to ½ teaspoon)
Cooking Oil	5½ tablespoons
Sesame Oil	2 teaspoons (optional)

AHEAD OF TIME:

Partially defrost *frozen chicken* just long enough to slice following these directions:

20 minutes or more to partially thaw meat at room temperature
5 minutes or more to partially thaw meat in a 250°F/120°C oven
35 seconds or more to partially thaw meat in a microwave oven

PREPARATION: 20 minutes

COOKING: 8 minutes

Preparation:

1. Cover tree ears with plenty of boiling water, and let soak for 15 minutes.
2. With *Steel Blade* in place, finely chop ginger and garlic. (To chop by hand see page 14.) Transfer to a small bowl.
3. With *Medium Slicing Disk* in place, slice water chestnuts, and transfer to a bowl. (To slice by hand see page 14.)
4. Cut chicken breast into halves crosswise, and pack them in the feed tube with cut side down. Slice with *Medium Slicing Disk*. (To slice by hand see page 14.) Transfer to a bowl, and mix with the marinade.
5. Cut broccoli flowerets into 1¼-inch/3¹/₅-cm lengths and ½ × ½-inch/1½ × 1½-cm on the tops. Cut red bell pepper into ½-inch/1½-cm squares. Put them in a bowl together.
6. Drain and rinse the softened tree ears, and cut to smaller pieces by hand or by *Steel Blade,* then put them in the same bowl with water chestnuts.
7. Mix the sauce ingredients in a small bowl. §

Have Ready Before Cooking:

1. Bottle of cooking oil
2. Bowl with red pepper and broccoli
3. Bowl with tree ears and water chestnuts
4. Bowl with chicken mixture
5. Dry hot pepper or crushed pepper on a small piece of foil
6. Small bowl with minced garlic and ginger
7. Bowl with sauce ingredients
8. Sesame oil, 2 teaspoons (optional)
9. Serving platter

Cooking:

1. Heat the wok over medium-high heat, then heat 1 tablespoon oil. Add red pepper and broccoli, stirring to coat them with oil. Cover the wok and cook for 1 minute. Then stir and add tree ears and water chestnuts. Cook, stirring, for another minute. Remove from the wok.

2. Heat the wok over high heat, then heat 3 tablespoons oil until very hot. Add chicken, and stir-fry very quickly until chicken just changes color, about 2 minutes. Remove from the wok.

3. Clean and dry the wok over heat. Heat 1½ tablespoons oil over medium-high heat. Cook dry hot pepper for 30 seconds or until lightly brown. Add chopped ginger and garlic, and cook for 20 seconds, then return the chicken and vegetables to the wok.

4. Turn heat to high. Give the cornstarch mixture a good stir, and pour into the wok. Stir and mix until the sauce thickens. Add the sesame oil (optional), and serve immediately.

Variations:

1. Substitute 4 dry Chinese mushrooms for the tree ears.

2. Substitute ½ carrot for the red pepper, thinly sliced by hand or by the *Fine Slicing Disk.*

SLICED CHICKEN IN OYSTER SAUCE (see page 92)
燒油雞片   Hao-you-ji-pian

Substitute chicken for beef in the recipe.

SLICED CHICKEN IN BLACK BEAN SAUCE (see page 111)
豆豉雞片   Dou-chi-ji-pian

Substitute chicken for pork in the recipe.

CHICKEN IN BIRD'S NEST

雀巢雞片   Que-chao-ji-pian

Serves 2 to 3

This is a dish that will surely win your praises as a great cook. The shredded potato nest is impressive looking, and its crunchy texture will enhance the taste of any dish used to fill its cavity. It is also a delight to anyone who wants to do as little as possible during the party, for the bird's nest can be made several weeks ahead, and rewarmed in the oven just before serving. Preparation of the chicken can be done half a day ahead, and last-minute cooking only takes a few minutes.

The bird's nest is excellent with Chicken in Spicy Garlic Sauce, both for its divine taste and its brilliant color. However, you can fill the nest with any of your favorite stir-fried dishes. Chicken and seafood are more delicate than a meat dish.

If you have a Julienne Disk or a Fine Slicing Disk, use either one of them instead of the Medium Slicing Disk to shred the potatoes, for your nest will look and taste more delicate.

Sliced Chicken in Spicy Garlic Sauce	1 recipe (see page 144)

Bird's Nest:

Potatoes	¾ pound/340 g (if Julienne or Fine Slicing Disk is used)
	1 pound/450 g (if Medium Slicing Disk is used)
Cornstarch	2 tablespoons
Cooking Oil	6 cups/1½ L or enough to fry the nest

PREPARATION OF THE BIRD'S NEST: 12 minutes

COOKING THE BIRD'S NEST: 5 to 10 minutes depending on the heat of your burner

PREPARATION OF SLICED CHICKEN IN SPICY GARLIC SAUCE: 20 minutes

LAST MINUTE COOKING: 10 minutes

Preparation of the Bird's Nest:

1. Wash and peel the potatoes. Shred them with the *Julienne Cutter*. Or slice and then shred with either the *Fine* or *Medium Slicing Disk*. Or shred potatoes by hand to ¹/₁₂-inch thick strips.

2. To save time, you can heat the oil for deep-frying while preparing the potatoes. (Heat the oil in a wok or a pot that will fit the 8-inch/20-cm strainer for shaping and cooking of the nest.)

3. Spread the potato shreds on paper towels, and blot them dry with more paper towels.

4. Place the shreds in a bowl, then toss and coat them evenly with cornstarch.

5. Line potato shreds in an 8-inch/20-cm strainer, and spread them out in the shape of a nest.

Cooking the Bird's Nest:

1. When the oil is very hot, about 400°F/205°C, lower the strainer gently into the deep fat. Fry, turning if necessary, until the nest is golden and crisp on all sides.

2. Carefully remove the nest from the strainer and drain on paper towels. Makes a 6-inch/15-cm nest. §

Preparation of Sliced Chicken in Spicy Garlic Sauce:

Can be done half a day ahead, following the steps given in the recipe. §

Last Minute Cooking:

1. Preheat oven to 300°F/150°C, then recrisp the bird's nest for 10 minutes. (This is not necessary if the nest is just freshly fried.) Do not overheat, or the nest will get too brown.

2. Follow the direction for cooking the chicken dish. When the chicken is done, place the hot bird's nest on a serving platter, fill the nest with the chicken, and serve immediately.

Tips:

The fried nest can be kept in the refrigerator for 7 to 9 days, and in the freezer for several weeks. It is very fragile, so it should be put away carefully.

Variation:

You can use a 5-inch/13-cm strainer, and make the potato shreds into three 4-inch/10-cm nests to be served individually.

DEEP-FRIED PEANUT CHICKEN

花生雞   Hua-sheng-ji

Serves 2 to 3 ‡

This crunchy and nutty-flavored chicken can be served as an appetizer or as a main course. As a single main dish, serve with fried rice and a vegetable salad.

Skinless Raw Peanuts (from Oriental or health food stores)	1¾ cups/4 dL
Chicken Breast	1 whole, skinned and boned
Marinade:	
Salt	1 teaspoon
Ground Pepper	¼ teaspoon
Dry Sherry	1 teaspoon
Egg White	2
Cornstarch	4 tablespoons
Cooking Oil	3 cups/¾ L

PREPARATION: 25 minutes

COOKING: 12 minutes

Preparation:

1. With *Steel Blade* in place, place half of the peanuts in the beaker. With quick on/off turns, chop until they are the size of large whole peppercorns. Remove from the beaker, and repeat with the other half. (To chop by hand see page 14.)

2. Cut chicken into 1 × 2-inch/2½ × 5-cm pieces (1 × 1 inch/2½ × 2½ cm for appetizers), then mix with the marinade.

3. Beat the egg whites lightly, and mix well with the cornstarch.

4. Dip chicken in the egg white mixture, then coat with chopped peanuts. Place them on a plate or a tray, making sure the coated pieces don't overlap each other. (It is not necessary, but the nuts will adhere better to the chicken if they are refrigerated for 1 or more hours before frying.) §

Cooking:

Heat oil to 350°F/180°C. Drop chicken pieces in the oil one by one, and deep-fry until light brown on both sides (about 2 minutes on each side). Remove from oil and drain on paper towels. Place on a serving platter and garnish with parsley sprigs. §

Serve with Szechuan peppercorn salt (under Chinese Ingredients) or Worcestershire sauce as dips. Yes! Worcestershire sauce, since the Chinese long ago adopted this as a condiment sauce.

Tips:

Deep-fried foods taste best when freshly cooked. However, when you are doing several dishes at the last minute, this chicken can be cooked ahead and refrigerated for 1 to 2 days. Rewarm in a 350°F/180°C oven for 10 minutes or until heated through (place them on a rack over a baking pan), turning once. Do not over heat, or chicken will get dry and tough.

Variation:

DEEP-FRIED ALMOND CHICKEN
杏仁雞 Xing-ren-ji

Substitute slivered almonds for peanuts in the above recipe, and chop the almonds with *Steel Blade*.

HACKED CHICKEN IN SPICY SAUCE

棒棒雞   Bang-bang-ji

Serves 2 as a main course ‡
Serves 4 to 6 as an appetizer ‡

This is a popular cold dish from Szechuan. You'll find it on the menu of every Szechuan or Hunam restaurant. It is often served by the Chinese restaurants here as one of the assorted cold appetizers at the beginning of a dinner banquet. The advantage of making this dish yourself is that you can make it mildly hot or as spicy as you like. Everything can be made ahead, and it is an especially good warm-weather dish. It is an easy and delicious meal served with Pita bread.

Chicken Breast	1 large, with bone and skin on
(or Shredded Cooked Chicken Meat)	(2 cups/½ L)
Cucumber	1
Salt	½ teaspoon

Sauce Mixture:

Szechuan Peppercorn	¼ teaspoon (optional)
Fresh Ginger	½-inch/1½-cm cube
Garlic	1 clove, peeled
Scallion	1, cut into 2-inch/5-cm sections
Soy Sauce	2½ tablespoons or to taste
Chinese Red Vinegar	1 tablespoon
(or Wine Vinegar)	(to taste)
Sugar	1 teaspoon
Sesame Seed Oil	1 tablespoon
Hot Chili Oil	½ teaspoon or to taste (see Variation)
(or Tabasco Sauce)	(to taste)
Water	1 tablespoon
Chinese Sesame Seed Paste	3 tablespoons
(or Creamy Peanut Butter)	

PREPARATION AND COOKING: 20 minutes with cooked chicken, 35 minutes with raw chicken breast

Preparation and Cooking:

1. Boil 2 quarts of water in a saucepan. Add chicken breast, and bring the water back to boil. Turn fire to low, and let simmer very slowly for 25 minutes. Then immediately remove the breast, and rinse it thoroughly in cold water. This can be done 1 or 2 days ahead, and on the day of serving, remove the meat from the bone and skin. Use your fingers to shred the chicken or cut with a knife to julienne strips. The slicing disk of the processor will not slice cooked meat neatly. §

If you have a microwave oven, you can save time on cooking the chicken. Lay the chicken breast flat (breast with bone and skin on will give you more juicy and tender meat) on a pyrex pie plate or a deep platter suitable for use in microwave ovens. Cover the pie plate loosely with wax paper. Cook on high for 2½ minutes. Then turn the breast upside down and cook for another 2 minutes. Let stand for 5 minutes to finish cooking. (A smaller breast will take less time. Do not overcook.)

2. Peel cucumber, and cut it lengthwise into two halves, and then cut into lengths shorter than the feed tube. With *Medium Slicing Disk* in place, wedge them compactly in the feed tube and slice. (To slice by hand see page 14.) Transfer cucumber to a bowl and sprinkle with ½ teaspoon salt. Toss to mix, and let stand for 15 minutes.

3. Dry the beaker and the cover well with paper towels. With *Steel Blade* in place, grind Szechuan peppercorn for a few seconds or until you can smell its distinguished fragrance. Add ginger, garlic, and scallion to the beaker. Process until they are finely minced. Add the remaining ingredients for the sauce mixture. Process until they are well mixed. (To prepare without the food processor, mince the ginger, garlic, and scallions by hand or in a blender. Then combine them with the remaining sauce ingredients.) More water can be added if the sauce is too thick. The sauce should be fairly thin but thick enough to coat the back of a spoon. If the sauce is too thin add more sesame paste or peanut butter. §

To Serve:

Drain cucumber very well and place in a salad bowl or serving dish, then top the cucumber with chicken strips. Pour the sauce over, and toss to serve.

Variation:

Commercial or homemade chili oil varies in hotness—for those who don't like it spicy, leave the hot oil out of the sauce mixture (it still tastes very good), and let each one add to taste at the last minute.

Szechuan peppercorn is not hot but has a special fragrance.

CHICKEN VELVET

芙蓉雞   Fu-rong-ji

Serves 2 to 3

This is a very attractive and delicate Northern dish often served at banquets. Traditionally, the chicken is chopped and minced by cleaver until it forms a smooth puree. The technique of pureeing is most time-consuming, but the smoother the puree, the better the dish. You can see why people don't cook this for an ordinary family meal. However, with the food processor, you can achieve a better and smoother paste in seconds at home. The puree can be made ahead of time, and kept in the refrigerator until cooking time.

Dried Chinese Mushrooms	4
Cooked Smithfield Ham (or Prosciutto Ham)	2 ½-inch/1½-cm cubes (2 tablespoons finely minced)
Water Chestnuts	5
Fresh Snow Peas	25, ends and strings removed

Chicken Mixture:

Chicken Breast	1 whole, boneless, skinless (about 8 ounces/225 g), cut into 1-inch/2½-cm cubes
Dry Sherry	1 tablespoon
Cornstarch	2 teaspoons
Salt	1 teaspoon or to taste
Sugar	¼ teaspoon
Sesame Oil	1 tablespoon (optional)
Chicken Broth	¼ cup/½ dL
Egg Whites	6
Fresh Ginger	1 slice
Chicken Broth	¾ cup/1¾ dL
Dry Sherry	1 tablespoon
Cornstarch	2 teaspoons in 2 tablespoons Chicken Broth
Salt	to taste
Sesame Oil	1 tablespoon (optional)
Cooking Oil	3 cups/¾ L

AHEAD OF TIME:

1. Snap the stems off the Chinese mushrooms. Soak the mushrooms in boiling water to cover for 20 minutes, or until soft.

2. If *frozen chicken* is used, defrost for 20 minutes or more at room temperature.

PREPARATION: 15 minutes

COOKING: 12 minutes

Preparation:

1. Squeeze mushrooms dry. Cut to smaller pieces, and place them in the same bowl with snow peas.

2. With *Steel Blade* in place, and the motor running, drop ham cubes through the feed tube, process until finely minced. (To mince by hand see page 14.) Remove ham and wipe the beaker clean with a paper towel.

3. With *Medium Slicing Disk* in place, slice water chestnuts and transfer to the bowl with snow peas and mushrooms. (To slice by hand see page 14.)

4. With *Steel Blade* in place, put chicken in the beaker and process until chicken becomes a puree. Add remaining ingredients for chicken mixture, processing until mixture becomes creamy and smooth (or puree using the blender). §

Have Ready Before Cooking:
1. 3 cups/¾ L cooking oil
2. Chicken puree
3. Strainer or colander
4. Bowl with vegetables, put ginger slice on top
5. Bowl with chicken broth and sherry
6. Bowl with cornstarch in chicken broth
7. Sesame oil (optional)
8. Small bowl with minced ham

Cooking:

1. Heat oil to 300°F/150°C over medium heat (about 4 minutes). An electric wok is very good for this, as one can set the oil at a desired temperature. However, you can do this in a regular wok or saucepan. The oil should not be too hot, as the chicken should be snow-white not golden yellow after cooked.

Pour the chicken puree into the oil, gently stir and cut the mixture with a spatula to smaller pieces. As soon as the chicken turns white, remove it with a slotted spoon or strainer. Leave in the strainer or colander to drain off excess oil.

This step can be prepared several hours ahead, leaving the cooked chicken at room temperature. §

2. Remove all but 1 tablespoon oil from the wok, fry ginger for 30 seconds over medium heat and discard the ginger. Add vegetables and stir-fry for 1 minute. Return chicken to the wok. Add chicken broth and sherry mixture, and bring to a boil. Give the cornstarch mixture a good stir, pour into the wok, and stir until sauce becomes a clear glaze. Add salt to taste. Remove wok from the heat. Add 1 tablespoon sesame oil (optional). Transfer to serving platter. Sprinkle with minced ham and serve immediately.

Variations:

1. Substitute 4 large fresh mushrooms (sliced) for Chinese mushrooms.

2. Substitute half a package of frozen snow peas (not as crisp) for the fresh ones.

SLICED BEEF WITH STIR-FRIED EGGS

滑蛋牛肉   Hua-dan-niu-rou

Serves 2

This simple dish can be ordered as a one-dish meal in the Cantonese restaurants. It is usually served over a dish of boiled rice. Traditionally, the Chinese eat it for lunch or supper, and it is usually a very inexpensive meal. However, you may like to serve this dish in place of your Western-style eggs for Sunday breakfast or brunch. The tender and moist stir-fried beef and the seasonings impart a delicious flavor to the eggs.

My son, Ted, who has an adventuresome palate and loves interesting food, has a new culinary suggestion for you: Serve this dish with a dash of Worcestershire sauce!

Boneless Beef	4 ounces, precut to fit feed tube and frozen
Fresh Ginger	½-inch/1½-cm cube
Scallion	1, in 2-inch/5-cm sections

Marinade for Beef:

Soy Sauce	2½ teaspoons or to taste
Dry Sherry	1 teaspoon
Cornstarch	1 teaspoon

Eggs	4
Soy Sauce	2 teaspoons or to taste
Cooking Oil	3 tablespoons

AHEAD OF TIME:

Partially defrost *frozen beef* just long enough to slice following these directions:

   20 minutes or more to partially thaw meat at room temperature
   10 minutes or more to partially thaw meat in a 250°F/120°C oven
   20 seconds or more to partially thaw meat in a microwave oven

PREPARATION: 7 minutes

COOKING: 5 minutes

Preparation:

   1. With *Steel Blade* in place, chop ginger until finely minced. (To mince by hand see page 14.) Transfer to a bowl large enough for marinating beef.

   2. Replace *Steel Blade,* and process scallion until finely chopped. (To chop by hand see page 14.) Transfer to a small dish.

3. With *Medium Slicing Disk* in place, slice beef across the grain. To slice by hand see page 14.) Mix with minced ginger and the marinade.

4. In a bowl beat the eggs with 2 teaspoons soy sauce until well mixed. §

Have Ready Before Cooking:
1. Bottle of cooking oil
2. Bowl with beef
3. Bowl with beaten eggs
4. Bowl with chopped scallion

Cooking:
1. Heat the wok over high heat, then heat 1 tablespoon oil. Cook beef over very high heat for 1 minute or until it is no longer red. Pour the cooked beef into the beaten eggs.

2. Heat 2 tablespoons oil in the same wok, and cook scallion for 30 seconds. Then pour in the egg and beef mixture. Stir and cook until eggs are set. Transfer to a serving platter, and serve hot.

CHOPPED PORK WITH STIR-FRIED EGGS

肉末炒蛋   Rou-mo-chao-dan

Serves 2

We often had this dish in Shanghai when unexpected guests were staying for dinner. Our chef would improvise the meal by taking a small amount of the meat from another dish, and cooking it with eggs to create an extra dish. You may like to borrow this idea from the Chinese for your impromptu meals (or use Sliced Beef With Stir-fried Eggs). You can also serve this dish for breakfast, Western-style, in place of bacon and eggs.

Fresh Ginger	½-inch/1½-cm cube (optional)
Scallions	2

Pork Mixture:

Boneless Pork	4 ounces/115 g
Cornstarch	2 teaspoons
Soy Sauce	2 teaspoons
Dry Sherry	2 teaspoons
Eggs	4 large
Soy Sauce	1 tablespoon
Cooking Oil	4 tablespoons

AHEAD OF TIME:

If *frozen pork cubes* are used, thaw partially or completely following these directions:

> 20 minutes or more to partially thaw meat at room temperature
>
> 10 minutes or more to partially thaw meat in a 250°F/120°C oven
>
> 30 seconds or more to completely thaw meat in a microwave oven

PREPARATION AND COOKING: 10 minutes

Preparation and Cooking:

1. With *Steel Blade* in place, finely mince ginger and scallion. (To mince by hand see page 14.) Remove from the beaker.

2. Replace the *Steel Blade,* and add pork and the marinade to the beaker. Process with quick on/off turns until pork is evenly chopped. Do not over process. (To chop by hand see page 14.)

3. Beat eggs with 1 tablespoon soy sauce until well mixed. §

4. Heat the wok, then heat 2 tablespoons oil. Fry chopped scallions and ginger for 30 seconds, then add chopped pork, stirring until pork is no longer pink. Remove from the wok.

5. Heat the wok, then heat 2 tablespoons oil. Pour the eggs into the wok. Cook stirring until eggs are almost set, and return cooked pork to the wok. Stir to mix, and cook until eggs are set. Serve hot.

STIR-FRIED EGG YOLKS

溜黄菜   Liu-huang-cai

Serves 1 to 2

This is a good way to use up leftover egg yolks. Raw egg yolks can be kept in the refrigerator covered with water for 3 to 4 days. Leftover egg whites can be frozen for several months. Once defrosted, they can be used in any recipe calling for egg whites. The recipe can be doubled and cooked in one batch.

Cooked Smithfield Ham (or Regular Ham)	2 ½-inch/1½-cm cubes (use double amount)
Scallion	1 small, in 2-inch/5-cm sections
Water Chestnuts	3
Egg Yolks	4
Chicken Broth	4 tablespoons
Cornstarch	¾ teaspoon
Salt	⅛ teaspoon or to taste
Cooking Oil	2 tablespoons

PREPARATION: 3 minutes

COOKING: 3 minutes

Preparation:

With *Steel Blade* in place, process ham until finely minced. Add scallion and water chestnuts, process until minced. Add the remaining ingredients except cooking oil, and process to mix. Do not overprocess. (To prepare by hand see page 14.) §

Cooking:

Heat the wok, then heat two tablespoons oil over medium-high heat. Add the egg yolk mixture, stirring back and forth until the mixture is set but still soft in texture. Serve immediately.

Variation:

Instead of ham, you can use 1 tablespoon dried shrimp. Pour boiling water over them to soak for 15 minutes before using.

Seafood

Fish and seafood are abundant and popular in China, especially along the Southern and Eastern coastlines. And the people in many inland areas find plentiful supplies of fresh water fish and shellfish from the numerous lakes and rivers in China.

Fish are mostly served whole, with head and tail included. Large fish are cut and sold in parts, but nothing goes to waste; even the big fish head is made into a popular fish head casserole. These dishes, however, are not applicable to the food processor.

The processor is wonderful as far as chopping shrimp and pureeing fish, for they used to be such tedious and time-consuming jobs. And as with minced pork, I find that the minced shrimp mixture produced by the food processor has a lighter texture than the same mixture mixed by hand. Traditionally, such light texture can only be achieved by adding a good portion of pork fat to the shrimp mixture.

Buying seafood is as important as not overcooking them, for freshness is the most crucial factor in the success of a good seafood dish. They should have the fresh ocean smell, and absolutely no fishy odor! Once they lose the freshness, no amount of skill can restore that sweet and delicate flavor. The Chinese have an ingenious way of seasoning seafood with wine, ginger, and scallions, for they are also used to mask the fishy smell.

Frozen seafood is not used in China. However, people there do eat many forms of dried or salted seafood, which are cooked and treated very differently from fresh seafood.

Unfortunately, really fresh shrimp are hard to get in the United States. But you can find them in some of the seafood markets. Yet, many people have the misconception that shrimp from the supermarket seafood counters are fresh. (They are usually defrosted from frozen packages.) Some are of very good quality, while others may not be so, although in general they are better than the frozen, shelled, and deveined ones in the plastic bags.

In selecting shrimp, you should choose them with stiff and shiny shells, and meat that is translucent and firm, not opaque and spongy. If you find fresh shrimp (it has never been frozen before) in your seafood market, you can freeze them up to 2 weeks without losing their flavor.

You'll find the freshness of the seafood can make a big difference in the taste of your dish. In China, the fish and shrimp are often still wriggling and alive after they are brought home from the market.

FRIED CRAB CLAWS ★

炸蟹鉗   Zha-xie-qian

Makes 15 ‡

This is an elegant banquet dish from the Southern region. It is also good as an appetizer. As a single main dish, serve them with fried rice, or Ginger and Scallion Lo-mein, and a green vegetable.

Ingredients for Fried Crab Patties	1 recipe (page 164)
Crab Claws (Pasteurized Cocktail Claws *or* cooked Crab Fingers)	15, shells removed, except the tip

PREPARATION: 45 minutes

COOKING: 15 minutes

Preparation:

Prepare as you would for Fried Crab Patty to step 3. It is not necessary, but you'll find that it will be easier to shape if you let the mixture refrigerate for 2 hours. Use 2 tablespoons of the mixture on each claw. Using wet hands, shape the mixture smoothly around the claw, and leaving the tip as a handle. Dip it in and coat it evenly with bread crumbs. Can be prepared half a day ahead. §

Cooking:

Heat oil in a wok or a 9-inch/23-cm skillet to 350°F/180°C. Drop a small piece of bread in the hot oil; if it browns in 1 minute, the oil is ready. Fry crab claws on both sides for 5 to 6 minutes until cooked inside and golden brown outside. Do not overcook. Drain on paper towels, and garnish with parsley sprigs. Serve with Szechuan peppercorn salt (see Chinese Ingredients) or light soy sauce. §

Tips:

Cooked crab claws can be kept in the refrigerator for 2 to 3 days, or in the freezer for a month. Rewarm in a 350°F/180°C oven for about 20 minutes, or until heated through. Do not overcook.

Variation:

You'll get a delicious crunchy crust if you use coarse, fresh bread crumbs. Use 6 slices of fresh white bread with the crust trimmed off. Process 2 slices at a time, cut each into quarters before processing. With *Steel Blade* in place, coarsely crumble the bread. Do not over process! Shape as you would in the preparation above, but use 2 level tablespoons or 1 heaping tablespoon of the mixture on each claw. You can get about 20 fried crab claws in this way.

FRIED CRAB PATTY ★

炸蟹餅   Zha-Xie-bing

Makes 15 to 20 1½ × 2-inch patties ‡

This is a very delicate dish. Both shrimp and crab should be very fresh. Fresh blue crab meat can be purchased at seafood markets, and is best. You can substitute with pasteurized fresh crab meat or frozen king crabs, but definitely don't use canned crabs.

They make a delicious first course, Western style. As a single main dish, serve them with fried rice and a green vegetable.

Shrimp Mixture:

Shrimp in Shells	1 pound (40 to 50 shrimp per pound) or ¾ pound (20 to 30 shrimp per pound)
Fresh Ginger	½-inch/1½-cm cube
Scallion White Top	2, in 1-inch/2½-cm sections
Water Chestnuts	half of an 8-ounce/225-g can
Egg White	1
Salt	1½ teaspoons or to taste
Sugar	1 teaspoon
Cornstarch	2 teaspoons
Sesame Oil	1 tablespoon
Dry Sherry	1 tablespoon

Crab Mixture:

Fresh Blue Crab Meat	½ pound/225 g
Egg White	1
Salt	¼ teaspoon
Sesame Oil	1 tablespoon
Dry Sherry	1 teaspoon

Bread Crumbs   6 tablespoons
(see Variation)
    Cooking Oil   2 or 3 cups/½ to ¾ L

PREPARATION: 40 minutes

COOKING: 12 minutes

Preparation:
1. Shell and devein the shrimp. Wash, drain, and then pat dry with paper towels. Cut into 1-inch/2½-cm pieces.
2. With *Steel Blade* in place, chop ginger and scallions until finely minced. Add water chestnuts to the beaker, give 2 quick on/off turns. Add shrimp and the remaining ingredients of the shrimp mixture to the beaker. Process with on/off turns until the mixture is finely minced but not pureed. (To mince by hand see page 14.)
3. Add ingredients of the crab mixture to a large bowl. Mix gently. Then add shrimp mixture, and mix lightly with a spatula, so it will not break up the tender blue crab meat. §
4. It is not necessary, but you'll find that it will be easier to shape the patty if you let the mixture refrigerate for 2 hours. Using wet hands, shape 2 tablespoons of the mixture into a 1½ × 2-inch/4 × 5-cm patty. Coat the patty completely with bread crumbs. Repeat the process, and arrange patties on a platter. (This can be done half a day ahead and kept in the refrigerator.) §

Cooking:
Heat oil in a wok or a 9-inch/23-cm skillet to 350°F/180°C. Test the oil by dropping a small piece of bread in the hot oil; if it browns in about 1 minute, the oil is ready. Fry the patties on both sides until golden brown, about 3 to 4 minutes. Do not overcook. Garnish serving platter with parsley. §
This is delicious with Chinese red vinegar as a dip. Or serve with soy sauce, Worcestershire sauce, or Szechuan peppercorn salt. (See under Chinese ingredients.)

Tips:
Cooked patties can be kept in the refrigerator for 2 to 3 days or in the freezer for a month. Rewarm in a 350°F/180°C oven for about 20 minutes. Do not overcook.

Variation:
You'll get a delicious crunchy crust if you use 1½ cups/3½ dL coarse fresh bread crumbs. Use 6 slices of fresh white bread with the crust trimmed off. Process 2 slices at a time, cut each into quarters. With *Steel Blade* in place, coarsely crumble the bread. Do not over process!

FISH BALLS ★

魚丸子   Yu-wan-zi

Makes 15 balls ‡

Fish balls can be used in soup, or cooked with other ingredients as a main dish. They are low in calories and cholesterol, but high in protein. Cooked fish balls can be kept in the refrigerator for 4 to 5 days, and in the freezer for 2 to 3 months.

Fresh Ginger	½-inch/1½-cm cube
Scallion, White Part	1, in 1½-inch/4-cm sections
Fish Fillet (flounder, sole, cod, or halibut)	½ pound/225 g, cut into 1-inch/2½-cm squares
Cornstarch	1 tablespoon
Dry Sherry	1 tablespoon
Salt	1½ teaspoon or to taste
Sugar	1 teaspoon
Egg White	1
Sesame Oil	2 tablespoons
Water	2 tablespoons

PREPARATION: 8 minutes

SHAPING AND COOKING: 16 minutes

Preparation:
    1. With the *Steel Blade* in place, and the machine running, drop ginger through feed tube, and process until finely minced. Add scallion, and process until minced. (To mince by hand see page 14.)
    2. Add fish to the minced ginger and scallion in the beaker. Process until fish becomes a paste, then add the remaining ingredients, and process until the mixture is completely smooth (or puree using the blender). §

Shaping and Cooking:
    With your wet hands, shape mixture into walnut size balls, and drop them in a pot of cold water as you finish making each one. When all the balls are formed, bring the water to a boil, and simmer for 2 minutes. Remove the fish balls with a strainer, they are now ready for use. §

SHRIMP BALLS WITH BROCCOLI

芥蘭蝦球   Gai-lan-xia-qiu

Serves 2 to 3

Steamed or Fried Shimp Balls (Frozen ones can be used without thawing)	1 recipe (see page 75)
Dry Chinese Mushrooms	4 (optional)
Fresh Broccoli	½ pound/225 g
Chicken Broth	½ cup/1 dL
Dry Sherry	1 tablespoon
Sugar	½ teaspoon
Cornstarch	1 tablespoon in ¼ cup/½ dL chicken broth
Cooking Oil	1 tablespoon
Sesame Oil	1 tablespoon (optional)

AHEAD OF TIME:

Snap the stems off of the Chinese mushrooms. Soak the mushrooms in boiling water to cover for 20 minutes, or until soft. Drain and squeeze dry. This can be done any time before the preparation begins.

PREPARATION: 6 minutes

COOKING: 7 minutes

Preparation:
1. If mushrooms are large, cut them into halves or quarters.
2. Wash the broccoli. Cut off flowerets from the large stems to about 1½ inches/4 cm in length, and cut the large flowerets smaller, about 1 × ¾ inches/2½ × 2 cm on the top. Cut off the tough bottoms of the stems; scrape and peel off the hard skin. They can be sliced by hand. Or using the *Medium Slicing Disk,* place stems flat side down and against the right side of the feed tube and slice.
3. Mix the chicken broth, sherry, and sugar in a bowl.
4. Mix cornstarch with ¼ cup/½ dL chicken broth. §

Cooking:
1. Heat 1 tablespoon oil in a wok over medium-high heat. Add broccoli and mushrooms to the wok, stir-frying for 1 to 2 minutes. Remove from the wok.
2. Add shrimp balls and the chicken broth mixture to the wok. Bring to a boil; cover the wok and let simmer for 2 minutes or until shrimp balls

are heated through. Add salt to taste. (Simmer longer if the shrimp balls are frozen.)

3. Return the vegetables to the wok, stirring to mix. Give the cornstarch mixture a good stir, and pour into the wok, stirring constantly until sauce becomes translucent. Add sesame oil (optional). Transfer to a serving platter and serve.

Variations:

1. Substitute 1 recipe cooked fish balls for shrimp balls.
2. Use a combination of shrimp and fish balls.
3. Other vegetables can be used: canned baby sweet corn, sliced bamboo shoots, sliced water chestnuts, sliced fresh mushrooms.

SHRIMP BALLS WITH SNOW PEAS
雪豆蝦球 Xue-dou-xia-qiu

Substitute 30 fresh snow peas (ends and strings removed) for broccoli.

SHRIMP BALLS WITH BOK-CHOY
白菜蝦球 Bai-cai-xia-qiu

Substitute ¾ pound/340 g Bok-choy for broccoli. Cut vegetables into 2-inch/5-cm long sections, then cut into ½-inch/1½-cm widths. Follow the above procedure for cooking. Bok-choy releases more water than broccoli, so use only 2 tablespoons chicken broth to combine with cornstarch in the above recipe. Or if the sauce is too thin, thicken it with more of the cornstarch mixture.

FRIED WONTON AND SHRIMP IN SWEET AND SOUR SAUCE

甜酸蝦仁餛飩   Tian-suan-xia-ren-hun-tun

Serves 3

This lovely dish can be a treat for the family or a special company meal. The crunchy wontons and the tender shrimps are bathed in a gingery sweet and sour sauce.

The advantage of the dish is that most of the preparations can be done ahead. The fried wontons can be made several weeks ahead, or, when making them for appetizers, prepare an extra two dozen for this dish, and place them in the freezer. The shrimp and the sauce ingredients can be done half a day ahead, for last minute cooking takes only a few minutes. The dish is delicious with boiled rice.

Fried Wontons	24 (see page 77)
Frozen Green Peas	½ cup/1 dL, thawed
Medium Shrimp	¾ pound/340 g, as fresh as possible

Marinade:

Salt	¼ teaspoon
Cornstarch	2 teaspoons

Fresh Ginger	½-inch/1½-cm cube
Scallion White Tops	2, in 2-inch/5-cm sections

Sauce Ingredients:

Soy Sauce	2 tablespoons
Wine Vinegar	3 tablespoons or to taste
Ketchup	4 tablespoons
Sugar	½ cup/1 dL or to taste
Salt	1 teaspoon
Water	1 cup/¼ L
Cornstarch	2 tablespoons mixed with 4 tablespoons water
Cooking Oil	2 tablespoons

PREPARATIONS: 20 minutes

COOKING: 6 minutes

Preparation:

1. If you are doing the preparation just before cooking, heat the oven to 350°F/180°C. Recrisp and reheat the fried wontons on a rack over a baking pan while you are preparing the following steps. If the preparation is done half a day ahead, then 20 minutes before serving, reheat the wontons in a preheated 350°F/180°C oven.

2. Defrost peas if they are frozen.

3. Shell and devein the shrimp, then wash and rinse with cold water. Pat them very dry with paper towels. Mix with the marinade.

4. Finely mince the ginger and scallions with *Steel Blade* or by hand, and transfer to a small bowl. (To mince by hand see page 14.)

5. Mix the ingredients for the sweet and sour sauce except the cornstarch mixture in a saucepan.

6. Mix the cornstarch mixture in a small bowl. §

Have Ready Before Cooking:

1. Bottle of cooking oil
2. Bowl with minced ginger and scallions
3. Bowl with shrimp
4. Saucepan with sweet and sour sauce
5. Bowl with cornstarch mixture
6. Bowl with thawed peas
7. Serving platter

Cooking:

1. Heat the wok, then heat 2 tablespoons oil. Cook minced ginger and scallions for 30 seconds. Add shrimp, and cook over high heat for 1 to 2 minutes depending on the size of the shrimp or until they are no longer translucent. Do not overcook, and remove from the wok. §

2. Heat the sweet and sour sauce in the saucepan, and bring to a boil. Give the cornstarch mixture a good stir, and gradually add to the sauce, stirring all the time until sauce thickens. §

3. Add the cooked shrimp and peas to the bubbling sauce, and stir to heat through. Pour the shrimp and sauce over the hot wontons in a serving platter and serve immediately.

Tips:

You can cook steps 1 and 2 half a day ahead. Reheat the wontons in a 350°F/180°C oven 20 minutes before serving. And 3 minutes before serving, reheat the sweet and sour sauce, then add the cooked shrimp and peas to heat through. Pour them over the hot wontons, and serve immediately.

You can double or triple the recipe.

Variations:

1. Substitute 8 ounces/225 g of thawed king crab meat for shrimp. Since they are already cooked, they don't have to cook as long, or just to heat through.

2. You can also serve the dish without using the shrimp or crab. In this case, omit cooking step 1, and 20 minutes before serving, heat up the sauce and thicken with cornstarch. Add peas just to heat through, then pour over the wontons, and serve immediately.

3. If you like spicy food, add hot chili oil or Tabasco sauce to taste to the sweet and sour sauce at the end of cooking step 2.

SHRIMP IN LOBSTER SAUCE

豆豉蝦   Dou-chi-xia

Serves 3

There is no lobster in this dish. It got the name from its sauce, which is used in cooking the Lobster Cantonese. Serve with plain boiled rice, and a vegetable salad such as cucumber or watercress.

Boneless Pork	4 ounces/115g
Shrimp in Shell	1 pound/450 g (20 to 25 shrimps)
Garlic	2 cloves
Scallion	1, in 2-inch/5-cm sections
Salted Black Beans	1 tablespoon
Cornstarch	2 tablespoons in 4 tablespoons water
Egg	1, lightly beaten
Cooking Oil	2 tablespoons

Sauce Mixture:

Soy Sauce	2 tablespoons
Dry Sherry	2 tablespoons
Sugar	½ teaspoon
Chicken Broth	⅔ cup/1½ dL

AHEAD OF TIME:

If *frozen pork cubes* are used, thaw partially or completely following these directions:

20 minutes or more to partially thaw meat at room temperature

10 minutes or more to partially thaw meat in a 250°F/120°C oven

30 seconds or more to completely thaw meat in a microwave oven

PREPARATION: 16 minutes

COOKING: 10 minutes

Preparation:

1. Shell and devein the shrimp. Rinse with cold water and drain. Pat the shrimp very dry with paper towels.

2. With *Steel Blade* in place, process garlic and scallion until finely chopped. Add black beans to the beaker, coarsely chop the beans with 2 quick on/off turns. (To chop by hand see page 14.) Transfer garlic, scallion, and black beans to a small bowl.

3. Replace the *Steel Blade,* and coarsely chop pork with quick on/off turns. (To chop by hand see page 14.)

4. Mix cornstarch with water in a small bowl.

5. Combine sauce mixture in a bowl. §

Have Ready Before Cooking:

1. Bottle of cooking oil
2. Bowl with shrimp
3. Bowl with garlic, scallion, and black beans
4. Bowl with chopped pork
5. Bowl with sauce mixture
6. Bowl with cornstarch mixture
7. Bowl with 1 lightly beaten egg
8. Serving bowl

Cooking:

1. Heat the wok over high heat, then heat 2 tablespoons oil. Add the shrimps, and stir-fry over high heat until shrimp is just cooked, about 2 minutes. Remove from the wok.

2. Heat 1 tablespoon oil in the wok. Stir-fry garlic, scallion, and black beans for about 30 seconds. Then add pork, and stir-fry until it is no longer pink.

3. Add sauce mixture to the wok, and bring to a boil. Add shrimp to the sauce, and bring it back to a boil. Give the cornstarch mixture a good stir, and gradually pour into the sauce, stirring constantly until the sauce is thickened.

4. Pour and spread the egg over the sauce, and cook for about 30 seconds or until the egg is partially set. Stir to mix. Transfer to the serving bowl, and serve immediately.

Note: Depending on the heat of your stove, the consistency of the sauce may vary. The sauce should be thick, but not runny or pasty. Before proceeding to step 4, adjust the sauce to the right consistency by adding more of the cornstarch mixture if it is too thin, or add more water if it is too thick.

LOBSTER CANTONESE

豆豉龍蝦   Dou-chi-long-xia

Serves 2

This is the most popular and best-known lobster dish from the Southern region. The tiny salted black beans and the fresh garlic are a perfect seasoning match. They are essential to the sublime flavor of the lobster sauce. Using coarsely chopped pork here gives the sauce a more interesting texture than that of regular ground pork.

The sauce is delicious on plain boiled rice. As a single main dish, serve with a stir-fried vegetable such as broccoli.

Boneless Pork	4 ounces/115g in 1-inch/2½-cm cubes
Live Lobster	1 (1¼ to 1½ pounds/565 to 675g)
Garlic	2 cloves, peeled
Scallion	1, in 2-inch/5-cm sections
Salted Black Beans	1 tablespoon
Cornstarch	4 teaspoons in 3 tablespoons water
Egg	1 large
Cooking Oil	2 tablespoons

Sauce Mixture:

Soy Sauce	2 tablespoons or to taste
Dry Sherry	2 tablespoons
Sugar	½ teaspoon
Chicken Broth	1 cup/¼ L

AHEAD OF TIME:

If *frozen pork cubes* are used, thaw partially or completely following these directions:

> 20 minutes or more to partially thaw meat at room temperature
>
> 10 minutes or more to partially thaw meat in a 250°F/120°C oven
>
> 30 seconds or more to completely thaw meat in a microwave oven

PREPARATION: 18 minutes

COOKING: 8 minutes

Preparation:

1. You can either kill the lobster yourself or have the seafood market do it for you. To do it yourself, use a sharp knife or cleaver to separate the head from the body. Or plunge the lobster into a large pot of boiling water for about 1 minute, and drain the lobster immediately. Then separate the head from the body with a sharp knife.

2. Cut off the claws, the legs, and throw away the small hairy legs. A kitchen shear can be very handy for cutting up the lobster. Cut the body and the tail in half lengthwise. Remove the vein, and cut crosswise into 1-inch/2½-cm pieces. Then cut the head lengthwise into halves. Cut off the eyes and antennae, and discard the stomach. Cut the remaining parts into 1-inch/2½-cm pieces. Put the lobster pieces in a bowl. The cutting of the lobster can be done half a day ahead. Cover the lobster with plastic wrap and keep it in the refrigerator. §

3. With *Steel Blade* in place, process garlic and scallion until finely chopped. Briefly rinse black beans and drain, then add to the beaker. Chop coarsely with 2 quick on/off turns. (To chop by hand see page 14.) Transfer garlic, scallion, and black beans to a small bowl.

4. Replace the *Steel Blade,* coarsely chop the pork with quick on/off turns. (To chop by hand see page 14.)

5. Mix cornstarch with water in a small bowl.

6. Lightly beat the egg in a small bowl.

7. Combine sauce mixture in a bowl. §

Have Ready Before Cooking:

1. Bottle of cooking oil
2. Bowl with garlic, scallion, and black beans
3. Bowl with chopped pork
4. Bowl with lobster
5. Bowl with sauce mixture
6. Bowl with cornstarch mixture
7. Bowl with the lightly beaten egg
8. Serving bowl

Cooking:

1. Heat the wok, then heat 2 tablespoons oil over moderate heat. Fry garlic, scallion, and black beans for 30 seconds.

2. Add pork, and stir-fry over high heat until it is no longer pink.

3. Add lobster to the wok, and cook over high heat for 2 minutes.

4. Add the sauce mixture, and bring to a boil. Cover the wok, and cook over medium heat for 2 more minutes or until lobster is cooked. Do not overcook.

5. Give the cornstarch mixture a quick stir to recombine it, and gradually pour into the wok, stirring constantly until the sauce is thickened.

6. Pour the egg into the wok, spreading it over the lobster, and cover the wok. Then remove the wok from the heat, and let stand covered for 2 minutes. The heat in the dish will finish cooking the eggs. Transfer to the serving bowl and serve immediately.

Note: Depending on the heat of your stove, the consistency of the sauce may vary. The sauce should be thick, but not runny or pasty. Before proceeding to step 6, adjust the sauce to the right consistency by adding more of the cornstarch mixture if it is too thin, or add more water if it is too thick.

Variation:

Frozen lobster tails can be substituted, but they will not have the sweet, firm texture of fresh lobster.

Vegetables

Vegetables play very important roles in Chinese cooking. Not only are they used with meat and chicken dishes, and in soup, but one or two pure vegetable dishes are also served with the daily meal.

Buddhism is the major religion in China. Many Buddhists would eat only vegetables as a sacrifice on certain days such as birthdays of important deities or anniversaries of their deceased relatives. Some are pure vegetarians who, like the Buddhist monks, would eat only vegetarian food—non-meat dishes—for their entire lives. Therefore, it is not surprising that the best vegetarian food in China is served at Buddhist temples.

Most cooked Chinese vegetables are characterized by their bright color and crispness. The vegetables are cooked very quickly in hot oil until almost tender but still crunchy. I would like to mention that some vegetables are cooked non-crunchy, often in a casserole or braising dish, such as Lion's Head. In this dish the cabbages are braised for a long period, so they are soft but they have also absorbed the savory juice of the meat balls.

When buying vegetables, choose the freshest from the market. Green vegetables should not have any yellow parts, and crunchy vegetables should be firm with smooth skins. Do not wash vegetables until you are ready to use them, as they will keep longer this way.

STIR-FRIED BROCCOLI

                                                    Chao-gai-lan-cai

Serves 4

This is a simple, tasty, and nutritious dish—very popular in my classes. Here again, by not overcooking the vegetable, broccoli retains its natural color and flavor, so very little seasoning is needed. It will complement both Chinese and American meals.

Fresh Broccoli	1 pound/450 g
Cooking Oil	1 tablespoon
Salt	½ teaspoon or to taste
Sugar	½ teaspoon
Water	1 tablespoon

PREPARATION: 4 minutes

COOKING: 4 minutes

Preparation:
   1. Wash the broccoli under cold running water. Cut off flowerets from large stems, about 2 inches/5 cm long. Cut the large flowerets smaller, about 1 × ¾ inches/2½ × 2 cm on top.
   2. Cut off the tough bottoms of the stems. Scrape and peel off hard skin. With *Medium Slicing Disk* in place, place stems flat-side down and wedge tightly in the feed tube. Slice. Or you can slice by hand. §

Cooking:
   Heat wok over medium-high heat, then add oil and salt. When oil is hot, add broccoli, and stir-fry for about 1 minute. Add sugar and water, and stir to mix. Cover the wok and let simmer over medium heat for 2 to 3 minutes, or until vegetables are tender but still crisp to taste. Stir once or twice during cooking.

Variations:
   1. Add sliced water chestnuts.
   2. Add 1 red bell pepper cut into 1½ × ½-inch/4 × 1½-cm strips, and season to taste.

EGGPLANT IN SPICY GARLIC SAUCE

魚香茄子   Yu-xiang-qie-zi

Serves 3 to 4

This dish has the characteristic flavor of many Szechuan dishes. The Chinese call it "Yu-xiang," which literally means "fish-flavored," though there is really no fish in it. It is the marvelous combination of hot pepper, fresh ginger, and garlic, with a subtle sweet and tangy taste. It is a most delicious way to cook eggplants, which if properly cooked should be smooth and soft, not mushy. The dish should be quite dry. If you have a lot of liquid in yours, you've overcooked the eggplant!

Boneless Pork	4 ounces/115 g, in 1-inch/2½-cm cubes
Scallion	1, in 2-inch/5-cm sections
Fresh Ginger	3 ½-inch/1½-cm cubes
Garlic	3 cloves, peeled
Eggplant	1 pound/450 g, peeled

Sauce Mixture:

Soy Sauce	2 tablespoons
Sugar	2 tablespoons or to taste
Salt	⅛ teaspoon or to taste
Dry Sherry	1 tablespoon
Chicken Broth	¼ cup/½ dL
Cornstarch	1½ teaspoons
Cooking Oil	1 cup/¼ L
Red Pepper Flakes	¼ to ½ teaspoon or to taste
Wine Vinegar	1½ teaspoons or to taste
Sesame Oil	1½ teaspoons

AHEAD OF TIME:

If *frozen pork cubes* are used, thaw partially or completely following these directions:

20 minutes or more to partially thaw meat at room temperature
10 minutes or more to partially thaw meat in a 250°F/120°C oven
30 seconds or more to completely thaw meat in a microwave oven

PREPARATION: 15 minutes

COOKING: 10 minutes

Preparation:

1. Finely chop scallion by hand into ⅛-inch/½-cm sections for garnish, or you can chop them with the *Steel Blade.* Hand chopped ones are more uniform looking.

2. With *Steel Blade* in place, finely chop ginger and garlic. (To chop by hand see page 14.) Transfer to a small bowl.

3. Replace the *Steel Blade.* Process pork cubes with quick on/off turns until they are evenly chopped, then remove pork. (To chop by hand see page 14.)

4. If you have a *French Fry Cutter,* use this to cut the eggplant into strips 2 inches/5 cm long and ¼ inch/¾ cm thick. Otherwise use the *Medium Slicing Disk* to slice the eggplant first, and then reprocess the slices to get shreds. (These shreds are thinner than those from the French Fry Cutter, so they should be cooked for less time than indicated in cooking step 1.) Or cut eggplant by hand into shreds 2 inches long and ¼ inch thick.

5. Mix the sauce ingredients in a bowl. §

Have Ready Before Cooking:

1. Bottle of cooking oil
2. Shredded eggplant
3. Small bowl with ginger and garlic
4. Bowl with chopped pork and red pepper flakes
5. Bowl with sauce mixture
6. Vinegar, 1½ teaspoons
7. Sesame oil, 1½ teaspoons
8. Chopped scallions
9. Serving bowl

Cooking:

1. Heat 1 cup/¼ L oil in a wok or a large pot. (You can use ½ cup/1 dL oil, but the cooked eggplant will not be as smooth.) When oil just starts to haze, add eggplant, stirring to coat each piece with oil. Cook until eggplant is just tender but not wilted, about 2 to 3 minutes. At the beginning the eggplant will absorb all the oil, but as it starts to soften, it will release the excess oil. Drain through a colander.

2. Heat 2 tablespoons oil in the same wok or pot. Saute ginger and garlic for 30 seconds, then add the red pepper flakes and the chopped pork. Cook, stirring, until meat is no longer pink.

3. Add the sauce mixture to the wok, heat to a boil. Return the well-drained eggplant to the wok, and cook quickly over high heat until the sauce is absorbed by the eggplant, about 1½ minutes. Do not overcook.

4. Add vinegar and sesame oil to the dish, and stir to mix. Transfer to the serving bowl, and garnish with chopped scallions. Serve immediately.

Variation:

Although not traditional, this dish is also delicious served cold.

STIR-FRIED CELERY

炒芹菜   Chao-qin-cai

Serves 3 to 4

This dish is good served warm or cold.

Celery Hearts	1 pound/450 g
Cooking Oil	1 tablespoon
Salt	½ teaspoon or to taste
Sugar	½ teaspoon

PREPARATION: 8 minutes

COOKING: 4 minutes

Preparation:

1. Wash the celery thoroughly, and peel off outer layer with a potato peeler to remove tough strings.

2. Cut off the root ends, then cut stalks (in bunches) to a length shorter than the feed tube. Wedge them tightly and vertically in the feed tube and slice with the *Medium Slicing Disk*. (To slice by hand see page 14.) There should be about 3½ cups/⁴/₅ L. §

Cooking:

Heat the wok over medium-high heat, then heat the oil. Add celery and salt, stir-fry for 1 minute. Add sugar and stir-fry for another minute until the celery turns an icy green color. It should be still crisp to the taste. §

Variations:

1. Add 5 sliced water chestnuts.
2. Add 4 sliced fresh mushrooms.

STIR-FRIED ZUCCHINI

炒綠瓜   Chao-si-gua

Serves 3 to 4

Zucchini	1 pound/450 g (not bigger than 1½ inch/4 cm in diameter)
Cooking Oil	1 tablespoon
Salt	½ teaspoon or to taste
Sugar	½ teaspoon

PREPARATION: 2 minutes

COOKING: 4 minutes

Preparation:

Wash zucchini. With *Medium Slicing Disk* in place, cut zucchini crosswise into halves, then place them vertically in the feed tube and slice. (To slice by hand see page 14.) §

Cooking:

Heat wok over medium heat, then add oil and heat until oil is hot. Add zucchini and stir until all the pieces are coated with oil. Add salt and sugar, and stir-fry for about 2 to 3 minutes or until vegetables are tender but still crisp to taste. Can be served hot or cold. §

Variations:

1. Use yellow squash in place of zucchini.
2. Use ½ pound/225 g of zucchini and ½ pound/225 g of yellow squash in the above recipe. It will make a colorful dish.

FRESH BEAN SPROUT SALAD

冷拌豆芽   Leng-ban-dou-ya

Serves 3 to 4 ‡

Fresh bean sprouts are now easily available in supermarkets, or you can grow your own from mung beans in 4 to 5 days. (See bean sprouts, page 273.) Low in calories but very high in vitamins and nutrients, they can be tossed with other vegetables or cooked meats and served as the main dish of a Chinese meal.

Scallions	4, cut into 1½-inch/4-cm sections
Fresh Bean Sprouts	1 pound/450 g
Sesame Oil	2 tablespoons or to taste
Soy Sauce	4 tablespoons or to taste

PREPARATION AND COOKING: 12 minutes

Preparation and Cooking:

1. Boil 2 quarts of water in a large pot. In the meantime, shred the scallions with the *Fine Slicing Disk* or by hand.

2. Plunge the bean sprouts into the boiling water, and let stand for 1 minute. Then quickly drain the sprouts in a colander, and rinse with plenty of cold water. Blanching the bean sprouts quickly removes the raw taste but retains their crispness. Drain them very well before using.

3. Placed the well-drained bean sprouts and shredded scallions in a salad bowl. They can be served now or kept in the refrigerator for later use. §

4. Just before serving, add sesame oil and soy sauce to taste, and toss well with the vegetables.

Variations:

1. Substitute 1 medium green bell pepper for the scallions. Seed and cut peppers lengthwise into 2-inch/5-cm sections. Then shred them with either the *Fine* or *Medium Slicing Disk*. (To shred by hand see page 14.)

2. Add 2 shredded egg sheets (see page 231).

3. Add ½ cup/1 dL cooked and shredded meat, ham, or chicken.

4. In China, water had to be boiled before drinking, so we always blanched the bean sprouts with boiling water. Here, in the United States, if you have very fresh bean sprouts, try serving the salad without blanching the bean sprouts. They give a refreshing and different taste.

5. When tossing the salad with soy sauce and sesame oil, add vinegar to your taste.

BROCCOLI SALAD

冷拌芥蘭菜   Leng-ban-gai-lan-cai

Serves 3 to 4 ‡

This is one of the favorite vegetable salads of my cooking classes. You can use either the flowerets or the stalks, or both. This recipe includes both.

If you follow the cooking directions below, you'll find the broccoli flowerets are soft but not limp. They are also very good served Western style as crudites with your favorite dip. (I find many people overcook them, and it is hard to pick up dips with limp vegetables.) The leftover stalks can be kept in the refrigerator much longer than the flowerets, and can be cooked as broccoli salad at a later date. When buying broccoli, make sure the flowerets are very green and not beginning to turn yellow.

Fresh Broccoli	1 pound/450 g (about half bunch)
Light Soy Sauce	1½ tablespoons or to taste
(*or* all-purpose soy sauce —light soy sauce is preferred for it will not mask the fresh green color of the broccoli)	
Sugar	1 teaspoon
Sesame Oil	1 tablespoon or to taste

PREPARATION AND COOKING: 12 minutes

Preparation and Cooking:
    1. Heat 2 quarts/2 L of water to boiling in a large pot while preparing broccoli.
    2. Wash broccoli under cold running water. Cut off flowerets from the stalks to about 2-inch/5-cm lengths. Cut the large flowerets smaller, to 1 × ¾ inches/2½ × 2 cm on the top. Then cut off the tough bottoms of the stalks. Scrape and peel off the hard skins.
    3. Cut the stalks into slices by hand or with the *Medium Slicing Disk.* If the processor is used, cut flat ends on the stalks, and make sure they are shorter than the feed tube, wedge them vertically in the feed tube and slice.
    4. By now the water should be boiling; add broccoli and bring the water quickly back to boiling. Immediately drain the vegetables into a colander, and rinse with lots of cold water. Drain as much water as possible. §
    5. Put the well-drained broccoli into a serving bowl. Add remaining ingredients to taste; mix thoroughly and serve. This can be prepared several hours ahead. §

CELERY SALAD

冷拌芹菜   Leng-ban-qin-cai

Serves 4 ‡

Celery	1 pound/450 g (or 8 large stalks)
Soy Sauce	3 tablespoons or to taste
Wine Vinegar	2 teaspoons
Sugar	2 teaspoons
Sesame Oil	1 tablespoon

PREPARATION: 10 minutes

Preparation:

1. Wash the celery thoroughly. Using a potato peeler, peel off outer layer to remove tough strings.

2. Cut off the root ends, then cut stalks (in bunches) to a length shorter than the feed tube. Wedge them tightly and vertically in the feed tube and slice with the *Medium Slicing Disk.* (To slice by hand see page 14.) There should be about 4 cups/1 L.

3. Transfer the celery to a serving bowl and mix with the remaining ingredients. This can be served right away, or kept in the refrigerator until serving time. §

Variations:

1. Add 2 finely chopped scallions.

2. Add 2 tablespoons dried shrimp. Place them in a small bowl, then pour boiling water over to cover and soak for 15 minutes. Chop coarsely and toss with the celery.

3. Add hot chili oil to taste.

CUCUMBER AND SCALLION SALAD

冷拌黄瓜   Leng-ban-huang-gua

Serves 2 to 3 ‡

Scallion	1, cut in 2-inch/5-cm sections
Cucumbers	2
Salt	¾ teaspoon
Sesame Oil	1 teaspoon or to taste

PREPARATION: 5 minutes

MARINATING TIME: ½ hour; *none,* if cucumbers are *thinly sliced*—see Variations

Preparation:
1. With *Steel Blade* in place, chop scallion with quick on/off turns. (To chop by hand see page 14.) Transfer to a small bowl.
2. Peel cucumber, and cut into halves crosswise. Slice with the *Medium Slicing Disk,* and transfer to a bowl. (To slice by hand see page 14.)
3. Add salt and mix with the cucumber. Let stand in the refrigerator for ½ hour, turning once or twice.
4. Drain the cucumber, then toss with scallions and sesame oil to serve. Or refrigerate until serving time. §

Tips:
The cucumber is easier to slice, and the salad will look prettier, if the diameter of the cucumber is less than 1½ inches/4 cm, or smaller than the feed tube.

Variations:
1. Slice cucumbers with the *Fine Slicing Disk.* The paper-thin cucumber slices can be tossed with chopped scallions, salt (⅜ teaspoon or to taste), and sesame oil, and served right away without marinating. It gives a different and interesting texture, and is most refreshing. But best of all, it is *so fast* to make!
2. Substitute zucchini for cucumbers.

SWEET AND SOUR CUCUMBER SALAD

甜酸黄瓜   Tian-suan-huang-gua

Serves 2 to 3 ‡

Cucumbers	2
Sugar	¼ cup/½ dL
White Vinegar	¼ cup/½ dL
Salt	½ teaspoon
Water	2 tablespoons

PREPARATION: 4 minutes

MARINATING TIME: 1½ hours; *none,* if cucumbers are *thinly sliced*—see Variations

Preparation:
    1. Wash the cucumbers, and cut into halves crosswise, or just shorter than the feed tube. Slice with *Medium Slicing Disk,* and transfer to a serving bowl. (To slice by hand see page 14.)
    2. Mix cucumbers with the remaining ingredients, and keep in the refrigerator for 1½ hours or longer, turning once or twice. Drain the cucumbers just before serving. §

Tips:
    The cucumber is easier to slice, and the salad will look prettier, if the diameter of the cucumber is less than 1½ inches/4 cm, or smaller than the feed tube.

Variations:
    1. Slice cucumbers with the *Fine Slicing Disk.* The paper-thin cucumbers can be mixed with the remaining ingredients, and served right away without marinating. They give a different and interesting texture, and is very refreshing. But best of all, it is *so fast* to make!
    2. Add ¼ teaspoon or more crushed red pepper flakes to the marinade.
    3. Substitute zucchini or yellow squash for cucumbers.

SPINACH SALAD

菠菜泥   Bo-cai-ni

Serves 2 to 3 ‡

Water	2 quarts/2 L
Fresh Spinach	10 ounces/285 g
Sesame Oil	1 tablespoon
Soy Sauce	1 tablespoon or to taste

PREPARATION AND COOKING: 12 minutes

Preparation and Cooking:

1. Heat water to boiling in a large pot. In the meantime, wash the spinach very well until it is free of sand.

2. Cook spinach for no more than 2 minutes after adding to the boiling water. Drain quickly in a colander, and rinse with cold water. Squeeze out the excess water.

3. With *Steel Blade* in place, chop spinach with quick on/off turns until coarsely chopped. Do not overprocess. You can chop by hand. §

4. Put spinach in a serving bowl. Toss with sesame oil and soy sauce until they are well mixed. This salad can be made ahead, and kept in the refrigerator until serving time. §

Variations:

1. Coarsely chop 6 water chestnuts with *Steel Blade,* and add them to the spinach salad.

2. Soak 2 tablespoons dry shrimps in boiling water, and let stand for 10 minutes. Drain and chop the softened shrimps with *Steel Blade,* then add to the spinach salad. Some dry shrimps are quite salty in taste even after soaking, so you may not need as much soy sauce for the spinach.

SZECHUAN PICKLED CABBAGE

辣白菜   La-bai-cai

Serves 4 to 5 ‡

Pickled cabbages are very popular in China, so home pickling is a common phenomenon in Chinese households. There are many different kinds, but all of them are refreshing and great as appetite enhancers. In fact, some Chinese restaurants start the dinner guests with a small dish of complimentary pickled cabbages, usually a house-specialty—a very clever idea! This recipe is a favorite from our household. It was originated in Szechuan, the Western region.

Szechuan Peppercorn	1 teaspoon
Fresh Ginger	2 ½-inch/1½-cm cubes
Celery Cabbage	1½ pounds/675 g
Salt	1½ tablespoon
Water	1 cup/¼ L
Sugar	4 tablespoons
White Vinegar	4 tablespoons
Cooking Oil	2 tablespoons
Crushed Red Pepper	½ teaspoon or to taste

PREPARATION: 12 minutes

MACERATING TIME: 2 hours

SEASONING: 5 minutes

MARINATING TIME: at least 1 day

Preparation:

1. With *Steel Blade* in place, process Szechuan peppercorns until they are crushed or when you can smell the distinct fragrance (about 8 seconds), or crush with a pestle or rolling pin. Transfer to a small bowl.

2. Replace the *Steel Blade.* With the machine on, drop the ginger through feed tube, and process until finely minced. (To mince by hand see page 14.) Transfer ginger to a small bowl.

3. Cut the celery cabbage into 2½-inch/6½-cm sections. Traditionally, it is shredded lengthwise. So keep this in mind when you are packing it into the feed tube. The sides of the cabbage should be touching or parallel to the slicing disk. It is easier to pack the first layer through the bottom of the feed tube, then place the cover over the processor. Now you can wedge a second layer of the cabbage through the top of the feed tube. Slice with the *Medium Slicing Disk.* (To slice by hand see page 14.)

4. Wash cabbage thoroughly and drain. Put it into a large bowl or pot. Add salt and water, and mix thoroughly. Place something heavy on top of the vegetables to press them down, and let stand for at least 2 hours. §

Seasoning:

1. Drain the cabbage in a colander, and rinse with cold running water. Squeeze the cabbage to expel any excess water. Wipe the bowl dry with paper towels, and return the cabbage to the bowl.

2. Sprinkle sugar, vinegar, and minced ginger over the cabbage.

3. Heat 2 tablespoons oil in a wok or a small saucepan over medium heat. Fry the crushed red pepper and Szechuan peppercorns for about 1 minute or until the red pepper flakes turn brown. Immediately pour the hot oil through a strainer and directly onto the cabbage. In this way, you will have the flavor of the Szechuan peppercorns, but will not get the hard husks into your mouth when you are eating. Toss and mix the cabbage thoroughly. Let it marinate in the refrigerator for at least a day before serving, turning the cabbage a few times. Serve cold. This dish can be kept in the refrigerator for several weeks. §

RADISH SALAD

 Tian-suan-hong-luo-bo

Serves 2 to 3 ‡

Radishes	2 6-ounce/180 g bags
Sugar	2 tablespoons or to taste
White Vinegar	2 tablespoons
Salt	½ teaspoon

PREPARATION: 7 minutes

MARINATING TIME: 1 hour

Preparation:

Wash and cut off ends of radishes. With *Medium Slicing Disk* in place, fill the feed tube with radishes and slice. Or slice by hand. When they are all sliced, remove to a serving bowl. Add remaining ingredients, and toss to mix. Let stand in the refrigerator for at least 1 hour, tossing once or twice. Drain and serve. §

Variations:

1. Add minced ginger. Before slicing the radishes, chop one ½-inch/1½-cm cube fresh ginger with *Steel Blade*.

2. Slice the radishes with *Thin Slicing Disk;* they will have a different texture.

SHREDDED TURNIP SALAD

葱油蘿蔔絲   Cong-you-luo-bo-si

Serves 4 ‡

Salt and sugar remove the pungent taste from the turnip, and turns this into a mild-tasting salad, refreshingly crunchy with a remarkable scallion flavor. It can be kept in the refrigerator for several days.

Scallions	2, cut into 2-inch/5-cm sections
Chinese Large White Turnips (*or* American Turnips)	1 pound/450 g
Salt	1 tablespoon
Sugar	1½ tablespoons or to taste
Cooking Oil	2 tablespoons

PREPARATION: 10 minutes

MACERATING TIME: 2 hours

COOKING: 4 minutes

MARINATING TIME: at least half a day

Preparation:

1. With *Steel Blade* in place, chop scallions and remove them from the beaker. (To chop by hand see page 14.)

2. With *Medium Slicing Disk* in place, cut turnips to the size that will fit the feed tube. Slice the turnips, and remove the slices from the beaker. Reprocess the slices to get shreds. Or you may shred the turnips with the *French Fry Cutter.* It will be faster, but the shreds will be coarser. Or shred by hand.

3. Transfer turnip shreds to a bowl, and sprinkle with salt. Mix thoroughly, and let stand for 2 hours or longer. §

Cooking:

1. Drain turnips in a colander, and rinse well with cold water. Squeeze out the water and drain well.

2. Put the turnips in a serving bowl. Sprinkle with sugar, and top them with chopped scallions.

3. Heat 2 tablespoons oil until it just reaches the smoking point. Pour the hot oil over the turnips. Toss and mix thoroughly. Let them marinate for at least a half day or longer, turning a few times. Keep in the refrigerator and serve cold. Can be kept for over a week. §

WATERCRESS SALAD

冷拌西洋菜   Leng-ban-xi-yang-cai

Serves 4 ‡

This is a refreshing salad. The watercress is blanched quickly in the boiling water to remove its bitter taste but still retain its crispy texture.

Water	2 quarts/2 L
Watercress	2 bunches
Sesame Oil	1 tablespoon
Light Soy Sauce	4 teaspoons or to taste
(*or* all-purpose soy sauce —light soy sauce is preferred here, as it will not mask the fresh green color of the watercress)	

PREPARATION AND COOKING: 8 minutes

Preparation and Cooking:

1. Heat water to boiling in a large pot. In the meantime, wash the watercress very well under running water. When the water in the pot comes to boiling, add watercress. Bring the water back to boiling, and let boil for 1 minute. Quickly drain the vegetable in a colander, and rinse with cold water. Squeeze out the excess water.

2. With *Steel Blade* in place, chop half of the drained watercress using 3 to 4 quick on/off turns or until coarsely chopped. Check carefully and do not overprocess. Remove the chopped watercress to a serving bowl, and repeat with the other half. (Discard any water collected in the beaker.) You may also chop the watercress by hand. §

3. Toss watercress with sesame oil and soy sauce until they are well mixed. This salad can be made ahead, and kept in the refrigerator until serving time. §

Variation:

Add ½ cup/1 dL finely minced fresh parsley. Using *Steel Blade*, mince parsley very finely in a dry beaker. Then without removing the parsley, add the first half of watercress to the beaker to chop. Proceed as in step 2.

Soup

Soup is an integral part of a traditional Chinese meal. It is usually placed in a large bowl and left on the table throughout the meal. You help yourself to a little soup from time to time, spooning it into your bowl, and drinking it as a beverage. Tea is usually not served until after the meal. At a formal dinner banquet, soup is served in the middle of the many courses.

A good soup depends on a good basic stock, and the best way is to make your own through the long simmering method. However, many people do not have time for such a long process. In this case, a light-colored, canned chicken broth, such as College Inn brand, is a good substitute. It is flavorful, clear, and free of residue.

Soup is a good way of using leftovers; use them as soup ingredients, or save your chicken, turkey, duck, and pork bones for making basic stock. Because of their strong flavor, lamb and beef bones are not used in basic stock.

Fresh green vegetables should not be added to the soup until a few minutes before it is to be served. Otherwise, they will lose their bright color.

BASIC CHICKEN BROTH *

清雞湯   Qing-ji-tang

Makes 10 cups

Use fowl to make the chicken broth, for it gives more flavor than the young tender chicken. If you don't have time to make your own chicken broth, you can substitute a light-colored canned chicken broth, such as College Inn brand.

Fowl	1 whole, cut into quarters
Water	3 quarts/2¾ L
Scallions	2 whole
Fresh Ginger	2 slices
Dry Sherry	2 tablespoons
Salt	to taste

PREPARATION AND COOKING: 4½ hours

Preparation and Cooking:
1. Put the fowl in a large pot, and cover with water. Bring to a boil, and cook for 2 minutes. Remove the bird, and rinse with cold water.
2. Discard the water in the pot, then rinse and clean the pot. Add 3 quarts/2¾ L of fresh cold water and return fowl to the pot. Bring the water to a boil. Add scallions, ginger, and sherry, and simmer the broth for 4 hours. Season to taste with salt and dash of pepper at the end of the cooking period.
3. Let cool, then strain the broth, and discard the fowl.
4. Refrigerate the broth, and just before using skim off the fat on the top. §

Tips:
The broth will keep in the refrigerator for 4 to 5 days. If you want to keep it longer, reboil the broth every 5 days, and replace it in the refrigerator.
Or you can measure the broth into 1- or 2-cup/¼- or ½-L portions, and keep in the freezer for over a year.

Variation:
You can use the bones from chicken breasts and pork, or carcasses from duck and turkey to replace the fowl. Save them in the freezer until you have enough to fill a large pot. Cover them with water, and cook for 2 hours. Strain and remove scum and bones. Return clear broth to the pot, and reduce to half its volume. Season to taste and refrigerate.

EGG DROP SOUP

蛋花湯   Dan-hua-tang

Serves 4 to 6 ‡

The best-known Chinese soup in the Western Hemisphere, this soup is delicate and nutritious, yet it is fast and easy to make. It is best tasting when the eggs are poured into the boiling soup and barely cooked just before serving.

Chicken Broth	5 cups/1¼ L
Scallions	2, cut into 2-inch/5-cm sections
Eggs	2
Cornstarch	2 tablespoons in 6 tablespoons water

PREPARATION AND COOKING: 6 minutes

Preparation and Cooking:

Heat the chicken broth in a saucepan. In the meantime, coarsely chop the scallions with *Steel Blade,* or by hand. Lightly beat the 2 eggs, and combine cornstarch with water.

Add chopped scallions to the boiling broth, and cook for 1 minute. Slowly pour the cornstarch mixture into the boiling broth, stirring constantly until the soup boils again. Pour the beaten eggs over the surface of the soup, and immediately remove the saucepan from the heat. Wait for 30 seconds, then stir once, and serve the soup in individual bowls or a tureen.

CHOPPED WATERCRESS AND EGG DROP SOUP

西洋菜蛋花湯   Xi-yang-cai-dan-hua-tang

Serves 4 to 5 ‡

Chicken Broth	5 cups/1¼ L
Watercress	4 ounces/115 g
Eggs	2
Cornstarch	2½ tablespoons in 4 tablespoons water or chicken broth

PREPARATION AND COOKING: 6 minutes

Preparation and Cooking:

1. Heat the chicken broth to boil in a saucepan. In the meantime, wash the watercress, and cut them into half lengths. By hand, or with *Steel Blade* in place, coarsely chop the watercress 2 cups/½ L at a time. Remove, and finish chopping the remaining watercress.

2. Lightly beat the 2 eggs. Combine cornstarch with water in a small bowl.

3. Add chopped watercress to the boiling chicken broth, and let simmer for 2 minutes. Give the cornstarch mixture a good stir, slowly pour into the soup, stirring constantly until the soup boils again. Pour the beaten eggs over the surface of the soup, and immediately removed the saucepan from the heat. Wait for 30 seconds, then stir up, and serve the soup in individual bowls or a tureen.

Variations:

1. Sprinkle 2 tablespoons finely minced Smithfield ham on top of the soup just before serving. Mince with *Steel Blade* before chopping the watercress.

2. Substitute 4 cups/1 L fresh spinach for watercress.

CHICKEN VELVET CORN SOUP

雞蓉粟米湯   Ji-rong-su-mi-tang

Serves 4 to 6 ‡

This is an elegant and delicious soup, one of the few thick Chinese soups. Traditionally, the chicken breast was pureed by the cleaver, but as you can see, it required time as well as patience. So this soup was traditionally served only by restaurants, and usually at dinner-banquets. However, with the advent of the food processor, this operation is reduced to seconds and now can be easily done at home.

Cooked Smithfield Ham	4 ½-inch/1½-cm cubes

Chicken Mixture:

Chicken Breast	half (or 4 ounces/115 g), boneless, skinless
Egg Whites	2
Cornstarch	1 teaspoon
Dry Sherry	1 teaspoon
Salt	¼ teaspoon or to taste
Water	2 tablespoons
Cream Corn	17-ounce/480-g can (or 2 cups/½ L)
Chicken Broth	2 cups/½ L
Salt	To taste
Ground White Pepper	¼ teaspoon or to taste
Cornstarch	1 tablespoon in 2 tablespoons water

AHEAD OF TIME:

If *frozen chicken* is used, thaw partially or completely following these directions:

20 minutes or more to partially thaw meat at room temperature
5 minutes or more to partially thaw meat in a 250°F/120°C oven
20 seconds or more to partially thaw meat in a microwave oven

PREPARATION: 5 minutes

COOKING: 6 minutes

Preparation:

1. With *Steel Blade* in a dry beaker, process the ham until finely minced. (To mince by hand see page 14.) Remove from the beaker and set aside. Clean the beaker out with a paper towel.

2. Replace the *Steel Blade.* Cut chicken into 1-inch/2½-cm pieces, and process until chicken is pureed. (To puree by blender see page 15.) Add the remaining ingredients for the chicken mixture, and process until it is creamy and smooth (or puree the chicken mixture using a blender). §

Cooking:

Combine cream corn and chicken broth in a pot, and bring to a boil. Season to taste, and let the soup simmer for 2 minutes. Give the cornstarch mixture a good stir, then add to the soup, stirring constantly until soup is thickened. Quickly stir the chicken mixture into the boiling soup, and disperse it evenly. Remove soup from the burner. The heat of the soup will finish cooking the chicken. This soup can be cooked ahead and reheated. §

Just before serving, sprinkle the minced ham on top of the soup.

Tips:

Smithfield ham is closest to the Chinese ham, for it is more salty and has much more flavor than the regular boiled and baked hams. Chinese food stores and many Western gourmet shops sell the Smithfield ham. Italian Prosciutto ham can be used as a substitute. The uncooked Smithfield and Prosciutto ham should be steamed for about 10 minutes. Let cool before mincing.

Variation:

CREAM OF CORN SOUP

                                                          Su-mi-tang

Serves 4 ‡

PREPARATION AND COOKING (5 minutes):

Substitute the chicken mixture in Chicken Velvet Corn Soup with 2 eggs slightly beaten with ¼ teaspoon salt. It is a quick, nutritious, and wonderful soup.

SLICED CHICKEN AND WATERCRESS SOUP

西洋菜雞片湯   Xi-yang-cai-ji-pian-tang

Serves 4 ‡

| Chicken Breast | half (4 ounces/115 g), boneless, skinless, and frozen |

Marinade:

Salt	¼ teaspoon
Cornstarch	1½ teaspoons
Dry Sherry	2 teaspoons

Fresh Watercress	4 ounces/115 g
Chicken Broth	4 cups/1 L
Salt	To taste

AHEAD OF TIME:
Partially defrost *frozen chicken* just long enough to slice following these directions:

20 minutes or more to partially thaw meat at room temperature
5 minutes or more to partially thaw meat in a 250°F/120°C oven
20 seconds or more to partially thaw meat in a microwave oven

PREPARATION: 4 minutes

COOKING: 5 minutes

Preparation:
With *Medium Slicing Disk* in place, cut chicken breast crosswise into halves. Fit the breast in the feed tube and slice. (To slice by hand see page 14.) Mix with the marinade in a bowl.

Wash and drain watercress. Cut off hard stems, then cut into halves lengthwise. §

Cooking:
Bring chicken broth to a boil. Add watercress, and bring the broth back to boil. Then add chicken slices, cooking over high heat until chicken just turns white. Remove from heat immediately. Add salt to taste and serve.

FISH BALL SOUP

魚丸湯   Yu-wan-tang

Serves 3 to 4 ‡

The soft white fish balls and the crisp green watercress give a contrast of color and texture to this light and refreshing soup. The Chinese often serve fish ball soup to convalescents, for it is high in protein and nutrients, low in fat, and easily digestible for the inactive person.

Chicken Broth	5 cups/1¼ L
Watercress	4 ounces/115 g
Cooked Fish Balls	Half a recipe (see page 166)
Salt	To taste
Ground Black Pepper	⅛ teaspoon or to taste

PREPARATION AND COOKING: 10 minutes

Preparation and Cooking:

1. Heat the chicken broth to boil in a saucepan. In the meantime, wash and drain watercress. Discard hard stems, and cut into 2-inch/5-cm sections.

2. Add fish balls to the boiling broth, and let simmer for 2 minutes. (Cook longer if fish balls are still frozen.)

3. Add watercress to the saucepan, and simmer for 2 more minutes. Season to taste with salt and pepper. Serve hot.

Variations:

1. Fresh spinach can be used in place of watercress.

2. Pork or shrimp balls can be used in place of fish balls, or you can use a combination of the two.

3. Sliced cooked Smithfield ham and Chinese mushrooms may be substituted for watercress, or added to the soup with watercress for additional flavors.

4. Fresh snow peas (ends and strings removed), sliced ham, and bamboo shoots can be substituted for watercress.

HOT AND SOUR SOUP

酸辣湯   Suan-la-tang

Serves 4 to 6 ‡

The name may scare away those with a timid palate. Given a chance to taste it, one would soon be attracted to its extraordinary and stimulating flavors—both spicy and pungent. This Northern soup is hearty and filling, and especially good for cold winter days. It has thus far become one of the most popular soups for Americans. And it makes a marvelous meal with Moo-shu Pork or dumplings.

Dry Chinese Mushrooms	4
Dry Tree Ears	2 tablespoons
Dry Tiger Lilies	14
Bean Curd	½ pound/225 g (or 2 3 × 3 × ¾-inch/8 × 8 × 2-cm pieces)
Scallion	1
Bamboo Shoots	4 ounces/115 g (1 cup/¼ L shredded)
Cooked Pork or Chicken	¼ cup/½ dL, in shreds
Eggs	2, lightly beaten
Cornstarch	2 tablespoons in 4 tablespoons water
Chicken Broth	4 cups/1 L
Soy Sauce	1 tablespoon or to taste
Ground Black Pepper	¼ to ½ teaspoon or to taste
Wine Vinegar	2 tablespoons or to taste
Sesame Oil	1 tablespoon

AHEAD OF TIME:

Snap stems off of the Chinese mushrooms. Place the mushrooms, tree ears, and tiger lilies in bowl. Pour 1½ cups/3½ dL of boiling water over them and let soak for 15 minutes.

PREPARATION: 15 minutes

COOKING: 10 minutes

Preparation:

1. Cut bean curd into 1 × 1 × ½-inch/2½ × 2½ × 1½-cm pieces.
2. Finely chop scallion either with *Steel Blade* or by hand. Transfer to a small bowl.
3. Slice bamboo shoots first, then cut into shreds. This can be done either by hand or with *Medium Slicing Disk.*
4. Shred the cooked meat by hand.
5. Lightly beat 2 eggs.

6. Drain mushrooms, tree ears, and tiger lilies. Cut mushrooms into shreds. Cut tree ears to smaller pieces by hand or by *Steel Blade*. Cut tiger lilies into 2 sections.

7. Combine cornstarch with water in a small bowl. §

Cooking:

1. Heat chicken broth to boil in a 3-quart/2¾-L saucepan. Add bean curd, bamboo shoots, meat, mushrooms, tree ears, tiger lilies, and soy sauce. Boil again, and let simmer for 2 minutes.

2. Add ground pepper and vinegar to the soup. Give the cornstarch mixture a good stir, and slowly pour into the saucepan, stirring constantly until soup boils again.

3. Slowly pour the beaten eggs into the soup, stirring gently a few times. Remove from the heat.

4. Add sesame oil and sprinkle with chopped scallions for garnish. Serve in a soup tureen or individual soup bowls.

Tips:

Eggs are lighter and more fluffy when freshly cooked. Vinegar and ground pepper lose their strength from prolong cooking, so you can pre-cook the soup to step 1, and do the rest just before serving to get the best results.

Leftover soup can be reheated; you may have to add more vinegar and pepper to restore its taste.

Offer hot chili oil to those who like additional spice.

Variation:

You can use 4 ounces/115 g of shredded raw meat in place of the cooked meat. Mix the raw meat with 1 teaspoon each of cornstarch, sherry, and soy sauce. The soup tastes good even without the meat.

PORK BALL AND CELLOPHANE NOODLE SOUP

粉絲肉丸湯   Fen-si-rou-wan-tang

Serves 4 to 6 ‡

Cellophane Noodles	2 ounces/60 g
Steamed Pork Balls	1 recipe (see page 79)
(frozen pork balls can be used without defrosting)	
Chicken Broth	4 cups/1 L
Salt	To taste

AHEAD OF TIME:

Put cellophane noodles in a bowl, then cover and soak with boiling water. Let stand for 15 minutes.

PREPARATION AND COOKING: 5 minutes

Preparation:

Heat the chicken broth to a boil. Drain the cellophane noodles in a colander. Add the noodles and the meat balls to the broth, and bring it back to a boil. Let simmer for 3 minutes (cook a little longer if the meat balls are frozen), and taste for seasoning. Add salt to taste, and serve hot. It can be cooked ahead. §

SHRIMP BALL SOUP

蝦丸湯   Xia-wan-tang

Serves 3 to 4 ‡

This shrimp ball soup is delicate in taste and appearance. Select a cucumber no larger than 1½ inch/4 cm in diameter, so you will have perfect slices from the processor. If you have a thin slicer, use it instead of the medium slicer. Only chefs with great cutting skills and experience can cut such thin, even slices. The thin cucumber slices will look almost transparent after they are cooked, showing only the green skin which floats in the soup like thin emerald rings surrounded by the pinkish shrimp balls. Serve 2 to 3 balls and a few cucumber slices in each individual soup bowl.

Steamed Shrimp Balls (frozen shrimp balls can be used without defrosting)	Half recipe (see page 75)
Cucumber	½, cut crosswise
Chicken Broth	4 cups/1 L
Salt	to taste

PREPARATION AND COOKING: 8 minutes

Preparation and Cooking:

1. Wash the cucumber and scrub the skin. Scoop out the seeds with a small paring knife. With *Thin or Medium Slicing Disk* in place, place cucumber flat side down and against the right side of the feed tube wall, and slice. (To slice by hand see page 14.)
2. Bring the chicken broth to a boil. Canned broth is usually salty enough; if homemade broth is used, adjust the seasoning to taste.
3. Add the shrimp balls, and bring the broth back to a boil, then let it simmer for 2 minutes. (If frozen shrimp balls are used, simmer them longer or until heated through.) Add sliced cucumber. If thin slices are used, cook for 1 minute; cook 2 minutes for the thick slices. Serve hot.

Variations:

1. Fish balls can be used in place of shrimp balls. Or you can use both in the soup.
2. Substitute ¼ cup/½ dL bamboo slices and 4 softened dry Chinese mushrooms for the cucumber. This soup can be cooked ahead and reheated.
3. Add 12 fresh snow peas (ends and strings removed) to the bamboo slices and dry mushrooms soup in the above variation. Cook the snow peas at the last minute for about 2 minutes. Do not over cook.

SZECHUAN PRESERVED VEGETABLE SOUP

榨菜湯   Zha-cai-tang

Serves 4 ‡

Szechuan preserved vegetable usually comes in cans. It is both salty and spicy, and gives this soup a unique and refreshing taste.

Dry Cellophane Noodles	1 ounce/30 g (½ package)
Cooked Meat or Chicken	2 to 3 ounces/60 to 85 g
Szechuan Preserved Vegetable	2 ounces/60 g (½ cup)
Water	4 cups/1 L
Soy Sauce	2 teaspoons or to taste
Salt	if desired
Sesame Oil	1 tablespoon (optional)

AHEAD OF TIME:

In a bowl, cover cellophane noodles with boiling water, and let stand for 15 minutes.

PREPARATION AND COOKING: 7 minutes

Preparation and Cooking:

1. Bring the 4 cups/1 L of water to boil. In the meantime, shred the meat by hand into 2-inch/5-cm thin strips.

2. If you prefer to have the soup not so spicy, rinse away the chili powder coating on the preserved vegetable, and pat dry with paper towels. Otherwise, use it without rinsing. With *Medium Slicing Disk* in place, first slice and then shred the vegetable. (To slice and shred by hand see page 14.)

3. Drain the cellophane noodles in a colander.

4. When the water is boiling, add Szechuan preserved vegetable, cellophane noodles, meat, and soy sauce. Bring the soup back to boil, and let simmer for 2 minutes. Taste for seasoning, and add salt if desired. Add sesame oil just before serving. This soup can be made ahead, and rewarmed. §

VEGETABLE SOUP

素菜湯   Su-cai-tang

Serves 3 to 4 ‡

This clear and refreshing soup with lots of vegetables is best tasting when the tomato is red and ripe.

Chicken Broth	3 cups/¾ L
Carrot	1 large, peeled
Celery	1 large stalk, stringed
Onion	1 medium, peeled
Potato	1 small, peeled
Round Cabbage	½ pound/225 g
Ripe Tomato	1 large
Cooking Oil	2 tablespoons
Salt	to taste
Ground Black Pepper	to taste
Sesame Oil	1 tablespoon or to taste (optional)
Hot Chili Oil	to taste (optional)

PREPARATION AND COOKING: 20 minutes

Preparation and Cooking:

1. Bring the chicken broth to boil in a 3-quart/2¾-L saucepan. In the meantime, prepare the vegetables.

2. Cut carrot and celery to lengths shorter than the feed tube. Pack them in the feed tube and slice with *Medium Slicing Disk.* Cut onion and potato to fit the feed tube, then slice. (To slice by hand see page 14.) Add the vegetables to the hot broth.

3. Cut cabbage into 1-inch/2½-cm wedges, then cut the wedges into halves crosswise. Add to the hot broth.

4. Let the soup come to a boil, then simmer for 5 minutes or until vegetables are just tender. In the meantime, boil 2 cups/½ L water.

5. Pour the boiling water over to cover the tomato in a small deep bowl. Let soak for 1 minute, then remove tomato and peel off the skin. Cut it into 8 wedges and remove the seeds.

6. Heat 2 tablespoons oil in a wok or small saucepan. Stir-fry tomato wedges for 1 minute. Add the oil and tomato to the soup; this will enhance the appearance of the soup with the orange-colored oil floating over the surface. Let the tomato simmer for 1 minute. Season to taste with salt and pepper before serving. It can be cooked ahead and rewarmed. §

7. For individual flavor, you can add sesame or hot chili oil to suit individual tastes.

WONTON SOUP

錕飩湯   Hun-tun-tang

Serves 4 to 5 ‡

Some people like the thin wrappers, and others like the thick ones for wrapping the wontons. It is a matter of personal taste.

Uncooked Wontons   20 (frozen wontons can be used without thaw-
                     ing, see page 236)
   Chicken Broth   5 cups/1¼ L
      Watercress   4 ounces/115 g

PREPARATION AND COOKING: 10 minutes

Preparation and Cooking:
   1. In a large pot, bring 2 quarts/2 L of water to a boil.
   2. In another pot, heat 5 cups/1¼ L of chicken broth to boil.
   3. In the meantime, wash watercress and cut into halves lengthwise.
   4. When the water is boiled, add the wontons and bring the water back to boil. Cook over medium-high heat for 3 to 5 minutes (a little longer for frozen wontons). Wontons with thick wrappers should be cooked so that the wrappers are tender but still a little resistant to the bite. Drain the cooked wontons in a colander.
   5. While the wontons are being cooked, cook the watercress in the boiling chicken broth for 2 minutes, uncovered, over medium heat.
   6. Add the drained boiled wontons to the hot chicken broth and serve hot.

Variation:
Fresh spinach can be used in place of watercress.

MONGOLIAN FIRE POT

火鍋   Huo-guo

Serves 6

The Mongols introduced this cooking method to Northern China after their invasion in the thirteenth century. It is like Western fondue, and a fun activity for the family, especially on cold nights. In China, where most homes did not have central heating, eating around a blazing fire pot and cooking as one ate, was not only fun, it was also a means of keeping warm! Since all the food is cooked in boiling water or a broth, it is a very healthy and low-calorie meal. Another advantage of the Mongolian fire pot is that all the preparations can be done in advance, and the cooking is done at the table by the diners.

About the Meat:

The Mongols and the Northern Chinese use thinly sliced lamb or mutton as the major ingredient. As fire pot cooking spread throughout China, it was much refined, and less pungent meat such as beef, chicken, fish, shrimp, oyster, and clams were also used. However, the vegetables used in this dish are quite similar throughout the country.

You should slice the meat across the grain (and as thin as possible) in about 1½ × 4-inch/4 × 10-cm slices. Check with your butcher, for my butcher would partially freeze the meat, and then slice it paper-thin for me with his machine. He then places it on wrapping paper, with a little overlapping so each slice can be picked up individually and easily without sticking to the others. In this way, your major preparations are done.

If you are slicing the meat by hand, it is easier to slice it paper-thin if it's partially frozen.

When I serve the fire pot just for the family (this is our favorite Sunday dinner in the winter months), I am not concerned about the uniformity and smaller size of the meat; so I slice the meat with the food processor and use the Fine Serrated Slicing Disk. To get neat slices, the meat should be partially frozen until firm. The Fine Serrated Slicing Disk can slice the meat thinner than I can by hand. The Medium Slicing Disk does not work well, for the slices are too thick for this dish.

Cooking Equipment:

I found that an electric wok or deep electric skillet works more conveniently than the traditional, charcoal-burning fire pot, especially for a family dinner. A large-sized fire pot, the electric wok, or the electric skillet can cook for up to 8 people. For 2 to 3 persons only, a fondue pot functions quite well. A pot on a hot plate will also work.

The traditional fire pot is made of copper or bronze with a chimney rising through the center. The base is used for filling with hot charcoal. It is a very impressive looking utensil, and does give a very festive atmosphere to your table. They can be purchased in Chinatown and gourmet shops.

It is easier to heat up the charcoal first, preferably in a barbeque pit outdoors, and then to transfer it to the fire pot, which is already filled with hot water or broth. You should also have a reserve supply of hot charcoal, for those in the fire pot will lose their intensity.

Individual Place Setting:
- 1 plate
- 1 soup spoon
- 1 bowl for both dipping sauce and soup (or you can offer 2 separate bowls)
- a pair of chopsticks (or a fork) for eating
- 1 wire-mesh scoop for cooking meat. (A pair of chopsticks, or a fondue fork can be substituted.) The wire-mesh scoop is a relatively new innovation. It is like a little strainer holding and cooking the meat very well. Traditionally, a pair of chopsticks is used to hold the meat in the boiling broth until meat is cooked.

Boned Leg of Lamb	2 pounds/900 g
(Flank Steak or Sirloin Tip)	
Cellophane Noodles	4 ounces/115 g
Fresh Bean Curd	1 pound/450 g (optional)
Fresh Spinach	1 pound/450 g
Celery Cabbage	½ pound/225 g

*Sauce Ingredients for the
Master Sauce:*

Fresh Ginger	½-inch/1½-cm cube
Scallion	1, in 2-inch/5-cm sections
Soy Sauce	½ cup/1 dL
Sesame Oil	3 tablespoons
Chinese Vinegar	3 tablespoons
(*or* Wine Vinegar)	
Sesame Paste	3 tablespoons
(*or* Creamy Peanut Butter)	
Red Fermented Bean Curd	2 tablespoons
(*or* substitute 3 tablespoons Soy Sauce)	
Sugar	1½ tablespoons
Hot Chili Oil	1 teaspoon or to taste (optional)
(*or* Tabasco Sauce to taste)	
Sesame Seed Bread	18 (see page 255)
(*or* Pita bread—the small 4-inch/10-cm ones)	
Chicken Broth (or Water)	8 cups/2 L

AHEAD OF TIME:
If you are going to slice the meat yourself, do it either by hand or with the food processor. Freeze the meat until firm, 2 hours or more, depending on the size of the meat. For slicing with the food processor, cut the meat into feed-tube size before freezing.

PREPARATION: 20 to 40 minutes

Preparation:
1. Soak and cover the cellophane noodles in plenty of boiling water for about 15 minutes or until soft. Drain in a colander. Cut them into shorter lengths, and place in a serving bowl.
2. While the cellophane noodles are being soaked, you can prepare the other steps. Cut bean curd into 1-inch/2½-cm cubes, and place in a serving bowl in the refrigerator.
3. Wash, drain, and remove tough ends of the spinach. Place in a serving bowl.

4. Wash and drain the celery cabbage. With *Medium Slicing Disk* in place, cut and wedge cabbage into the feed tube and slice. (To slice by hand see page 14.) Transfer the cabbage to a serving bowl.

5. If you are to slice the meat yourself, do it by hand or with the processor. Use *Fine Serrated Slicing Disk* to slice with the processor.

6. Arrange the meat slices neatly and slightly overlapping the next slice on 3 large plates. For family meals, I often place all the layers on one plate, but each layer is separated by plastic wrap. Keep the meat slices in the refrigerator until serving time.

7. For the dipping sauce, you can either mix the ingredients together to make a master sauce, or let the diners mix their own sauce. For the latter, you should put each sauce ingredient in an individual bowl or container, about 3 to 4 times of the quantity indicated for making the master sauce. Finely mince the ginger and scallion, and thin the sesame paste with water so it is the consistency of a thick sauce.

8. To make master sauce, place *Steel Blade* in the clean beaker. Process ginger and scallion until finely minced. Add the remaining sauce ingredients to the beaker. (You can leave the hot oil out of the sauce mixture, and let each one add it according to taste at the last minute.) Process until mixed. (To prepare without the food processor, mince the ginger and scallion by hand or in a blender. Then combine them with the remaining sauce ingredients. You can leave the hot oil out of the sauce mixture and let each one add it according to taste at the last minute.) §

Cooking and Serving:

1. 10 minutes before serving, wrap the breads in aluminum foil, and heat in a 350°F/180°C oven. Or warm them in a bread warming basket.

2. Heat the chicken broth or water to a boil in the cooking equipment, which is placed at the center of the table, and keep it simmering throughout the meal. Arrange platters of meat, and sauce ingredients, or master sauce around the pot.

3. Seat the diners around the table. You can place 2 to 3 tablespoons of the master sauce in your bowl, or mix your own sauce.

4. You pick up 1 or 2 pieces of uncooked meat from the platter, and hold the meat in the simmering broth with the wire-mesh scoop, chopsticks, or fondue fork. When the meat is cooked to desired degree, remove it from the pot. Meat only takes a few seconds. Dip the cooked meat in the sauce in your bowl. It can be eaten by itself or with the warm bread. (Cut the bread in half, and fill the pocket of each half with the meat. Add more sauce or spices if desired.) If the simmering liquid is too quickly reduced in the cooking, add more water.

5. When the meat is finished, bring the vegetables, bean curd, and cellophane noodles to the table, and add to the simmering liquid, using one-third or one-half of these ingredients at a time. Cover the pot, and cook until the vegetables are tender. They can be served with the dipping

sauce or with the broth in the pot. The broth is served as the last course, for as you can see, the Chinese don't waste anything! This broth is usually very tasty, for it has by now incorporated all the flavors from the meat and the vegetables. Finish cooking all the vegetables, and then help yourself to the vegetables and the broth, which can be served in the same bowl that was used for the dipping sauce. Any extra sauce left in the bowl will also flavor the soup.

Tips:

The number of people served at this kind of meal will depend on the capacity of the cooking pot and the size of the table. When there are more people, just use more cooking pots and bring out more tables.

Variation:

Thinly sliced chicken, fish fillets, fresh oysters, and fresh clams can also be used to add more variety.

Rice, Noodles, and Other Wheat Products

With the exception of the Northern region, rice is the main staple of the Chinese. Because of China's geographic location, wheat grows much better than rice in the North, and so it has become the main staple of the Northerners. It is served as noodles, steamed buns, breads, and pancakes. For the rest of the country, these wheat products are eaten occasionally, and often as snacks.

RICE

Rice is so important to the Chinese that the word "rice" is often used to mean the meal itself. When a Chinese asks someone whether they have had their lunch or dinner, the question will be: "Have you had your rice?" Even in the Northern region, where wheat is the common staple, the question is still: "Have you had your rice?"

Be they rich or poor—and even in the North, the wheat region where my husband grew up—children are always taught at a very young age about the hard labor of the farmers in the rice fields, and that they must finish every grain of rice in the bowl.

Plain boiled rice (no butter or salt) is used to accompany the dishes at the daily meal. Fried rice is often served as a snack, or sometimes at the end of a formal banquet. Another way of cooking rice is to make it into rice soup or congee (rice cooked with a large amount of water). Both raw or cooked rice can be used. Congee and fried rice are both good ways of using leftover cooked rice. Plain congee is served as breakfast and is very bland, so it is usually accompanied by pickled and salty food, such as salted duck eggs, thousand year eggs, salted peanuts, or salted and pickled vegetables. These are an acquired taste; most Americans will not take to them easily.

Seasoned rice congee is often cooked with chicken, fish, or meat and served as a light meal or midnight snack. It is especially popular in the Southern region.

There are two kinds of rice to serve with the daily meal: a long-grain and an oval (or medium-grain) rice. The latter has a softer and stickier texture. The long-grain rice is better for fried rice; the medium-grain rice is better for congee. Both are good when the recipe calls for boiled rice; it is strictly a matter of personal preference.

The Chinese usually wash the rice several times before cooking it or until the water is clear. This is to remove any husks and to rinse off any loose starch, so each grain of rice will seperate after cooking. But since most of the rice now sold in American supermarkets is enriched and specially labeled "to retain vitamins, do not rinse before cooking," you can get pretty good results without rinsing it. This rice does not have as much superficial starch as Chinese rice, so if you want to save the vitamins or just save time, you can skip the washing.

BOILED RICE ★

白飯

You should cook rice in a heavy saucepan that is at least 4 times bigger than the volume of rice to be cooked. Be sure you have a tight-fitting cover for your pan.

If you choose to wash the rice, cover it with cold water in the saucepan that you are going to use for cooking. Stir the rice with water and then drain in a strainer. Repeat the process 2 to 3 times. Drain the rice thoroughly after the final washing.

Cooking (35 minutes):

For cooking, place the unwashed or the washed and well-drained rice in the saucepan, and add the appropriate amount of water given below. Place the uncovered saucepan on a burner over high heat. When it comes to a vigorous boil, turn the heat down immediately to very low and cover the saucepan. (For the *electric burner,* transfer the saucepan to another burner which is preheated at low, instead of leaving on the same burner and waiting for it to cool off.) Cook for 20 minutes undisturbed. Then immediately remove the saucepan from the heat, and let it stand for 10 minutes undisturbed. *Do not lift the cover* throughout the simmering and the standing period. The last step is important to achieve properly cooked rice, for during this standing period, the heat in the saucepan will finish cooking the rice and absorb the remaining moisture.

Fluff and stir the rice while it is hot, so each grain of rice will separate.

The ratio of rice to water is given below. If you prefer a softer rice, add a little more water; and if you like it firmer, use a little less. Long-grain rice takes more water than the medium-grain rice. One (1) cup/¼ L rice makes 3½ cups ⁴/₅ L cooked rice.

Long-grain rice	Water
1 cup/¼ L	1½ cups/3½ dL
2 cups/½ L	3 cups/¾ L
3 cups/¾ L	4 cups/1 L

Medium-grain rice	Water
1 cup/¼ L	1⅓ cups/3¼ dL
2 cups/½ L	2½ cups/6 dL
3 cups/¾ L	3½ cups/⁴/₅ L

Tips:

Freshly cooked rice will stay warm in the saucepan for a good 45 minutes. Or it can be transferred to a covered serving bowl and kept warm in a 200°F/95°C oven for 1½ hours.

If you eat rice frequently, it will save you both time and heat if you cook extra amounts of rice the first time. (But remember that the more raw rice you use, the less water you need for cooking.) Then the next time when you need rice, just reheat the cooked rice by steaming directly in a heat-proof serving bowl for 5 to 10 minutes depending on the amount of rice. Or reheat the rice covered in a microwave oven, about 1 minute for each cup of cold rice. (You can use a plastic wrap to cover the rice.)

Boiled rice can be kept in the refrigerator for 5 to 6 days, or it can be frozen, and reheated without defrosting.

You can also buy an *automatic rice cooker* from Oriental food stores or Chinatowns. It will cook the rice, then keep the rice warm in the cooker. It comes in various sizes, so you can select one to suit your needs.

FRIED RICE ★   *Good – I added Vegetables*

炒飯   /Chao-fan

Serves 2 to 3 ‡
as one-dish meal

One of the most important requirements for cooking good fried rice is to start with cold boiled rice, so it is a perfect way to use leftover rice, and leftover meat can also be used in the fried rice.

Fried rice is most versatile, for it can be served as a snack, a side dish, and a one-dish meal if you have a substantial amount of meat in it. You can use any kind of cooked meat, or just use scrambled eggs alone. These dishes are named according to the main ingredients, such as ham fried rice, shrimp fried rice, chicken fried rice, egg fried rice, or subgum fried rice. (Subgum means an assortment of ingredients in Cantonese.)

Scallion	1, in 2-inch/5-cm sections
Cooked Meat (Ham, Chicken, Shrimp, Crab Meat, Roast Pork)	1½ cups/3½ dL (use one or several kinds)
Eggs	2
Salt	¼ teaspoon
Cooking Oil	4 tablespoons
Cold Boiled Rice	4 cups/1 L
Cooked Green Peas	½ cup/1 dL (or frozen peas)
Soy Sauce	2 tablespoons or to taste

PREPARATION: 5 minutes

COOKING: 6 minutes

Preparation:

1. With *Steel Blade* in place, chop scallion coarsely and remove from the beaker.

2. Replace the *Steel Blade,* and coarsely chop the cooked meat.

3. Beat eggs with ¼ teaspoon salt. §

Cooking:

1. Heat the wok, then heat 1 tablespoon oil. Scramble the beaten eggs until they are set, and remove from the wok.

2. Heat the wok, then heat 3 tablespoons oil. Stir-fry chopped scallions for 30 seconds, then add the rice, stirring quickly until rice is well coated with oil. (If your peas are still frozen, add them now with the rice, otherwise, add them in step 3.)

3. Add chopped meat and green peas, and stir to mix and heat through. Then add 2 tablespoons soy sauce or to taste, cooking and tossing until the rice is evenly coated.

4. Return the eggs to the wok, breaking them into small pieces and mixing with rice. Serve hot. §

Tips:

The cooked rice can be kept warm covered in a serving bowl in a 250°F/120°C oven for half an hour.

Fried rice can be reheated in the wok on the stove top, or reheated in a covered heat-proof server in a 350°F/180°C oven for ½ hour or until heated through. (Peas are best added last minute to the rice, as they will look stale from prolonged heating.)

Microwave oven is excellent for warming fried rice about 1 minute per cup.

Leftover fried rice can be kept in the refrigerator for 4 to 5 days, or can be frozen.

Variations:

1. Chinese sausages are delicious with fried rice. Use 2 links for the above recipe. They should be steamed for 15 minutes, then sliced or chopped before cooking with the rice.

2. In the Eastern region, salt rather than soy sauce is used to season the rice, so the rice remains white after frying. You may like to try this variation. Adding soy sauce is the Cantonese style of cooking fried rice.

CHOPPED BEEF AND EGG FRIED RICE ★

牛肉末炒飯   Niu-rou-mo-chao-fan

Serves 2 ‡

This is a fast one-dish meal from the Southern region.

Lettuce	4 to 5 leaves

Beef Mixture:

Boneless Beef	6 ounces/180 g, in 1-inch/2½-cm cubes
Cornstarch	1½ teaspoons
Dry Sherry	2 teaspoons
Soy Sauce	1 tablespoon

Eggs	2 with 1 teaspoon soy sauce
Cooking Oil	5 tablespoons
Cold Cooked Rice	3½ cups/⁴/₅ L
Soy Sauce	2 tablespoons or to taste

AHEAD OF TIME:
  If *frozen beef cubes* are used, thaw partially or completely following these directions:
    20 minutes or more to partially thaw meat at room temperature
    10 minutes or more to partially thaw meat in a 250°F/120°C oven
    1 minute or more to completely thaw meat in a microwave oven

PREPARATION: 8 minutes

COOKING: 7 minutes

Preparation:
  1. Shred the lettuce leaves with *Medium Slicing Disk.* (To shred by hand see page 14.) You should have about 1½ cups/3½ dL shredded lettuce. Remove.
  2. With *Steel Blade* in place, add beef mixture to the beaker. Process until it is chopped. (To chop by hand see page 14.)
  3. Beat 2 eggs with 1 teaspoon soy sauce. §

Cooking:
  1. Heat the wok, then heat 1½ tablespoons oil. Stir-fry the eggs until set; remove from the wok.
  2. Heat the wok, then heat another 1½ tablespoons oil. Stir-fry beef until it is no longer red; remove from the wok.
  3. Heat the wok, then heat 2 tablespoons oil. Toss the rice in the hot

oil until it is coated with oil. Return the beef and eggs, and add the shredded lettuce. Toss to mix. Add soy sauce or salt to taste. Cook to heat through. §

Tips:

The cooked rice can be kept in the refrigerator for 4 to 5 days or can be frozen. (If you freeze it, don't add the lettuce to the rice.) The rice can be rewarmed in a 350°F/180°C oven, or by heating and tossing in a wok.

Microwave ovens are very good for rewarming fried rice; it takes about 1 minute per cup.

NOODLES

Because of their great length, noodles are looked upon by the Chinese as the symbol of longevity. It has been a faithful tradition to serve noodles on birthdays, and they are not to be cut or shortened on such occasions, for this would mean shortening one's life, so to say.

Chinese noodles come in all forms: dry, fresh, thin, wide, wheat, egg, rice, or transparent. The dry and brittle chow-mein noodles served by the Chinese-American restaurants are not known in China. (Chow-mein actually means fried noodles.)

Noodles are so versatile, for they can be cooked by many methods, and mixed with any variety of meat, seafoods, and vegetables. They can be served as a side dish, a snack, or a whole meal.

A good noodle dish should not be overcooked. Noodles will continue to cook in their own heat even after they are removed from the pot. Rinsing boiled noodles immediately with cold water prevents them from cooking further. If they are to be recooked again, they should be cooked only 80 percent the first time. The finally-cooked noodles should be tender but still somewhat chewy—or al dente.

The Chinese don't bother to make their own noodles, for ready-made fresh noodles are always easily available. Even in the United States, you can find them in Oriental food stores in the suburbs, or food stores located in Chinatowns of major cities. Some American supermarkets now also stock them.

The fresh egg noodles (see recipe, page 234) can be kept 2 to 3 days in the refrigerator after purchasing, or in the freezer for 5 to 6 months. You can substitute dry thin or extra thin spaghetti from American supermarkets for the fresh noodles. You may also use any homemade noodles.

NOODLES WITH MANDARIN MEAT SAUCE

炸醬麵   Zha-jiang-mian

Serves 3 to 4 ‡

This is a popular one-dish meal in China. Although it was originated in the North, I remember we often had this meal in Shanghai (in the Eastern region), especially in the summer. The savory and spicy (not hot) meat sauce, contrasting with the soft bland noodles and the refreshing and crisp vegetables, not only enhanced the appetite on a hot and humid day, but it also relieved our chef from sweating in a hot kitchen. Often we would eat this meal outdoors under a shady tree to catch a few evening breezes, as central air-conditioning was rather rare in those days.

Usually the food is placed in the middle of the table, and you mix your noodles with meat sauce and vegetables, according to individual tastes. This adapts beautifully to busy American households, where eating hours may be different for family members. You can have everything prepared in advance, and let family members help themselves at convenient eating times.

Since this dish can be cooked in large quantities, with almost everything cooked ahead, I have used it many times for informal entertaining. The meat sauce can be cooked several days ahead, and kept in the refrigerator. For a cold meal, just bring it back to room temperature. The noodles and the vegetables can be prepared half a day ahead, then you can have the rest of the day free to enjoy your party.

For a hot meal in cold weather, you can reheat the meat sauce, and it also keeps well on a hot tray. To prepare warm noodles, you can cook them just before serving, or cook them ahead. Rewarm by plunging the cooked noodles into a large pot of boiling water, and heat just to warm through. Both sauce and noodles can be rewarmed in a microwave oven. In any case, don't overcook the noodles. The vegetables are usually served cold.

Coarsely chopped pork gives the sauce a more interesting texture than that of regular ground pork.

Fresh Bean Sprouts	4 cups/1 L
Cucumber	1

Meat Sauce:

Boneless Lean Pork	¾ pound/340 g, in 1-inch/2½-cm cubes
Scallions	2, in 2-inch/5-cm sections
Water Chestnuts	8 large
Brown Bean Sauce (or Soy Sauce to taste)	5 level tablespoons or to taste

Hoisin Sauce	3 level tablespoons
Sugar	1 teaspoon or to taste
Dry Sherry	1 tablespoon
Water	½ cup/1 dL

Cooking Oil	2 tablespoons
Cornstarch	1 tablespoon in 2 tablespoons water
Fresh Egg Noodles	1 to 1¼ pounds/450 to 565 g
(*or* Dry Thin Spaghetti)	
Sesame or Cooking Oil	2 tablespoons

AHEAD OF TIME:

If *frozen pork cubes* are used, thaw partially or completely following these directions:

    20 minutes or more to partially thaw meat at room temperature

    10 minutes or more to partially thaw meat in a 250°F/120°C oven

    1 minute or more to completely thaw meat in a microwave oven

PREPARATION: 14 minutes

COOKING: 14 minutes

Preparation:

1. Boil 1½ quarts/1½ L of water for blanching bean sprouts. In the meantime, peel cucumber, cut in 2-inch/5-cm lengths or largest size that will fit the feed tube horizontally. Slice first and then shred with *Medium Slicing Disk*. (To slice and shred by hand see page 14.) Transfer to a serving bowl.

2. Soak bean sprouts in boiling water for 45 seconds. Drain and rinse with cold water. Drain well and place bean sprouts in a serving dish.

3. Use a paper towel to dry the beaker well, and put *Steel Blade* in place. Prepare meat sauce by chopping scallions first and removing from the beaker. Chop water chestnuts coarsely and transfer to a small bowl. (To chop by hand see page 14.)

4. Chop pork with a few quick on/off turns, checking carefully so the texture is coarser than that of the regular ground meat. (To chop by hand see page 14.) §

Cooking:

1. To save time, boil 3 quarts/2¾ L of water while making the meat sauce.

2. Heat 2 tablespoons oil in a wok, then add scallions, and cook for 1 minute.

3. Add pork and water chestnuts to the wok, and cook over high heat, stirring until the meat loses its pink color. Add the remaining 5 ingredients for the meat sauce. Stir to mix, and bring the sauce to a boil.

4. Give the cornstarch mixture a good stir, and pour into the sauce, stirring to mix until the sauce becomes translucent. Simmer the sauce over medium heat until most of the liquid has evaporated. The meat sauce can be served either hot or at room temperature. §

5. When the water in the pot is boiling, add the noodles. Cook fresh noodles for 1 to 2 minutes or until al dente. (Cook spaghetti according to the package directions.) When the noodles are ready, add 1 cup of cold water to the pot to slow down the cooking, and immediately drain the noodles in a colander. Drain very well, then toss the noodles with 2 table-spoons sesame or cooking oil to keep them from sticking together. If noodles are to be served cold or for later use, rinse with cold water and drain very well before tossing with the oil. §

To Serve:

The only dish you'll need for each person is a soup bowl or a dinner plate with a pair of chopsticks. (A fork and knife can be used in place of chop-sticks.) Place noodles and meat sauce in separate serving bowls or platters, and put them with the shredded cucumbers and the bean sprouts in the middle of the dining table, or line them up on a buffet table.

You help yourself to the noodles by placing them in a soup bowl or din-ner plate, then spoon the meat sauce and the vegetables on top of the noodles. Mix them to your taste, and eat. Additional brown bean sauce or soy sauce may also be served with the noodles.

Variations:

1. Beef may be used in place of pork.

2. If you cannot get fresh bean sprouts (see page 268 to grow your own), use more cucumber shreds or substitute shredded iceberg lettuce. Canned bean sprouts do not add crispness to this dish.

SOFT-FRIED NOODLES WITH BEEF

牛肉炒麵   Niu-rou-chao-mian

Serves 2 to 3

These delectable noodles are inexpensive, filling, and great one-dish meals served by Chinese restaurants, but they are especially tasty at those small, unpretentious Cantonese noodle shops. The secret of cooking these dishes is not to overcook the noodles, which should be al dente. Fresh egg noodles are especially good; they cook very quickly, in about 1 to 2 minutes.

Dry Chinese Mushrooms	4
Flank Steak	½ pound/225 g, cut to fit feed tube and frozen

Marinade

Cornstarch	1½ teaspoons
Dry Sherry	2 teaspoons
Soy Sauce	1 tablespoon

Celery Cabbage (*or* Bok Choy)	½ pound/225 g
Fresh Egg Noodles (*or* dry Thin or Extra Thin Spaghetti)	½ pound/225 g
Cooking Oil	6 tablespoons
Salt	¼ teaspoon
Oyster-Flavored Sauce (*or* Soy Sauce)	2 tablespoons (to taste)
Soy Sauce	1 tablespoon

AHEAD OF TIME:

1. Snap stems off Chinese mushrooms. Soak the mushrooms in boiling water to cover for 20 minutes, or until soft.

2. Partially defrost *frozen beef* just long enough to slice following these directions:

> 20 minutes or more to partially thaw meat at room temperature
> 10 minutes or more to partially thaw meat in a 250°/120°C oven
> 35 seconds or more to partially thaw meat in a microwave oven

PREPARATION AND COOKING: 25 minutes

Preparation and Cooking:

1. To save time, you can start heating the water to cook the noodles, while doing the other preparations.

2. With *Medium Slicing Disk* in place, slice beef across the grain. (To slice by hand see page 14.) Mix with the marinade in a bowl.

3. Wash cabbage, and cut off tough ends. Cut to fit the feed tube, and slice with *Medium Slicing Disk*. (To slice by hand see page 14.)

4. Drain the soften mushrooms, squeeze out the water, and cut into shreds. §

5. Cook egg noodles in the boiling water (cook spaghetti according to its package direction), stirring occasionally for about 2 minutes. Do not overcook; it should be al dente. Rinse in cold water immediately, and drain again. Cut noodles to a shorter length so you can cook them more easily. If they are not to be used right away, toss and coat noodles with 1 or more tablespoons of oil to prevent noodles from sticking, then set aside. §

6. Heat the wok, then heat 1 tablespoon oil over medium-high heat. Add ¼ teaspoon salt, and stir-fry cabbage and mushrooms for about 2 minutes. Remove from the wok.

7. Heat the wok over high heat, then heat 2 tablespoons oil. Stir-fry beef quickly for about 2 minutes or until meat loses its red color. Remove from the wok.

8. Rinse, then heat and dry the wok over the burner. Heat 3 tablespoons oil over medium-high heat. Toss and stir the noodles in the hot oil until they are coated with oil and heated through, about 2 minutes. Return the vegetables and beef, then add oyster-flavored sauce and soy sauce. Stir to mix until noodles become one even color. Serve immediately.

Tip:
The dish can be reheated by the microwave oven.

Variations:
Substitute fresh mushrooms for dry Chinese mushrooms, or omit the mushrooms.

SOFT-FRIED NOODLES WITH CHICKEN
雞片炒麵 Ji-pian-chao-mian

Follow the directions for Soft-fried Noodles With Beef, but substitute one whole boneless, skinless, and frozen chicken breast for the beef. Defrost just long enough to slice by *Medium Slicing Disk,* or slice by hand.

NOODLES IN SESAME SAUCE, SZECHUAN-STYLE

芝蔴醬拌麵   Zhi-ma-jiang-ban-mian

Serves 3 ‡

This is very refreshing and a great one-dish meal for the summer. Everything can be cooked ahead in large quantities. The sesame sauce is often served with just the noodles (with or without the fresh bean sprouts) as a snack or side-dish, and is equally delicious this way.

Chicken Breast	1 large, with bone and skin
(*or* **Cooked Chicken**)	(2 cups/½ L)
Fresh Bean Sprouts	4 cups/1 L
(*or* **Cucumbers**)	(2)

Sauce Ingredients:

Fresh Ginger	3 ½-inch/1½-cm cubes
Scallions	3, in 2-inch/5-cm sections
Sugar	4 teaspoons
Sesame Paste	¼ cup/½ dL
(*or* Creamy Peanut Butter)	
Soy Sauce	½ cup/1 dL
Chinese Vinegar	6 tablespoons
(*or* Wine Vinegar)	(¼ cup/½ dL)
Sesame Oil	2 tablespoons
Water	3 tablespoons
Hot Chili Oil	to taste
(*or* Tabasco Sauce)	
Fresh Egg Noodles	1 pound/450 g
(*or* dry extra thin Spaghetti)	(¾ pound/340 g)
Sesame or Cooking Oil	2 tablespoons.

PREPARATION AND COOKING: 45 minutes; 30 minutes *if* chicken was cooked ahead

Preparation and Cooking:

1. Boil 2 quarts/2 L of water in a 3-quart/2¾-L saucepan. Add chicken breast, and bring the water back to a boil. Turn heat to low immediately, and simmer very slowly for 25 minutes. (For the electric stove, set one burner on high and one on low, so the saucepan can be transferred from high to low immediately.) At the end of the 25 minutes, immediately remove the breast from the saucepan, and rinse thoroughly with cold water. (You'll find that chicken cooked by this Chinese method is tender and juicy, for it is not overcooked.) The chicken can be cooked one or two days ahead. §

Note: If you have a microwave oven, you can save time on cooking the chicken. Lay the chicken breast flat (breast with bone and skin on will give you more juicy and tender meat) on a pyrex pie plate or a deep platter suitable for use in microwave ovens. Cover the pie plate loosely with wax paper. Cook on high for 2½ minutes. Then turn the breast upside down and heat for another 2 minutes. Let stand for 5 minutes to finish cooking. (A smaller breast will take less time. Do not overcook.)

2. While the chicken is being cooked, boil 3 quarts/2¾ L of water for cooking noodles, and boil another 1½ quarts/1½ L of water for blanching bean sprouts. Let bean sprouts soak in boiling water for 45 seconds, then drain immediately and rinse with cold water. Drain them very well, and place in a serving bowl. §

3. Or *if* cucumbers are used, peel them and cut into 2-inch/5-cm lengths or the largest size that will fit the feed tube horizontally. Slice first and then shred with the *Medium Slicing Disk.* (You may save time by shredding the cucumber with *French Fry Cutter,* but the shreds will not be as refined looking.) Or you may slice and shred them by hand. Transfer cucumber shreds to a serving bowl. §

4. Dry the beaker and its cover with paper towels. With *Steel Blade* in place, chop ginger and scallions for the sauce until finely minced. Add the remaining ingredients for the sauce mixture (except the chili oil) to the beaker. Process until mixed. (To prepare without the food processor, mince the ginger and scallions by hand or in a blender. Then combine them with the remaining sauce ingredients.) Add the hot chili oil to taste. The sauce should be fairly thin, but thick enough to coat the back of a spoon. If it is too thick, more water or soy sauce can be used to thin it down. If it is too thin, thicken it with more sesame paste or peanut butter. Transfer the sauce to a sauce bowl. (You can leave the hot oil out of the sauce mixture, and let each one add it to taste at the last minute.) §

5. Remove the skin and bone from the cooked chicken breast. Cut with knife or tear the meat into julienne strips by hand, and place them in a serving bowl. §

6. Add egg noodles to the boiling water (or cook spaghetti according to the package directions), boil 1 to 2 minutes or until noodles are al dente. Do not overcook. Rinse well in cold water; toss and drain as dry as possible. Toss them with 2 or more tablespoons of sesame or cooking oil, making sure all the noodles are coated with the oil, so they will not stick to each other on standing. Place them on a serving platter. §

To Serve:

The only dish you'll need for each person is a soup bowl or a dinner plate with a pair of chopsticks (a fork and knife can be substituted). Place noodles, shredded chicken, vegetables, and sauce in the middle of the dining table, or line them up on a buffet table. Also place chili oil on the table for some people may like the noodles more hot and spicy.

You help yourself to the noodles by placing them in a soup bowl or on a dinner plate; then add the chicken, vegetables, and sauce to the noodles. Mix them well.

Variations:

1. Chopped roasted peanuts, shredded ham, shredded scallions, or shredded egg sheets (see recipe below) may also be served with the noodles.

2. All vegetables used in the dish should be fresh. Shredded iceberg lettuce, though not traditional, can be used as a substitute for the bean sprouts or the cucumbers.

3. Szechuan peppercorns can also be used in the sauce. Grind them with the *Steel Blade* first before making the sauce in step 4.

EGG SHEETS

蛋皮 Dan-pi

Makes 2 sheets ‡

Eggs   2
Cooking Oil   2 teaspoons

Heat a wok or a 10-inch/25-cm skillet, then heat 1 teaspoon oil over medium heat. Add 1 beaten egg, and swirl the wok to spread the egg, so it forms a 9-inch/23-cm, thin pancake. Cook until the egg is set on the surface. Lift the egg sheet (pancake) from the wok. Repeat the process with the other egg. §

To shred the egg sheets, cut the cool egg sheets into halves, then cut them crosswise into julienne strips. §

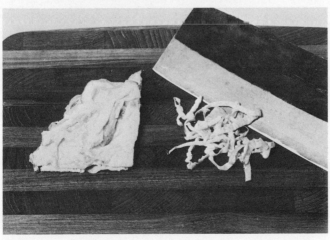

GINGER AND SCALLION LO MEIN

葱薑撈麵   Cong-jiang-lao-mian

Serves 3 ‡

"Lo Mein" means tossed noodles in Cantonese. This is good as a snack or served in place of boiled rice.

Fresh Ginger	½-inch/1½-cm cube
Scallions	5, in 2-inch/5-cm sections
Cooking Oil	1½ tablespoons
Chicken Broth	2 tablespoons
Sugar	½ teaspoon
Soy Sauce	1 tablespoon
Oyster Sauce	1 tablespoon or to taste
(*or* Soy Sauce)	(to taste)
Fresh Egg Noodles	½ pound/225 g
(*or* dry Thin or	
Extra Thin Spaghetti)	
Sesame Oil	1 tablespoon (optional)

PREPARATION AND COOKING: 12 minutes

Preparation and Cooking:
1. Heat 2 quarts/2 L of water to a boil. In the meantime, prepare other ingredients.
2. With *Steel Blade* in place, finely mince ginger. Then coarsely chop scallions with ginger still in the beaker. (To mince and chop by hand see page 14.)
3. Heat 1½ tablespoons oil in the wok. Stir-fry ginger and scallions over medium heat for 1 to 2 minutes, then add chicken broth, sugar, soy sauce, and oyster sauce. Stir to mix and set aside.
4. When the water is boiled, cook noodles for about 2 minutes. They should be still chewy inside. Add 1 cup/¼ L cold water to the pot to stop the water from boiling, and quickly drain the noodles.
5. Toss the well-drained noodles with 1 tablespoon sesame oil, then toss with the ginger and scallion sauce, and serve.

Tips:
The noodles can be reheated in a microwave oven.

NOODLES WITH FRIED ONIONS

洋蔥麵   Yang-cong-mian

Serves 3 to 4 ‡

This noodle dish is especially appetizing served cold on a summer day. It can be cooked ahead, served as a snack or served in place of boiled rice.

Dry Shrimp	¼ cup/½ dL (optional)
Scallions	8, in 2-inch/5-cm sections
Onions	4 medium
Cooking Oil	4 tablespoons
Soy Sauce	3 tablespoons or to taste
Dry Sherry	6 tablespoons ⎱(only if dry shrimp is used)
Water	2 tablespoons ⎰
Fresh Egg Noodles	½ pound/225 g
(*or* dry Thin or Extra Thin Spaghetti)	
Sesame Oil	1 tablespoon or to taste (optional)

PREPARATION AND COOKING: 45 minutes

Preparation:

1. If dry shrimp are used, soak them in ½ cup/1 dL boiling water and 2 tablespoons dry sherry for about 20 minutes.

2. Chop scallions coarsely with *Steel Blade,* and remove from the beaker. Or chop by hand.

3. Peel and quarter onions. Chop one onion at a time, and remove before adding the next one. Overloading the beaker will make the chopped onions too watery.

4. Heat the wok, then add and heat 3 tablespoons oil. Fry the chopped scallions and onions slowly over medium heat, stirring every once in a while. Cook until most of the moisture in the onions has evaporated, making sure that the vegetables do not burn. If the heat is too strong, lower it. The cooking takes about 30 minutes. Add 2 tablespoons soy sauce and continue cooking, stirring occasionally until there is almost no sizzling sound and the onions are almost dehydrated. Yields about 5 to 6 tablespoons. §

5. While the onion is cooking, boil 2 quarts /2 L of water. Cook the fresh noodles for only about 2 minutes. They should be soft outside but still chewy inside (or cook spaghetti according to package directions). Drain immediately in a colander, and rinse with cold water. Drain the noodles very well. §

6. If dried shrimps are used, drain the softened shrimp. Chop them coarsely with the *Steel Blade,* using on/off turns. Or chop by hand. In a wok or small saucepan, heat 1 tablespoon oil, and fry the dried shrimp for 1 minute. Add 4 tablespoons dry sherry and 2 tablespoons water, and cook on medium heat until all the liquid has evaporated. Remove from heat, and add 1 tablespoon sesame oil (optional). §

7. Transfer noodles to a serving bowl, and add the cooked onions and dried shrimps and 1 tablespoon soy sauce or to taste. Toss and mix thoroughly. Serve warm or at room temperature. §

EGG NOODLES, WONTON, CANTONESE EGG ROLL, and CANTONESE STEAMED DUMPLING WRAPPERS★

蛋麵, 餛飩皮, 廣東春捲皮, 燒賣皮

Dan-mian, Hun-tun-pi, Guangdong-chun-juan-pi, Shao-mai-pi

Makes 1 pound dough

All-purpose Flour   2 cups/½ L
Salt   ½ teaspoon
Egg   1 large
Water   7 to 8 tablespoons, or more if needed
Cornstarch   For dusting

PREPARATION OF THE DOUGH: 6 minutes

RESTING: 30 minutes

ROLLING: 10 minutes

STANDING: 20 to 60 minutes

SHAPING: 10 to 30 minutes

Preparation:

1. With *Steel Blade* in place, add flour and salt to the beaker, and mix with 1 quick on/off turn.

2. Add egg, and with machine running, pour 6 tablespoons water through the feed tube. Then dribble in only enough remaining water until ball of dough forms on the blade. (You may not need all the water.) Let the machine run for another 30 seconds. The dough will be a little sticky but should not be wet.

3. Remove the dough, and knead on a lightly floured surface for 1 to 2 minutes until smooth.

(To prepare without the food processor, mix all ingredients together by hand until a dough is formed. Knead for 10 minutes until the dough is smooth.)

Resting:

Transfer the dough to a bowl, and cover with a damp cloth. Let it rest for 30 minutes.

Rolling:

Dust the working surface with cornstarch (it is better than flour to prevent dough from sticking, and roll the dough out to $^1/_{16}$ inch/¼ cm thick or as thin as you desire. You can also divide the dough into 2 portions, and roll out one portion at a time.

Standing:

Let the sheet stand in the air for ½ to 1 hour (depending on the moisture in the air) to dry to a semi-stiff state. The sheet should not be limp and stretchable, yet it should not crack when folded. It can be hung over the back of a chair to free the working surface.

Shaping:

Using a sharp knife or cookie-cutter, cut 7-inch/18-cm squares for Cantonese egg roll wrappers; 3-inch/8-cm squares for wonton wrappers; 3 or 4-inch/8 or 10-cm rounds for Cantonese steamed dumpling wrappers. Sprinkle a little cornstarch in between the pieces before stacking them. They are now ready for using.

For noodles, dust both sides of the dough with cornstarch. Fold them accordion style in folds about 3 inches/8 cm wide. Use a sharp knife to shred straight across these folds into $^1/_{16}$-inch/¼-cm strips or to your desired width, making sure to cut all the way through. Unfold the strips by fluffing up with your fingers. They are now ready to be cooked. If the noodles are not to be used right away, sprinkle them with more cornstarch to prevent sticking.

Tips:

1. The wrappers and the noodles can be stored in well-sealed plastic bags in the refrigerator for 2 to 3 days, or in the freezer for several months.

2. Left-over dough can also be kept in the refrigerator or in the freezer, dusting it with plenty of cornstarch before putting in a tightly-sealed plastic bag. Let the dough come to room temperature before using.

3. If you have a pasta machine, it will save you time when you shape the wrappers and make the noodles.

WONTONS★

飩餛   Hun-tun

Wontons are found in every region of China. The Chinese make them at
home, but also enjoy eating them in restaurants. They are popular snacks
that can be purchased from street vendors who wander about day and night
with their portable kitchens.

These Chinese cousins of the Italian ravioli are one of the most versatile
foods. They can be served as soup, snack, appetizer, a main course, or as a
one-dish meal.

About the Wrappers:

In China, the wonton wrappers are available all the time, so no one
makes them at home. Here you can purchase them in Chinatowns or Oriental food stores. Some American supermarkets now also stock them. The
wrappers can be refrigerated for few days and frozen for 1 to 2 months in a
tightly sealed plastic bag. If you cannot find them in your area, you can
make your own (see page 234). Wonton wrappers are made in different
thicknesses. For the fried-wontons, the thin wrappers are much lighter and
therefore better. For the other kinds, the thickness of the wrapper largely
depends upon your personal preference and taste.

Filling for Boiled Wontons:
Makes 45 ‡

Boneless Pork	½ pound/225 g, in 1-inch/2½-cm cubes
Shrimp in Shell	¼ pound/115 g, shelled, deveined, cleaned, dried, and cut into 1-inch/2½-cm sections
Dry Sherry	1 tablespoon
Soy Sauce	1 tablespoon or to taste
Salt	½ teaspoon
Sugar	½ teaspoon

PREPARATION: 7 minutes

Preparation:

With *Steel Blade* in place, chop the pork cubes with 3 quick on/off turns.
Then add the remaining ingredients to the beaker. Use quick on/off turns
until the mixture reaches the texture of ground meat. Do not over process.
(To chop by hand see page 14.) It can be refrigerated for a half day. §

Variations:

1. Use all pork without the shrimp, add 2 more ounces/60 g of pork.
2. Substitute 2 chopped scallions and 6 chopped water chestnuts for the
shrimp.

3. Substitute 3 ounces/85 g of crab meat for shrimp.

Shaping Wontons (30 minutes for experienced cooks; 1 hour for the less experienced):

Wonton Wrappers   45
Filling for Wontons   1 recipe
1. Place 1 teaspoon filling in the center of the wrapper.
2. Fold over at the center, and seal the edge with a little water.
3. Fold it in half again.
4. Pull the two corners (on the stuffing side) together, overlapping one over the other, and sealing them together with a little water. The finished wonton looks like a nun's hat. §

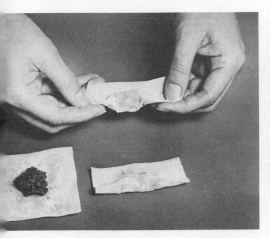 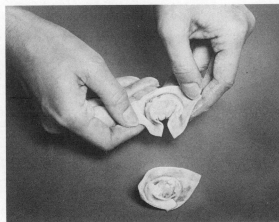

Tips:
You can wrap the wontons half a day ahead, and place them on a plate dusted with flour to prevent them from sticking, and keep them in a single layer. Cover with plastic wrap and refrigerate. Uncooked wontons can also be frozen, provided the raw meat and shrimp have never been frozen before. Freeze them individually on a tray; then you can wrap them in a well-sealed plastic bag, and keep them in the freezer for future use.

The frozen wontons can be cooked without thawing; just boil them a little longer. Stock them up in the freezer; they are a good short-notice meal.

BOILED WONTONS (Snack or one-dish-meal)

煮餛飩   Zhu-hun-tun

Serves 3 to 4 as a meal ‡

They are good as lunch or supper. The thicker wrappers will make a more filling meal. You can serve them cold or warm. Cold ones are good for the summer, and you can cook them ahead.

Uncooked Wontons	45
Scallions	2, finely chopped
Sesame Oil	2 tablespoons
Soy Sauce	2 tablespoons or to taste

Cooking (10 minutes):

In a large pot, bring 3 quarts of water to a boil. Add the wontons, and bring the water back to boil. Cook the wontons over moderate heat for 3 to 5 minutes until the meat is cooked. Wontons with thick wrappers need to cook longer or until the wrappers are tender, but still a little resistant to the bite. Drain in a colander. To serve, toss with chopped scallions, sesame oil, and soy sauce.

PAN-FRIED WONTONS (Snack or one-dish-meal)

煎餛飩   Jian-hun-tun

Serves 2 as a meal

Left-over or cold boiled wontons can be served pan-fried. They are very tasty. Wontons with the thicker wrappers are better for pan-frying. Be sure they are *well-drained and cold* before cooking.

Cold Boiled Wontons	20
Cooking Oil	2 tablespoons

Cooking (6 minutes):

Heat 2 tablespoons oil in a 10-inch/25-cm skillet, add the wontons and spread them out in a single layer. Cook over medium-high heat until both sides are browned. Add a little more oil if dough sticks to the skillet.

Serve hot with Chinese vinegar and soy sauce or a mixture of the two. If you like spicy food, use hot oil also. Worcestershire sauce, which has been adopted especially by the Southern chefs, makes a good and interesting condiment.

WONTONS IN SOUP AS A MEAL (One-dish-meal)

湯餛飩   Tang-hun-tun

This is a very common lunch in China. Cook it as you would for the Wonton Soup (see recipe, page 210), but cook 12 to 15 wontons for each serving. Serve them in a large bowl with 1 cup chicken broth, and place cooked meat and vegetables on top of the wontons. (You can use any or few of the following ingredients: sliced ham, roast pork, roast duck, cooked chicken, cooked shrimp, bamboo, and mushrooms.)

WONTON SOUP (as a soup), see recipe, page 210.

餛飩湯   Hun-tun-tang

FRIED WONTONS (as appetizers), see recipe, page 77.

炸餛飩   Zha-hun-tun

FRIED WONTON AND SHRIMP IN SWEET AND SOUR SAUCE (as a main course), see recipe, page 169.

甜酸蝦仁餛飩   Tian-suan-xia-ren-hun-tun

YEAST DOUGH

發麵

Makes 16 ‡

This is very much like the Western yeast bread dough. The traditional Chinese kitchen does not have an oven, so Chinese buns are steamed, not baked. Steamed buns are white in appearance, and may looked uncooked to Westerners.

There are plain steamed buns, and buns stuffed with savory fillings which can be either salty or sweet. Stuffed buns are for lunch or snacks.

Dry Yeast	1 teaspoon
Lukewarm Water	3 tablespoons
Sugar	2 teaspoons
All-purpose Flour	2½ cups/355 g
Vegetable Shortening	1½ tablespoons
Lukewarm Water	⅔ cup/1½ dL
Baking Powder	1 teaspoon

PREPARATION: 15 minutes

RISING TIME: 1 to 2 hours

SECOND KNEADING: 5 minutes

Preparation:

1. Sprinkle yeast over 3 tablespoons lukewarm water, then sprinkle sugar over the yeast. Let stand for 5 minutes, or until yeast bubbles up and doubles in volume.

2. With *Steel Blade* in place, put the flour in the beaker. Add vegetable shortening and process until they are well mixed. Add the yeast mixture, and process until mixed. With the machine running, pour ⅔ cup/1½ dL of lukewarm water through the feed tube. Add more water if needed. Process until ball of dough forms on the blades.

3. Turn dough out onto a lightly-floured surface and knead for 2 to 3 minutes. Transfer to a bowl at least twice the size of the dough, and cover with plastic wrap. (To prepare without the food processor, mix flour, vegetable shortening, yeast mixture, and water together. Knead for 10 minutes until dough is smooth. Transfer to a bowl at least twice the size of the dough, and cover with plastic wrap.) Let rise in a warm (between 78 and 82°F/26 and 28°C.) place until double in bulk. The time varies from 1 to 2 hours, depending on the yeast and the surrounding temperature.

4. Remove dough from the bowl. Add baking powder and knead for 2 to 3 minutes until the baking powder is well incorporated. If necessary, sprinkle more flour while kneading. The dough is now ready for shaping.

PLAIN STEAMED BUNS ★

饅頭   Man-tou

Makes 16 ‡

The Northerners eat these plain steamed buns in place of rice to accompany cooked dishes. You just help yourself to a chopstickful of the dish and take a bite from the bread, then a chopstickful of the next dish and some more bread. Traditionally, there is always a soup to accompany the meal.

Since they can be frozen and reheated by steaming or in the microwave oven without thawing, these buns are handy when there is no time to cook rice. Ready-made buns can be purchased at Oriental food stores.

Yeast Dough   1 recipe
Wax Paper   16   2-inch/5-cm squares

SHAPING: 5 minutes

RISING: 20 minutes

STEAMING: 20 minutes

Shaping:
Divide the yeast dough into halves, and roll each into a cylinder about 1-inch/2½-cm in diameter. Cut the cylinder into 8 equal portions, and put a piece of wax paper under each portion. Repeat with the other half.

Rising:
Set the buns on the steamer or steamer tray about 2 inches apart, and let rise for 20 minutes.

Steaming:
Bring the water in the steamer to a rolling boil, and steam the buns over high heat for 20 minutes. §

Tips:
The steamed buns can be kept in the refrigerator for several days, and in the freezer for several months.

To reheat the buns in the microwave oven, place the buns on a plate covered with plastic wrap. One bun takes about a minute to be reheated. Do not overheat, as it will get hard and dry.

MINCED MEAT AND VEGETABLE STEAMED BUNS ★

菜肉龟   Cai-rou-bao

Makes 16 ‡

These stuffed buns are popular snacks in the Eastern region. In the North, they are often served with a soup as lunch.

Filling Mixture:

Bok Choy	1 pound/450 g
Fresh Ginger	½-inch/1½-cm cube
Scallion	1, cut into 2-inch/5-cm sections
Boneless Pork	½ pound/225 g, in 1-inch/2½-cm cubes
Salt	2½ teaspoons or to taste
Sugar	1 teaspoon
Cornstarch	2 tablespoons
Soy Sauce	1 tablespoon
Sesame Oil	2 tablespoons

Yeast Dough	1 recipe (see page 240)
Wax Paper	16 2-inch/5-cm squares

PREPARATION AND RISING TIME OF YEAST DOUGH: 1½ to 2½ hours

PREPARATION OF THE FILLING: 17 minutes

SHAPING: 25 minutes

RISING: 20 minutes

STEAMING: 20 minutes

Preparation:

1. Boil 2 quarts/2 L of water and, in the meantime, wash the Bok Choy thoroughly until it is free of sand. Drain and cut into 2-inch/5-cm sections. Cook in boiling water for 2 minutes. Drain in a colander, and rinse with cold water. Drain and squeeze dry.

2. With the *Steel Blade* in place, chop ginger and scallion until finely minced. Add pork to the beaker, chop with 2 quick on/off turns, then process for about 5 seconds until pork is chopped. (To chop by hand see page 14.) Remove pork to a mixing bowl.

3. Replace *Steel Blade,* add the well-drained Bok Choy to the beaker,

and process until it is coarsely chopped, using quick on/off turns. Do not over process, or it will turn into puree. (To chop by hand see page 14.) Drain and squeeze the chopped Bok Choy very dry. Makes about 1¼ cups/3 dL.

4. Mix pork, Bok Choy, and the remaining ingredients of the filling mixture in the bowl. Can be made 1 day ahead and kept in the refrigerator. §

Shaping:

1. Divide the yeast dough into 2 halves. Roll each into a cylinder 1½ inches/4 cm in diameter on a lightly-floured surface. Cut the cylinder into 8 equal portions. Flatten each portion with the palm of your hand. On a lightly-floured surface, roll each into a 4-inch/10-cm circle.

2. Place 1 heaping tablespoon of the filling in the center of each round. With your fingers, gather the edge of the dough up and around the filling in folds. Bring the folds to the top and the center of the bun. Close the top by twisting the folds together. Place the bun with the folded side up on a 2-inch/5-cm square wax paper.

Rising and Steaming:

Let the buns rise for 20 minutes. Bring the water for steaming to a rolling boil, and place buns on the bamboo steamers or steamer rack about 2 inches/5 cm apart. Steam over high heat for 20 minutes. They can be refrigerated or frozen, and resteamed to serve. §

Variation:

Swiss chard or 1 cup/¼ L thawed, squeezed-dry, frozen chopped collard greens can be used in place of Bok Choy.

MANDARIN PANCAKES ★

                                                    Bao-bing

Makes 16 ‡

These pancakes are served with the famous Peking Duck as well as the popular Moo-shu Pork (see recipe, page 113).

This pancake dough is made with boiling water, so it is usually very hot to handle. Here's where the food processor is very helpful, because it cuts down the kneading time. The amount of water for the dough will vary somewhat with different brands of flour.

All-purpose Flour	1¾ cups/4 dL
Boiling Water	¾ cup/1¾ dL
Cooking Oil	1½ tablespoons

PREPARATION: 5 minutes

RESTING: 15 minutes

SHAPING: 30 minutes

COOKING: 16 minutes

Preparation and Resting:

With the *Steel Blade* in place, put flour in the beaker. Start the machine, then pour the boiling water through the feed tube. Leave the machine on until a ball of dough has formed. The dough will be a little sticky but should not be wet. Let the machine run until the dough is smooth, about 30 seconds. There may be small pieces in the bottom of the beaker; just add them to the ball when you remove it.

If the dough is too wet during processing, add more flour. Place the dough in a bowl and cover the bowl with a damp.kitchen or paper towel. Let it rest for 10 to 15 minutes.

(To prepare without the food processor, mix the flour and boiling water together using a wooden spoon. Knead together until the dough is smooth. If the dough is too wet, add more flour. Place the dough in a bowl and cover the bowl with a damp kitchen or paper towel. Let it rest for 10 to 15 minutes.)

Shaping:

Shape the dough into a sausage about 1½ inches/4-cm in diameter. With a knife, cut the dough into 16 equal pieces. Flatten one piece and roll out to a 2½-inch/6½-cm circle on a lightly floured surface. Brush the top side with oil. Flatten a second piece, and roll to another 2½-inch/6½-cm circle. Lay it over the oiled piece.

On a lightly floured board, roll the pair into an 8-inch/20-cm circle. (Rotate the sandwich an inch or so in a clockwise direction as you roll, in this way, the circle will keep its shape.) Repeat the process until all the pieces are rolled out in this sandwich style.

Cooking:

Heat an ungreased 10-inch/25-cm skillet over medium heat, and cook the double pancakes in the heated skillet, one at a time. Turn them over as they puff up, and when little bubbles appear on the surface. Regulate the heat so the pancakes become speckled with light brown spots after cooking for ½ to 1 minute on each side. Let cool slightly, and while they are still warm, use your fingers to pull the pancakes apart into 2 single pancakes. (If the pancakes tend to stick to each other, you'll need more oil in between the pancakes before rolling.)

Repeat the process until all the pancakes are cooked and separated. §

Tips:

The cooked pancakes can be kept in the refrigerator for 3 to 4 days, and in the freezer for 2 to 3 months, making sure that they are wrapped in a tightly sealed plastic bag.

To Serve:

Just before serving, steam the pancakes for 10 minutes or until they are hot.

PAN-FRIED DUMPLINGS, MANDARIN-STYLE ★

鍋貼   Guo-tie

Makes 24 ‡

These juicy and irresistible dumplings are often served as a meal in Northern China. In Shanghai, we ate them for snacks. Here in the United States, many Chinese restaurants serve them as hot appetizers. They are popular with the Chinese as well as with the Americans. The pan-fried dumplings are always served with the crisp brown side facing up, and the soft side facing down. If the dumpling is properly made and cooked, a delicious juice will squirt out when you take your first bite.

As a meal serve 10 dumplings for average appetites. You can also serve a soup with them.

The Dough ★:

All-purpose Flour	2 cups/½ L
Cold Water	½ cup/1 dL plus 2 to 4 tablespoons

AHEAD OF TIME:

If *frozen pork cubes* are used, thaw partially or completely following these directions:

20 minutes or more to partially thaw meat at room temperature

10 minutes or more to partially thaw meat in a 250°F/120°C oven

55 seconds or more to completely thaw meat in a microwave oven

PREPARATION OF THE DOUGH: 10 minutes

PREPARATION OF THE FILLING: 20 minutes

SHAPING THE DUMPLINGS: 45 minutes

COOKING: 15 minutes

Preparation:

The amount of water required depends on the humidity in the kitchen, and varies with the different brands of flour. Start with ½ cup/1 dL and 2 tablespoons of water, and you can add more water if the dough doesn't form a ball. If the dough is too sticky, add more flour.

With the *Steel Blade* in place, put flour in the beaker. Start the machine, and pour the water through the feed tube. Leave the machine on until a ball of dough has formed. The dough will be a little sticky but not wet.

(To prepare without the food processor, mix the flour with ½ cup/1 dL water, adding more water if necessary, and shape into a ball. If the dough is too sticky, add more flour.)

To develop more gluten in the dough, knead it with hands for 3 to 4 minutes (or, without the food processor, for 10 minutes, or until smooth). Put the dough in a bowl, and cover with plastic wrap. Let stand for at least 15 minutes or longer. The dough can be refrigerated in a tightly sealed plastic bag for 1 or 2 days. Dust with plenty of flour before storing. Or it can be frozen for a few weeks. Defrost completely before using. §

The Filling:

Boneless Pork	½ pound/225 g in 1-inch/2½-cm cubes
Celery Cabbage	½ pound/225 g
Fresh Ginger	½-inch/1½-cm cube
Soy Sauce	2 tablespoons
Dry Sherry	1 tablespoon
Salt	¾ teaspoon or to taste
Sugar	1 teaspoon
Sesame Oil	2 tablespoons

Preparation:

1. Cut the cabbage into 2-inch/5-cm sections. Cook them in 2 quarts/2 L of boiling water over medium heat for 5 minutes. Drain quickly and rinse with cold water.

2. While the cabbage is being cooked, place *Steel Blade* in the beaker. With the machine running, drop ginger through the feed tube, and process until finely chopped. Add pork cubes, and process with 3 quick on/off turns. Then add the last 5 ingredients for the filling mixture, and process with quick on/off turns until the meat reaches the texture of ground pork. (To prepare by hand see page 14.) Transfer the mixture to a large bowl.

3. Replace the *Steel Blade,* and add the well-drained cabbage to the beaker. Process until the vegetable is coarsely chopped. (To chop by hand see page 14.) Remove from the beaker, and squeeze out as much water as possible, making about 1 cup/¼ L. Add the cabbage to the pork mixture. Mix thoroughly, and set aside until ready to use. (You may find it easier to wrap the dumplings if the filling is refrigerated for a few hours, or until it is firmer to handle.) Can be kept in the refrigerator for 1 day. §

Shaping the Dumplings:

Turn the dough out onto a lightly floured surface, then divide it into 4 equal portions. Put 3 portions back into the bowl and cover with plastic wrap.

Shape the one portion into a cylinder, and cut into 6 equal pieces. Take one piece at a time, form into a ball, and press with the palm of your hand to flatten it. Roll it out with a lightly-floured rolling pin, turning clockwise a quarter turn, as you roll, to keep the shape round until it is about 3½ inches/9 cm in diameter.

1. Put 1 level tablespoon of the filling in the center of the circle.

2. Fold the dough in half, and pinch the 2 semi-circles together at the center along the edges.

3. Starting at one end, with your forefinger and thumb, make 2 to 3 pleats on the back side, then pinch them together with the front side of the dough to seal the filling in.

4. Do the same at the other end until the opening is completely closed.

Wetting the inside edge of the dough may help in sealing the edges. Press and pinch the edges to seal tightly, so the juice of the filling will not leak out during cooking.

Arrange the finished dumplings on a well-floured tray, and cover with a dry cloth. Do not have the dumplings touching each other or they will stick together. §

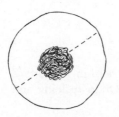 

Cooking:

1. Heat a 10-inch/25-cm skillet over medium-high heat, then add 3 tablespoons vegetable oil. When oil is hot, arrange dumplings with sides just touching and pleated side up in a winding circle. You can fit about 12 dumplings around the side of the skillet, and 2 or 3 more in the center. Cook about 2 minutes or until the bottoms of the dumplings are golden.

2. Add ¾ cup/1¾ dL of water to the skillet, and cover with the lid immediately. Simmer on medium heat for 10 minutes. If the water is evaporating too fast, add a little more during cooking. At the end of the period, the water will be almost all evaporated. Uncover and cook until the dumplings have a golden brown crust on the bottom. If the bottoms of the dumplings stick to the pan, usually they are not crisp enough, so cook a little longer.

3. Carefully free the dumplings from the pan, and don't break the skin, or you will lose the nice juice from the filling. Serve the dumplings brown side up. Use Chinese vinegar (or wine vinegar), soy sauce, and hot oil for dipping.

Tips:

Both cooked and uncooked dumplings (only if the uncooked meat has not been frozen before) can be frozen. I prefer to freeze the uncooked ones for future use. You can cook them without defrosting, and still have the juicy stuffing which is lost in the recooked ones.

Freeze the uncooked dumplings on a well-floured tray, so they are not touching one another. Then transfer them to a well-sealed plastic bag. They can be frozen for 1 to 2 months.

Variations:

1. Use pork only without the celery cabbage.
2. Add some crab meat to the filling.

SPRING ROLLS ★ (Known as Egg Rolls by Americans)

春捲   Chun-juan

Makes 12 ‡

The Chinese often serve them as mid-afternoon snacks for company. Cut into halves, they make excellent appetizers, Western style. As a main course (the recipe will serve 2 to 3 persons), served with a soup such as the hearty Hot and Sour Soup, they will make a very satisfying meal.

The authentic Chinese versions are called Spring Rolls, but there is no egg in them whatsoever. It is still a mystery to us, how Americans originated the name of "Egg Rolls"!

Spring rolls are very delicate, for their skins are glassy, very light, and very crisp. They are very much unlike their American cousins, which are heavy and doughy. But unfortunately, many Chinese restaurants still serve these Americanized egg rolls.

It is a Chinese tradition to serve spring rolls on New Year's Day because they resemble the gold bars of the old days, and therefore are symbols of prosperity. Many other foods are served at New Year's. Most of these foods symbolize tokens of long life, happiness, prosperity, and good fortune.

In Shanghai, my family always served spring rolls as one of the foods for our New Year's breakfast—and how I used to look forward to this very special feast. Here in the United States, we still keep the tradition of serving spring rolls in our household on the Chinese New Year. But since there is no holiday here for us, and since the Chinese New Year most often falls on a weekday, we often have our spring rolls at dinner time. But it is still one of our favorite foods!

About the Wrappers:

The authentic Shanghai spring roll wrappers are traditionally handmade by special professionals. It is a technique to be mastered only by experience, and not easy for a novice to attempt. In China, these wrappers are readily available, and can be purchased at any time, so no one makes them at home. It is the wrappers that largely determine the quality of these rolls. The Cantonese egg roll wrappers are machine-made egg noodle sheets cut into 8-inch/20-cm squares. They are much heavier than the spring roll wrappers, and unfortunately are more familiar to Americans. However, you can now find both wrappers in food stores in Chinatown or neighborhood Oriental stores.

If you don't live near any of these stores, don't despair! I have experimented and discovered that if you roll the Mandarin pancakes (see recipe, page 244) thinner than the recipe specifies, to at least 8½-inch/21½-cm in diameter or larger, you then will have excellent wrappers for the spring rolls. Remember, the thinner the wrapper, the lighter the roll.

I tested this by comparing the Mandarin pancake side-by-side with the Shanghai spring roll wrapper. The fried roll from the Mandarin pancake shows some tiny bubbles and is less glassy, but otherwise it gives the same delicate, light, and crisp texture as the spring roll. Although the two are made in different ways, each is made from cooked dough, and each dough is made from just flour and water. So if I were to make my own wrappers for the spring rolls, I would choose the paper-thin Mandarin pancakes, especially when the food processor can cut down the preparation time.

Spring rolls do take time to make, but the results are well worth the effort. The recipe gives indications that you can stop at different steps, and continue on at a later time, so you can work them out to suit your schedule.

Traditionally the stuffings in the spring rolls are all cut into shreds. However, I have found that by chopping the stuffings instead of shredding them in the food processor, I have saved preparation time, and it does not change the taste of the spring rolls. This is the time-saving method.

AHEAD OF TIME:

1. Snap the stems off the Chinese mushrooms. Soak the mushrooms in boiling water to cover for 20 minutes, or until soft.

2. If *frozen pork cubes* are used, thaw partially or completely following these directions:

> 20 minutes or more to partially thaw meat at room temperature
> 10 minutes or more to partially thaw meat in a 250° oven
> 55 seconds or more to completely thaw meat in a microwave oven

Dried Chinese Mushrooms	5 large (optional)
Fresh Bean Sprouts	½ pound/225 g
(*or* Canned Bean Sprouts)	(16 ounce/450 g can)
Bamboo Shoots	5 ounces/140 g
Scallions	2, cut in 2-inch/5-cm sections

Pork Mixture

Boneless Pork	½ pound/225 g in 1-inch/2½-cm cubes
(*or* 1 chicken breast, boneless, and skinless, cut into cubes)	
Cornstarch	2 teaspoons
Dry Sherry	2 teaspoons
Soy Sauce	2 teaspoons

Shrimp Mixture:

Shrimp with Shell	4 ounces/115 g, shelled and deveined
Cornstarch	½ teaspoon
Salt	¼ teaspoon
Dry Sherry	1 teaspoon
Cornstarch	1 tablespoon in 1½ tablespoons water
Sugar	1 teaspoon
Salt	½ teaspoon or to taste
Soy Sauce	2 tablespoons
Cooking Oil	2 cups/½ L plus 5 tablespoons
Wrappers	12

PREPARATION AND COOKING OF THE FILLING: 25 minutes. Allow 20 minutes or more to cool down the filling before wrapping.

ASSEMBLING THE SPRING ROLLS: 15 minutes

COOKING THE SPRING ROLLS: 10 minutes

Preparation of the Filling:

1. Boil enough water to blanch the fresh bean sprouts. (You do not have to blanch canned bean sprouts. Just rinse and drain them very well.) Cover fresh bean sprouts with boiling water and let stand for 1 minute. Immediately drain and rinse with cold water. Drain very well before cooking.

2. While you are boiling the water in step 1, you can prepare the other ingredients. Cut bamboo shoots into 1-inch/2½-cm cubes. Drain the softened mushrooms.

3. With *Steel Blade* in place, add bamboo shoots, mushrooms, and scallions to the beaker. Process until coarsely chopped. (To chop by hand see page 14.) Transfer to a bowl.

4. Replace the *Steel Blade,* add pork cubes to the beaker, process with 3 quick on/off turns. Add the remaining 3 ingredients for the pork mixture. Process until pork is chopped. (To chop by hand see page 14.) Transfer to a bowl.

5. Replace the *Steel Blade,* add the shrimp mixture to the beaker, and process until shrimp is coarsely chopped. (To chop by hand see page 14.)

6. Mix 1 tablespoon cornstarch with 1½ tablespoons water.

7. Combine 1 teaspoon sugar, ½ teaspoon salt (or to taste), and 2 tablespoons soy sauce in a bowl.

8. Squeeze out excess water from the well-drained bean sprouts, and add them to the bowl with chopped bamboo shoots. §

Have Ready Before Cooking:

1. Bottle of cooking oil
2. Bowl with pork mixture
3. Bowl with shrimp mixture
4. Bowl with vegetables
5. Bowl with soy sauce mixture
6. Bowl with cornstarch mixture

Cooking the Filling:

1. Heat wok over high heat, then add 3 tablespoons oil. When the oil is hot, stir-fry the pork mixture until pork is partially cooked. Add the shrimp mixture, and cook until pork loses its pink color. Remove from the wok.

2. Heat 2 more tablespoons oil in the wok, and stir-fry the vegetables for 2 minutes. Add the soy sauce mixture, and return the cooked meat, stirring to mix. Give the cornstarch mixture a good stir, and add to the

wok, stirring until all the liquid is absorbed by the ingredients. The filling mixture should be quite dry with no liquid left behind. Let the filling cool to room temperature before wrapping. It can be prepared 1 or 2 days ahead, and kept in the refrigerator. §

Variations:
1. You can use all meat or chicken without the shrimp.
2. Add some thinly shredded Smithfield ham.
3. Use shredded, blanched celery cabbage in place of the bean sprouts. Be sure to drain it very well, and give a good squeeze to get rid of most of the water. This way, the cooked filling will be quite dry with no liquid left behind.

Assembling:
To have good crisp spring rolls, it is very important that the filling be quite dry. If there is any liquid in it, drain the filling before wrapping. Otherwise, the liquid will soften the wrapper and make the roll soggy.
1. For each spring roll, use about ¼ cup/½ dL of the filling, and place it at the lower center of the wrapper. Shape the filling into a cylinder.
2. Lift the lower flap over the filling and tuck under.
3. Fold over the other two flaps on the sides to make an envelope.
4. Roll the wrapper into a neat package. With a little cold water, or a mixture of cornstarch and water, seal the edge of the roll. Place the sealed rolls on a plate with sealed side down. If they are not to be cooked right away, separate the layers with wax paper, and cover them with plastic wrap. Keep in the refrigerator. Can be made a few hours ahead. §

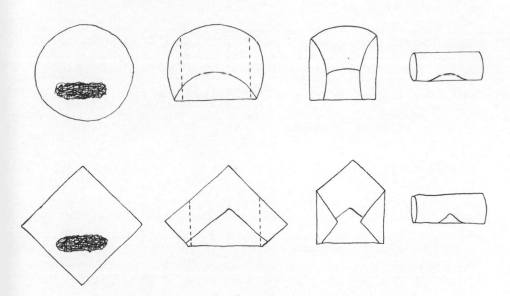

Cooking:

1. It is easier to cook them in a skillet than in a wok. Heat 2 cups/½ L oil in a 10-inch/25-cm skillet, or fill an electric skillet with ½-inch/1½-cm oil, and heat to 375°F/190°C. You can test the temperature by dropping a small piece of dough into the oil; if it turns golden brown in 1 minute, the oil is ready.

2. Fry the spring rolls for 3 to 5 minutes, turning once. When they are golden and crisp on both sides, remove and drain on paper towels. Serve at once, with Chinese vinegar, soy sauce or both. (I like them best with just Chinese vinegar.) §

Tips:

The cooked spring rolls can be refrigerated for 1 to 2 days, or frozen for a few weeks. The only way to recrisp the cooked spring rolls is by re-frying. (Crispness is the important quality for spring rolls.) Heating in a hot oven will not give the same result, and the filling tends to lose flavor. To defrost frozen spring rolls, remove them from the plastic wrap, and lay them out on a platter. Do not overlap them, and shake off any frost that may have collected during freezing. Refry until the wrappers are crisp again.

SESAME SEED BREAD ★

                                                    Shao-bing

Makes 12 ‡
(4-inch/10-cm rounds)

These typical Northern breads are served with the Mongolian fire pot or with other meat dishes. They are flat, about ¾-inch/2-cm thick, with a crusty outside and a soft inside. When cut into halves, each piece forms a pocket for a food stuffing. If you like to make bread, you would enjoy the nutty flavor of this Chinese bread. The Northerners also eat them for breakfast. The breads are traditionally baked in a pan over the burner since Chinese kitchens do not have ovens. However, they can be easily baked in the ovens of Western kitchens.

Warm Water	½ cup/1 dL
Active Dry Yeast	1½ teaspoons
Sugar	2 teaspoons
All-purpose Flour	3 cups/¾ L
Salt	1 teaspoon
Warm Water	½ cup/1 dL plus 1 to 2 more tablespoons
Sesame Paste	2 tablespoons
(*or* Creamy Peanut Butter)	
Salt	½ teaspoon
Corn Syrup	1 tablespoon mixed with 1 tablespoon water
White Sesame Seeds	½ cup/1 dL or more

PREPARATION OF THE DOUGH: 10 minutes

RISING: 30 minutes

SHAPING: 40 minutes

BAKING: 15 minutes if all the breads are baked at one time

Preparation of the Dough:

1. Sprinkle yeast in ½ cup/1 dL warm water, then sprinkle sugar over the yeast. Let stand for 3 to 5 minutes until yeast bubbles up and doubles in volume.

2. With *Steel Blade* in place, add flour and salt to the beaker. Give a quick on/off turn to mix. Add the yeast mixture to the flour, and with the machine running, add ½ cup/1 dL warm water through the feed tube. Then dribble in only enough of the remaining water until ball of dough

forms on the blades. Let the machine run for another 30 seconds. Remove the dough, and knead on a lightly-floured surface for 1 minute or until smooth. (To prepare without the food processor, mix flour, salt, yeast mixture, and water together. Knead for 10 minutes or until the dough is smooth.)

Rising:

Place the dough in a bowl, and cover with a damp cloth. Let it rise in a warm place for 30 minutes.

Shaping:

Knead the dough on a lightly-floured surface for 1 to 2 minutes. Divide it into 2 equal portions.

Roll out one portion at a time into a 15 × 8-inch/38½ × 20-cm rectangle.

Spread half of the sesame paste evenly over each portion of the dough. (The sesame paste should be the consistency of peanut butter; if it is too thick, thin it out with the oil in the bottle or with water. Then mix with

½ teaspoon salt.) Roll it into a 15-inch/38½-cm length jelly roll, and cut into 6 sections.

Seal each section at both ends by pulling and pinching the outer dough.

Roll each section with rolling pin into a 4-inch/10-cm diameter round.

Brush the top of the dough with the corn syrup and water mixture. Dip the top into the sesame seeds, and press lightly.

Baking:

Place 6 shaped doughs in a 12-inch/30-cm skillet or 4 in a 10-inch/25-cm skillet.

The bread can be baked right after they are shaped, or wait until the other half of the dough is shaped. They are not supposed to rise a lot before baking.

To bake, cover the skillet and let cook on low heat for about 5 minutes. Then turn heat to medium, and bake for another 5 minutes until the bottom is golden in color. Turn the breads over, cover, and bake until the sesame seeds are golden, about 3 to 4 minutes. Serve hot.

To bake in the oven: Place the shaped doughs in a large pan at least 1-inch/2½-cm deep. Cover the pan with aluminum foil, and bake in a preheated 450°F/230°C oven for 15 minutes or until the bottoms of the bread are golden brown. §

Tips:

1. These breads should be served warmed. They can be kept in the refrigerator for 3 to 4 days in a well-sealed plastic bag, or in the freezer for 2 to 3 months.

2. They can be rewarmed in a covered skillet on low heat, or wrapped in foil and rewarmed in a 350°F/180°C oven for 15 minutes. They can also be rewarmed, covered with plastic wrap, in a microwave oven, but do not overheat.

Variation:

Pita bread can be used as substitute.

Chinese Sweets

I know many Americans find a meal incomplete without dessert, but the Chinese custom is to end a meal with hot tea and fresh fruit. So you, too, can conclude your meal with a platter of seasonal fruits, or chilled Chinese canned fruits such as lychee, loquat, or Mandarin oranges.

Chinese sweets are eaten as snacks, except at dinner banquets where a sweet dish or a sweet soup is served in-between dishes or at the end of the dinner. The sweet soups are often made from ground nuts, and many sweet things are stuffed with red bean paste or date puree. They are very different from Western desserts.

Interestingly, though Chinese genius does not express itself in sweet things, several American food writers have given the Chinese credit for discovering ice cream. But I am always puzzled by such claims, for China is not a dairy country. We have always considered ice cream as something Western that has been adopted into our cuisine. Yet, I don't know of a single Chinese who doesn't like ice cream, for as far back as I remember as a child, we always had ice cream in big cities like Shanghai. But we ate it more as a snack than as a dessert, unlike the way Chinese restaurants here in the United States serve it. However, ice cream does make a refreshing dinner ending, so you can serve it with your Chinese meal at home. Or for a party, use assorted flavors and colors, and shape the ice cream into balls before the guests arrive. Refrigerate a platter of Chinese canned fruit, or combine them with chunks of fresh fruit. At serving time, just arrange the ice cream balls on top of the fruit and serve.

In this chapter, I have included the Chinese sweets that are popular with Americans, and also time-saving when prepared using the food processor. All the recipes can be prepared ahead, and will adapt well as Western desserts.

Modern Chinese families sometimes serve Western pastries and cakes after an informal dinner, especially for birthday celebrations. Now, by adopting the Western custom of serving birthday cake along with the traditional longevity noodles, they have been Westernized!

But East and West do meet. If dessert is dear to your heart, why not make a meal taking the best of the two worlds? Many Western desserts will make a nice ending to a Chinese meal.

ALMOND COOKIES

杏仁餅   Xing-ren-bing

Makes 32 2½-inch/6½-cm cookies
or 16 3½-inch/9-cm cookies ‡

Rich in almond flavor, light and crisp in texture, these cookies are easy and
fast to make with the food processor.

Lard	6 tablespoons
Vegetable Shortening	6 tablespoons
Large Egg	1
Sugar	¾ cup/145 g
Almond Extract	2 teaspoons
All-purpose Flour	1½ cups/215 g
Baking Powder	1 teaspoon
Baking Soda	½ teaspoon
Salt	⅛ teaspoon
Skinless Whole Almonds	16 to 32, whole or cut into halves
Egg (for glazing)	1 (optional)

PREPARATION: 15 to 18 minutes

BAKING: 15 minutes

Preparation:

1. With *Steel Blade* in place, put lard, vegetable shortening, egg, sugar,
and almond extract in the beaker. Use 7 on/off turns or until they are just
mixed. (To prepare without the food processor, cream the ingredients
together with an electric mixer until well blended.)

2. Add flour, baking powder, baking soda, and salt to the beaker. Process, using 7 on/off turns or until the last bit of flour just disappears. Do
not overprocess. (To prepare without the food processor, sift the flour, baking powder, baking soda, and salt together twice. Then mix with the egg
mixture and work into a dough.)

3. Preheat oven to 400°F/205°C.

4. Transfer dough onto a lightly-floured surface. Divide the dough into
2 equal portions, and roll each into a cylinder. For *2½-inch/6½-cm cookies:*
Roll each cylinder to 1¼ inches/3¹/₅ cm in diameter, then cut each into 16
equal pieces. Lay all 16 of them on an ungreased cookie sheet.
For *3½-inch/9-cm cookies:* Roll each cylinder 2 inches/5 cm in diameter, cut
each into 8 equal pieces. Lay the 8 pieces well apart from each other on an
ungreased cookie sheet.

5. Press whole or half almonds firmly in the center of each cookie.

6. If desired, brush the cookies with 1 beaten egg for glazing.

Baking:

Bake the cookies in a preheated 400°F/205°C oven for 12 to 14 minutes or until they are golden yellow. Let cool, and remove from the cookie sheets. §

Tips:

Almond cookies can be kept for several weeks in an air-tight container at room temperature.

Variation:

You can substitute vegetable shortening for lard.

SESAME COOKIES

芝蔴餅   Zhi-ma-bing

Makes 60 1½-inch/4-cm cookies ‡

These small and very crunchy cookies have a delicate and nutty flavor. You may find them in Chinatown grocery stores; they are packed in cellophane bags imported from Hong Kong.

Vegetable Shortening	⅓ cup/¾ dL
Sugar	⅔ cup/235 g or to taste
Egg	1 large
All-purpose Flour	1 cup/140 g
Baking Powder	1 teaspoon
White Sesame Seeds	½ cup/70 g

PREPARATION: 35 minutes

BAKING: 20 minutes

Preparation:

1. With *Steel Blade* in place, add vegetable shortening, sugar, and egg to the beaker. Process until they are well blended. (To prepare without the food processor, cream the ingredients together with an electric mixer until well blended.)

2. Add flour to the beaker, and then sprinkle the baking powder over the flour. Process until the dough forms a ball above the blades. Do not over process. There may be small pieces in the bottom of the beaker; just add them to the ball when you remove it. (To prepare without the food processor, sift the flour and baking powder together twice. Then mix with the egg mixture and work into a dough.)

3. Divide the dough into 2 equal portions. Roll each into a cylinder ¾ inch/2 cm in diameter. Cut into 30 ¼-inch/¾-cm-thick pieces.

4. Place each piece, one piece at a time, in the sesame seeds, and press down firmly so the seeds will adhere to the dough. Turn over, and repeat with the other side. You should have a 1-inch/2½-cm circle generously coated with sesame seeds on both sides. (If the sesame seeds are not sticking well to the dough, wet the surface of the dough with a very small amount of water before pressing.) Place all 30 cookies on an 11 × 16-inch/28 × 40-cm cookie sheet. Repeat the process with the other portion of the dough.

Baking:

Bake the cookies in a preheated 325°F/165°C oven for 20 minutes until they are light yellow in color. §

Tips:

The cookies can be kept for several weeks in an air-tight container at room temperature.

STEAMED CAKE*

黄鬆糕   Huang-song-gao

Serves 10 to 12

This cake is often served in Cantonese teahouse restaurants, or it can be purchased at Chinese bakeries. Because traditional Chinese kitchens do not have an oven, the cake is cooked by steaming, and usually served warm, but it's just as good when cold. It makes a good snack with tea and milk.

The food processor cuts down ⅔ of the normal preparation time.

All-purpose Flour	1½ cups/215 g
Baking Powder	3 teaspoons
Baking Soda	½ teaspoon
Salt	½ teaspoon
Dark Brown Sugar	1½ cups/275 g, very well packed
Cooking Oil	6 tablespoons
Vanilla Extract	1 teaspoon
Large Eggs	4
Milk	¼ cup/½ dL
Cake Pan	1 9-inch/23-cm, well-greased, spring-form pan

PREPARATION: 15 minutes

STEAMING: 1 hour

Preparation:

1. With *Steel Blade* in place, add flour, baking powder, baking soda, and salt to the beaker. Process for few seconds or until they are well mixed. Remove from the beaker. (To prepare without the food processor, see below.)

2. Set up the steamer, heat the water for steaming while preparing the cake batter.

3. Replace the *Steel Blade,* add sugar, oil, and vanilla to the beaker, and process until mixed.

4. Add 2 eggs to the beaker, and process until the mixture is smooth. Repeat with the other 2 eggs.

5. Add milk to the beaker, and process to mix.

6. Add the flour mixture to the beaker. Use quick on/off turns until the flour is well incorporated. Pour the batter into the well-greased cake pan.

(To prepare without the food processor, sift the flour, baking powder, baking soda, and salt together three times. Set aside. Mix the dark brown sugar, cooking oil, vanilla extract, eggs, and milk together using an electric mixer and beat until smooth. Gradually sift in the flour mixture, mixing lightly until the flour is completely incorporated. Pour the batter into the well-greased cake pan.)

Steaming:

Place the cake pan in the bamboo steamer or on a steamer rack. Steam over boiling water and on high heat for 10 minutes. Then steam on medium heat for 50 minutes. Check occasionally to see if more boiling water should be added to the steamer. Do not let the water run dry.

Remove the cake pan from the steamer, and let the cake cool for few minutes. Then remove the cake from the cake pan, and serve warm. §

Tips:

The cake can be kept in the refrigerator for 4 to 5 days, or in the freezer for 2 to 3 months. It can be rewarmed by steaming, or served at room temperature.

EGG TARTS*

蛋撻   Dan-ta

Makes 10 3-inch/8-cm tarts ‡

Since the traditional family kitchen is not equipped with an oven, the baked goods are usually made at the baker's. These sweet pastries are served by the Cantonese teahouse restaurants, or the Chinese buy them at their bakeries. They are usually served warm, although you can eat them cold. You can bake them in plain large muffin tins, however, traditionally fluted molds are used to make them look prettier. The tarts will be smaller in the muffin tin, so cut the pastry into circles that are smaller than specified in the recipe.

Small Fluted Molds (Brioche Molds or Large Muffin Tins)	10 3½-inch/9-cm-diameter and 1½-inch/4-cm-deep

Filling:

Sugar	½ cup/100 g plus 3 tablespoons
Water	6 tablespoons
Milk	6 tablespoons
Eggs	3 large

Pastry:

All-purpose Flour	1⅓ cups/190 g
Sugar	2 tablespoons
Vegetable Shortening	½ cup/1 dL
Water	4 tablespoons

PREPARATION: 30 minutes

BAKING: 1 hour

Preparation:

1. Make the filling mixture by first dissolving the sugar in 6 tablespoons water in a small pot over heat. When the sugar is all dissolved, set the solution aside to cool.

2. In the meantime, prepare the pastry dough. With *Steel Blade* in place, add flour, sugar, and shortening to the beaker. Process until mixture has the consistency of coarse meal, about 10 seconds. With the machine running, pour in the water in a steady stream through the feed tube, and process until a ball of dough forms above the blades (less than a minute). Do not over process. There may be small pieces in the bottom of the

beaker, just add them to the ball when you remove it. (To prepare without the food processor, cut the shortening into the flour and sugar with a pastry blender until the mixture resembles small peas. Then sprinkle 1 tablespoon of water at a time over the mixture. Gently mix with a fork. Add just enough water to moisten the dough. Gather up and form into a ball.) The dough can be used immediately.

3. On a lightly-floured surface or a pastry cloth, flatten the dough slightly, and roll into a square about 12×12 inches/30×30 cm. Using a large 4- to 4½-inch/10- to 12-cm round pastry cutter or a bowl of the same diameter as a guide, cut the pastry into circles. Fit each circle into a mold, and press the pastry snugly into the fluted areas of the mold. Push and anchor the pastry around the edges of the mold. Care must be taken not to break the pastry, and not to let the bottom part get too thin, for if the filling leaks under the pastry, you'll have difficulty removing the baked tart from the mold.

Combine the scraps of dough, and roll out to make more circles.

4. Now return to the filling mixture. Clean the beaker with a paper towel, and replace the *Steel Blade*. Place the cool sugar solution, 6 table-spoons milk, and 3 eggs in the beaker. Process for 5 seconds or until the mixture is just evenly mixed. Do not overprocess to create a lot of air bubbles. Pour the mixture through a strainer, and fill the pastry to $^7/_{10}$ full. (To prepare without the food processor, mix the cool sugar solution, milk, and eggs using an electric mixer. Beat at low speed just until all the ingredients are well mixed. Do not overbeat to create a lot of air bubbles. Pour the mixture through a strainer, and fill the pastry to $^7/_{10}$ full.)

Baking:

Place the molds on a large cookie sheet, and bake in a preheated 300°F/150° C oven for 1 hour or until a knife comes out clean when inserted into the filling. The tart shell has a pale yellow color. Remove tart from the mold before serving. §

Tips:

These tarts can be kept in the refrigerator for 2 to 3 days, or in the freezer for 2 to 3 months. Rewarm in a 300°F/150°C oven before serving.

Chinese Ingredients

BABY SWEET CORN
玉米筍 Yu-mi-sun

Packed in 15-ounce/425 g cans, only about 2 to 3 inches/5 to 8 cm long, it is tender and delicate, and can be used to add color and texture to any of the stir-fried dishes. Available in Oriental food stores and China-towns.

To store: After opening, store with its juice in a covered jar in the refrigerator. It will keep for a week.

BAMBOO SHOOTS:
筍 Sun

Ivory-colored shoots grown from bamboo stalks, they are available in cans, and add a crisp texture to dishes.

To store: After opening, drain and store in a covered jar filled with fresh cold water, and refrigerate. Change water every other day; in this way, they will keep for a few weeks.

BEAN CURD, FRESH:
豆腐 Dou-fu

This ivory-colored, smooth and custard-like product is made from soy-bean milk, and has been an important source of protein to Orientals. It is high in protein, but much less expensive than meat and poultry. Because it is low in cholesterol and calories, bean curd is beginning to gain popularity in the United States, and is now found in many American supermarkets. It is available in 3 × 3 × ¾-inch/8 × 8 × 2 cm individual pieces or in a 1-pound block, vacuum-sealed in a plastic container.

To store: The 3-inch/8 cm squares should be covered with fresh water after purchasing, and then stored in the refrigerator. By changing the water every day, they may be kept unspoiled for a week. A sour taste will develop when spoiling sets in. The unopened vacuum-sealed 1-pound block can be kept in the refrigerator for 1 to 2 weeks. Once opened, it should be treated as the 3-inch/8 cm squares.

BEAN SPROUTS:
綠豆芽 Lü-dou-ya

The sprouts from the mung beans (the Chinese call them green beans) are now available in fresh form in many American supermarkets. Be sure to buy only the white and plump-looking ones; when they turn brownish, they're no longer fresh. Bean sprouts are at their best when they are bought fresh and used the same day. High in nutrients and low in calories, canned bean sprouts taste quite different and lack the delicate and crunchy texture.

To store: Very dry fresh sprouts can be kept in the refrigerator for 2 to 3 days if kept away from moisture and placed in sealed plastic bags.

To grow your own bean sprouts: Wash and then soak ¼ cup dried mung beans overnight in warm water.

Place double layers of cheesecloth on a perforated pan, aluminum steaming tray or colander. Moisten the cloth thoroughly with warm water, then drain the mung beans and spread them over the cloth in a single even layer. Cover the beans with another double layer of cheesecloth. Sprinkle and moisten them with warm water. Place the pan or tray over a draining basin, and put in a dark place, such as a closet, at a temperature of about 68° to 75°F/20° to 24°C. *Yields 3 cups.*

Keep the cheesecloth moist by sprinkling with plenty of water at least once a day, and let the excess water drain off properly into the basin. The sprouts should be kept moist all the time, but don't let them soak in the water.

In 4 or 5 days, depending on the growing temperature, the bean sprouts will mature and be ready to eat. Immerse them in cold water in a large pot, and stir to let the green hulls float to the surface. Discard the green hulls, and drain the bean sprouts. They are now ready for cooking.

BLACK BEANS, SALTED:
豆豉 Dou-chi

One of the most interesting seasonings, they are salty with a distinct flavor. The beans are available in cans or plastic bags.

To store: Will keep indefinitely in a covered jar at room temperature. Tiny white-salt crystals may appear after a long period, but the beans will still be usable. Rinse briefly before using.

BOK CHOY:
白菜 Bai-cao

The Cantonese words for "white vegetable," Bok Choy has white stems with green leaves, and is now available in some American supermarkets. The small ones are more tender and, therefore, better than the large ones. Bok Choy has a taste similar to Swiss chard.

To store: Will keep for a week in the vegetable crisper of the refrigerator. (Keep it free from moisture.)

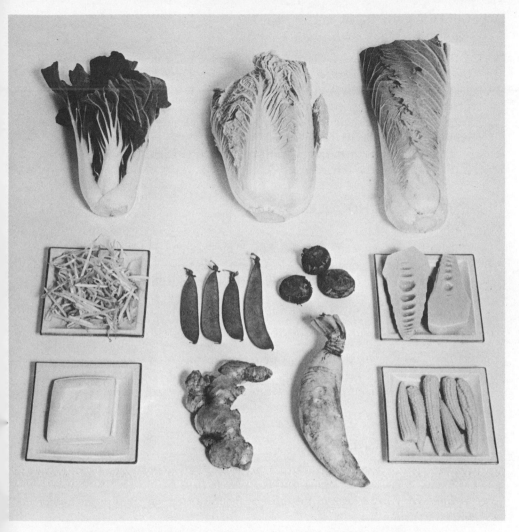

From left to right: (top) Bok choy, celery cabbage; (middle) bean sprouts, snow peas, water chestnuts, bamboo shoots; (bottom) bean curd, fresh ginger, Chinese turnips, baby sweet corn.

BROWN BEAN SAUCE:

原晒豉 Yuan-shai-chi

Made from fermented soy beans, salt, flour, and water, it is a salty, thick, brownish sauce. When the beans in the sauce are ground up, it is then called *ground* brown bean sauce. Both are sold in cans or jars, mostly used in the dishes from Northern and Western (Szechuan) regions.

To store: If the sauce is from a can, it should be transferred to a covered jar after opening, and kept in the refrigerator. It will keep for months.

269

CELERY CABBAGE:
黃芽白菜 Huang-ya-bai-cai

There are two kinds. The fatter and shorter ones are sometimes labeled by American supermarkets as Nappa cabbage. Their leaves are curlier and more tender than the long-headed, thinner varieties. The short ones are better for stir-frying, and the long ones are better for making pickled cabbage. Choose the long ones with pale green leaves, for they are more tender than the darker green ones.

To store: Wrap them in dry, well-sealed plastic bags. They will keep for 2 to 3 weeks in the refrigerator.

CELLOPHANE NOODLES:
粉絲 Fen-si

Also known as "transparent noodles" or "bean threads," they are made from mung beans, and sold in dried form as 2-ounce bundles.

To store: Dried cellophane noodles will keep indefinitely.

DUCK EGGS, SALTED:
鹹鴨蛋 Xian-ya-dan

They are uncooked duck eggs preserved in brine, so they are salty, and have to be cooked before serving.

To store: Will keep at room temperature for several weeks, or store in the refrigerator.

EGG NOODLES, FRESH:
蛋麵 Dan-mian

They are packed in 1-pound/450 g plastic bags.

To store: Can be kept in the refrigerator for 2 to 3 days and in the freezer for several months.

EGG ROLL WRAPPERS, CANTONESE:
廣東春捲皮 Guang-dong-chun-juan-pi

These 8-inch/20-cm squares are machine-made from egg, flour, and water, and sold in 1- to 2-pound/450 to 900 g packages. You can make your own. (See recipe, page 234, and check spring roll wrappers in this chapter.)

To store: To prevent them from drying out, keep in well-sealed plastic bags. Can be kept in the refrigerator for 3 to 4 days and in the freezer for 2 to 3 months. You may want to divide the 2-pound package into smaller packs before freezing.

Clockwise from bottom left (all items appear in and out of packages): Spring roll wrappers, fresh egg noodles, egg roll wrappers, wonton wrappers.

FERMENTED BEAN CURD (red and white):

 Fu-ru (Hong, Bai)

Both are pungent and salty in taste, and are used mostly for seasoning or as condiments for Chinese breakfast with the rice congee.

To store: Sold in cans or jars. If canned and opened, they should be transferred to a jar with a rust-proof cap and kept in the refrigerator. Will keep for several months.

GINGER, FRESH:

薑 Jiang

This gnarled, beige-colored root is indispensable in Chinese cooking. Now available in most American supermarkets, it flavors food and masks the fishy odor of seafood. Select the ones with firm skin, for when it looks wrinkly, the root is too old. *Do not use* ginger powder as a substitute; even canned ginger is a better replacement if the fresh is not available in your area.

To store: Peel off the skin with a potato peeler, then place the ginger in a jar covered completely with dry sherry and keep in the refrigerator. It will keep for several months.

GLUTINOUS RICE:

糯米 Nuo-mi

Also known as sweet rice, it has shorter grain than ordinary rice, and becomes sticky when cooked. Used in Pearl Balls (see recipe on page 120), sweet things, and stuffings.

To store: Can be kept for years in a covered container.

HOISIN SAUCE:

海鮮醬 Hai-xian-jiang

Thick, reddish brown sauce made from sugar, vinegar, soybean, salt, flour, fermented rice, chili, and spices. It is sold in cans or glass jars.

To store: If it is canned, transfer contents after opening into a glass jar. It will keep for many months in the refrigerator.

HOT CHILI OIL:

辣油 La-you

The most convenient way to spice up a dish is to use hot chili oil. It can be added during cooking, or at last minute, to your taste. It can also be used in salads and sauces. Commercial chili oil is red in color, and varies a great deal in spiciness, so always add just a little at a time until you reach the right taste. You can use Tabasco sauce as a substitute or make your own with the recipe below:

To make hot chili oil: Heat 1 cup vegetable oil in a small pot over medium heat. When oil is fairly warm but not hazing (for it will burn the peppers), add 30 hot dry red peppers (broken into halves, with seeds), and fry for about 1 minute or until the peppers turn black.

Remove from heat and cover the pot. Let the oil cool before straining it through a cheesecloth into a bottle. It should be golden yellow in color. *Yields* 1 cup.

Tips:

You can use 3 tablespoons crushed red pepper flakes as a substitute for the hot dry red peppers. These dry peppers also vary by package in spiciness, so the spiciness of the oil will vary. You can adjust the spiciness by using more or less of the peppers.

To store: It will keep for 6 months at room temperature. Any oil will turn rancid if kept on the shelf too long.

HOT DRY RED PEPPER (or *hot chili pepper*):

辣椒 La-jiao

About 1 to 2 inches long and red in color. They are available in Oriental or Italian food stores. They vary in spiciness from bag to bag, and are used to season the oil in the spicy stir-fried dishes. The longer you cook them in the oil, the spicier the oil gets. The peppers are also used in making hot chili oil.

To store: They will keep indefinitely in a covered jar at room temperature.

Tips:

You can substitute crushed red pepper flakes for them, about ¼ teaspoon for each whole pepper.

LOQUAT:
枇杷 Pi-pa

A small apricot-size, yellow-orange fruit, they are sold pitted in cans in Oriental stores and some gourmet shops.

To store: After removing from the can, they can be kept in a covered container for several days in the refrigerator.

LYCHEE:
荔枝 Li-zhi

A tropical fruit with rough red skin, white translucent pulp, and a brown pit. They are available fresh in the summer in some Chinatown groceries. Canned ones are sold in Oriental stores and many gourmet shops.

To store: After opening, the canned ones can be kept in a covered container for several days in the refrigerator. The fresh ones can be kept for a week if refrigerated.

MUNG BEANS:
綠豆 Lü-dou

These tiny green beans are available in Oriental groceries and health food stores. Fresh bean sprouts can be easily sprouted from them in 4 to 5 days (see bean sprouts). Another product made from mung beans is cellophane noodles. The Chinese also use them to make sweet snacks.

To store: Will keep indefinitely in a dry container at room temperature.

MUSHROOMS, DRIED CHINESE:
冬菇 Dong-gu

These brownish black dried mushrooms must be soaked for at least 20 minutes in boiling water to soften before using. But be sure to cut off the hard stems before cooking. Their lovely flavor and meaty texture enhance the color and taste of many dishes.

To store: Will keep indefinitely if stored in a dry, covered jar in the refrigerator.

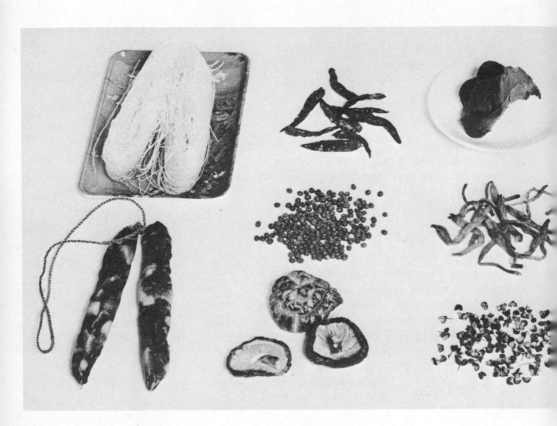

From left to right: (top) *cellophane noodles, hot dried peppers, Szechuan preserved vegetable;* (middle) *mung beans, tiger lilies;* (bottom) *Chinese sausage, dried Chinese mushrooms, Szechuan peppercorns.*

From left to right: (top) dried shrimp, salted black beans, salted duck eggs, white and red fermented bean curd; (bottom) black sesame seeds, tree ears.

OYSTER-FLAVORED SAUCE:
蠔油 Hao-you

A thick brown sauce sold in bottles, it is made from oyster extract, water, salt, and cornstarch. It enhances many dishes with a rich and subtle flavor. This sauce is used mostly in Cantonese cooking, often as an alternative seasoning to soy sauce.

To store: Will keep indefinitely in a dry container at room temperature.

RICE WINE:

Made from fermented rice, it is used as a table wine or for cooking. This wine can be purchased in Chinatown liquor stores. Dry sherry is a good substitute to use for cooking, and was used in all the recipes in this book. (See the chapter on Tea and Wine.)

To store: Keep in the refrigerator after the bottle is opened.

CHINESE SAUSAGES:
臘腸 La-chang

There are two kinds. One is made from pork (reddish color) and the other is made from liver (brownish color). The pork sausage has a sweet, delicate flavor. The sausages should be steamed for 10 to 15 minutes before eating. They can be served plain or used to enhance the flavor of the other dishes.

To store: Will keep in the refrigerator for several weeks.

SESAME OIL:
蔴油 Ma-you

This aromatic, golden-brown colored oil is made from roasted sesame seeds. It has a better nutty flavor than the light-colored sesame oil sold in health food stores. This oil is an excellent flavor enhancer when used in place of cooking oil in salads and cooked dishes. A small amount goes a long way, so it's an ideal salad dressing for the calorie-conscious. It comes from China or Japan, and is usually sold in bottles or cans.

To store: Will keep for at least 6 months or longer at room temperature without becoming rancid. It will keep longer in the refrigerator.

SESAME PASTE:
芝蔴醬 Zhi-ma-jiang

A dark brown paste made from roasted ground sesame seeds, it is sold in jars. Its oil tends to separate to the top, so stir well before using to recombine with the thick paste at the bottom. Creamy peanut butter mixed with a little sesame oil is a good substitute.

To store: Will keep for several months at room temperature.

SESAME SEEDS:
芝蔴 Zhi-ma

These tiny seeds are white or black. American supermarkets sell only the white seeds, but Oriental food stores carry both kinds.

To store: Keep in a covered jar. They will keep in the freezer for over a year, and for several months at room temperature.

SHRIMP, DRIED:
蝦米 Xia-mi

Dried, shelled, and salted shrimp must be soaked in hot water to soften before using.

To store: Can keep indefinitely if stored in a covered jar in the refrigerator.

SMITHFIELD HAM:
火腿 Huo-tui

This famous ham from Virginia is close in taste to Chinese ham. However, it is much more salty than regular ham. Chinese groceries do carry uncooked ham whole or by the slice, and cooked ones are available in some gourmet shops. Uncooked ham should be steamed in a bowl for 15 minutes before use. Prosciutto ham may be used as a substitute.

To store: Cooked ham will keep several months in the freezer in a well-sealed plastic bag.

SNOW PEAS
雪豆 Xue-dou

Flat and light-green peas are eaten with their pods. A better choice are the small, tender thin ones. The fresh peas are now available in many American supermarkets, but be sure to remove the strings before cooking. Frozen ones can be substituted, but they are not as crisp.

To store: They will keep for a week or more in a well-sealed plastic bag in the refrigerator, depending on how fresh they are to start with.

SOY SAUCE:
醬油 Jiang-you

This is the most important and distinctive seasoning in Chinese cooking. Sold in cans or bottles, it comes in many colors and many brands. Each brand varies in taste and saltiness, so the flavor of a dish will vary, depending upon the soy sauce that is used. Experiment until you find one you like best, then adjust the saltiness to taste.

But remember, good quality soy sauce is essential to good flavor. Imported soy sauce from the Orient is much better than the chemically processed brands made in the United States. The Oriental brands are made by natural fermentation and aging.

Kikkoman, the naturally brewed Japanese soy sauce, is a good all-purpose brand readily available in American supermarkets. All dishes in this book, unless otherwise noted, have been tested with Kikkoman soy sauce. This brand is available in bottles of various sizes, and also sold in ½- and 1-gallon cans in Chinatown groceries.

Imported Chinese soy sauce comes in light and dark colors.

LIGHT SOY SAUCE (or thin soy):
生抽   Sheng-chou

Is good for salad, dippings, or in stir-fried dishes when the natural color of the food is to be restained.

DARK SOY SAUCE (thick or black soy):
老抽   Lao-chou

With a slightly sweet taste, has caramel added for coloring. It is used in many slow-cooking or stir-fried dishes when a dark, rich color is desired.

Sometimes a dish is cooked with both light and dark soy sauce to achieve the desired color and flavor.

To store: Soy sauce will keep for a long time in bottles at room temperature.

SPRING ROLL WRAPPERS (Shanghai style):
上海春捲皮   Shanghai-chun-juan-pi

They are different from the egg roll wrappers (Cantonese), for they are much more delicate and crisp once fried. Unfortunately, they are confusingly labeled as "egg roll skins." Traditional spring roll wrappers come in 8-inch/20-cm rounds, usually sold in sealed plastic packs of 10. Use homemade Mandarin pancakes (see recipe, page 244) as a substitute.

To store: These wrappers dry out easily, and once dried, they are difficult to handle. Wrap them in another well-sealed plastic bag before freezing; then they will keep for 2 to 3 months without drying out. They will also keep in the refrigerator for 2 to 3 days. Thawed wrappers can be refrozen if they are not allowed to become dry, or thaw for too long.

SZECHUAN PEPPERCORN:
花椒   Hua-jiao

These reddish-brown peppercorns are not peppery hot, but have a distinctive aroma. Their husks are usually opened.

To store: They will keep indefinitely in a closed jar at room temperature.

SZECHUAN PEPPERCORN SALT:
椒鹽 Jiao-yan

It is usually served as a dip with deep-fried dishes. Szechuan peppercorns impart a special flavor to the roasted salt.

To store: It will keep for a long time in a tightly-covered jar at room temperature.

To make Szechuan peppercorn salt: Heat 4 tablespoons salt with 2 tablespoons Szechuan peppercorns in a dry pan for a few minutes, shaking the pan a few times until the salt turns light golden, and you can smell the fragrance from the peppercorns.

Remove the pan from the heat and let cool. Crush the salt mixture with the *Steel Blade* in the processor, then strain or remove the husks of the peppercorns before transferring to a tightly covered jar.

SZECHUAN PRESERVED VEGETABLE:
榨菜 Zha-cai

Both salty and spicy, this vegetable can be used as a seasoning and is sold in cans.

To store: After opening the can, it should be stored in a jar with a rust-proof cover. It will keep for a long time in the refrigerator.

TIGER LILIES (or golden needles):
金針 Jin-zhen

Pale golden in color, they have a delicate and distinct flavor and are 3 to 4 inches/8 to 10 cm long. They have to be softened by soaking in boiling water (about 10 minutes) before use, but lose flavor if oversoaked.

To store: They will keep indefinitely in a covered jar at room temperature.

TREE EARS (cloud ears or black fungus):
木耳 Mu-er

Dark brown to grayish black in color, tree ears have to be soaked in boiling water before use. They will expand to 3 to 4 times their original size. They have no flavor, but add color and a crunchy texture to dishes.

To store: They will keep indefinitely in a covered jar at room temperature.

TURNIPS, CHINESE, LARGE WHITE:
白蘿蔔 Bai-luo-bo

About 2 inches/5 cm in diameter and 8 to 10 inches/20 to 25 cm long, it is closer in taste to the Western radish.

To store: Will keep in the refrigerator, in a sealed plastic bag for 2 weeks.

VINEGAR, CHINESE RED:

大紅浙醋   Da-hong-zhc-cu

Made from rice, it has a delicate flavor and is milder in taste than Western vinegars. It is used in cooking, and is delicious as a dip, especially with dumplings and spring rolls. If you substitute wine vinegar, use a smaller amount.

To store: Will keep indefinitely at room temperature.

WATER CHESTNUTS:

荸薺   Bi-qi

Fresh water chestnuts have dark brown skins. Once you peel off the skins with a potato peeler, you'll discover an inside that is white, sweet, crunchy, and delicious. Water chestnuts are available in cans, but canned water chestnuts, despite their crunchy texture, have lost all flavor.

To store: Fresh water chestnuts are quite perishable, but will keep unpeeled from 1 to 2 weeks in the refrigerator. Canned water chestnuts, after opening, will keep for several weeks in a covered jar of fresh water in the refrigerator, if you change the water every other day.

WONTON WRAPPERS (3- × 3-inch/8- × 8-cm squares):

餛飩皮   Hun-tun-pi

There are thick and thin wonton wrappers, but both are sold in 1-pound/450 g packages. The Cantonese egg roll wrappers can be used as a substitute, if you cut each into 4 small squares before wrapping. Or you can make your own (see recipe, page 234).

To store: Do not let the wrappers become dried out. Wrap them in a tightly-sealed plastic bag. They can be kept in the refrigerator for 3 to 4 days, and will keep in the freezer for 3 to 4 months. You may want to divide them into smaller packages before freezing. The thawed wrappers can be refrozen if they are not allowed to dry out or thaw for too long.

Tea and Wine

TEA

The favorite and most common beverage in China, tea is something the Chinese drink all day instead of water. Whenever someone visits a home or business office, a cup of tea is served as a gesture of hospitality.

Contrary to what most Americans are accustomed to in Chinese restaurants, tea is rarely served during the meal at home, for soup is used as the beverage. A common custom is to serve hot tea after the meal, for tea soothes the stomach and helps digestion. It is always served plain, never with sugar or cream.

The quality of tea can vary a great deal, and good tea in China is like good wine in the Western world. The best is cherished by tea connoisseurs, and can be quite expensive. Tea is best stored in air-tight containers to preserve its freshness.

Because of the different methods of preparation, there are many varieties of Chinese tea. In general, they can be divided into three kinds:

1. *Unfermented Tea*—also known as *green tea*—is roasted immediately after picking. It has a pure and refreshing taste.
> Loong Ching—best known (phonetic translation of Dragon Well)
> Gunpowder
> Lu An
> Chrysanthemum (scented)

2. *Fermented Tea*—known as black tea in the Western world—but the leaves are black and the brew is red, so the Chinese call it red tea. The leaves are left in muggy air to ferment before roasting, so it has a full-bodied and stronger flavor than the green tea.
> Keeman—best known
> Lychee (scented)—has a sweet flavor
> Iron goddess of Mercy

3. *Semifermented*—made from partially fermented tea leaves—its flavor and color are in-between a green and a red tea.
> Oolong—best known
> Jasmine (scented)

The flavor of tea is a matter of personal taste, so you can serve any kind. Experiment to find your favorite.

How To Brew Tea

As a rule, tea should be steeped in porcelain or earthenware teapots or teacups—but avoid metal pots, for they will distort the flavor. The Chinese usually brew tea to individual taste, so if you find the tea too strong, it can be diluted with hot water.

For average taste, use 1 teaspoon tea leaves to 1 cup of boiling water. Pour freshly boiled water over the leaves and cover for 3 to 4 minutes before serving.

A Chinese family will often make a large pot of very strong tea in the morning. So whenever needed, it is diluted to individual taste with hot water in a cup or a glass. The leftover tea leaves may be used to make a second pot of tea. Just add a little more of the new leaves, and pour freshly boiled water over the leaves just as you did the first time.

WINES AND SPIRITS

Chinese wines and spirits are made of rice or other grains. The best known rice wine is named for Shaoshing, in the Eastern region, although Shaoshing wine is also called "yellow wine." Similar in taste to dry sherry, it is served warm at about 176°F/80°C. Low-grade Shaoshing wine is usually used in cooking but you can substitute a dry sherry.

Mao-tai, the well-known spirit from the Western region, is made from wheat and millet. It is colorless and very strong—even stronger than vodka! So drink it slowly, little by little. The Northern region is known for Kaoliang, made from sorghum. It's also very strong and ranges up to 60 percent alcohol.

Ng Gah Pei liqueur from the South is laced with herbs, and is drunk for its tonic effects as well. There are also fruit-flavored wines like the lychee and plum wines, but both are quite sweet. Lychee wine has a refreshing taste, and you may like it as a unique after-dinner treat.

Everyday meals are usually served without wine, but it is always served at dinner parties. A toast with wine is an important ritual, and it goes on for many rounds throughout the dinner. The Chinese drink their wine and spirits straight, but always at dinner with food, and not before dinner.

Many of these Chinese wines and spirits are now available in Chinatown liquor stores. Serving a warm Chinese rice wine may be an interesting experience, but to most Westerners it is an acquired taste that has to be developed.

Actually, any dry white wine goes very well with Chinese food. There is a popular French light wine, specially bottled to go with Chinese food, named "Wan Fu" (a "million blessings").

Some people like to drink beer with Chinese food. Since there is no hard and fast rule, it is really a matter of personal taste.

Sources for Mail Ordering

CALIFORNIA

Kwong On Lung Importers
680 North Spring Street
Los Angeles, 90012

The Chinese Grocer
209 Post Street
San Francisco, 94108

FLORIDA

South Eastern Food Supply
6732 N.E. 4th Avenue
Miami, 33138

GEORGIA

Asia Trading Company
2581 Piedmont N. E.
Atlanta, 30324

ILLINOIS

Dong Kee Company
2252 South Wentworth Avenue
Chicago, 60616

MASSACHUSETTS

See Sun Company
36 Harrison Avenue
Boston, 02111

MICHIGAN

Chinese Asia Trading Company
734 S. Washington Road
Royal Oak, 48067

NEW YORK

Kam Kuo Food Corporation
7 Mott Street
New York, 10013

OHIO

Soya Food Products
2356 Wyoming Avenue
Cincinnati, 45214

PENNSYLVANIA

Hon Kee Company
935 Race Street
Philadelphia, 19107

TEXAS

Oriental Import-Export Company
2009 Polk Street
Houston, 77003

WASHINGTON

Wak Yong Company
416 Eighth Avenue, South
Seattle, 98104

Metric Conversion Tables

TEMPERATURES

Fahrenheit°/Celsius°	(Actual Celsius°)	Fahrenheit°/Celsius°	(Actual Celsius°)
−5°F/−20°C	(−20.6°C)	180°F/82°C	(82.2°C)
32°F/0°C	(0°C)	190°F/88°C	(87.8°C)
37°F/3°C	(2.8°C)	200°F/95°C	(93.3°C)
50°F/10°C	(10°C)	205°F/96°C	(96.1°C)
60°F/16°C	(15.6°C)	212°F/100°C	(100°C)
70°F/21°C	(21.1°C)	225°F/110°C	(107.2°C)
75°F/24°C	(23.9°C)	228°F/109°C	(108.9°C)
80°F/27°C	(26.7°C)	238°F/115°C	(114.4°C)
85°F/29°C	(29.4°C)	250°F/120°C	(121.1°C)
100°F/38°C	(37.8°C)	275°F/135°C	(135°C)
105°F/41°C	(40.6°C)	285°F/140°C	(140.6°C)
110°F/43°C	(43.3°C)	300°F/150°C	(148.9°C)
115°F/46°C	(46.1°C)	325°F/165°C	(162.8°C)
120°F/49°C	(48.9°C)	350°F/180°C	(176.7°C)
125°F/52°C	(51.7°C)	375°F/190°C	(190.6°C)
130°F/54°C	(54.4°C)	400°F/205°C	(204.4°C)
135°F/57°C	(57.2°C)	425°F/220°C	(218.3°C)
140°F/60°C	(60°C)	450°F/230°C	(232.2°C)
150°F/66°C	(65.6°C)	475°F/245°C	(246.1°C)
160°F/71°C	(71.1°C)	500°F/260°C	(260°C)
165°F/74°C	(73.9°C)	525°F/275°C	(273.9°C)
170°F/77°C	(76.7°C)	550°F/290°C	(287.8°C)

POUNDS TO GRAMS AND KILOGRAMS

Pounds	Convenient Equivalent	Actual Weight
¼ lb	115 g	(113.4 g)
½ lb	225 g	(226.8 g)
¾ lb	340 g	(340.2 g)
1 lb	450 g	(453.6 g)
1¼ lb	565 g	(566.99 g)
1½ lb	675 g	(680.4 g)
1¾ lb	800 g	(794 g)
2 lb	900 g	(908 g)
2½ lb	1125 g; 1¼ kg	(1134 g)
3 lb	1350 g	(1360 g)
3½ lb	1500 g; 1½ kg	(1588 g)
4 lb	1800 g	(1814 g)
4½ lb	2 kg	(2041 g)
5 lb	2¼ kg	(2268 g)
5½ lb	2½ kg	(2495 g)
6 lb	2¾ kg	(2727 g)
7 lb	3¼ kg	(3175 g)
8 lb	3½ kg	(3629 g)
9 lb	4 kg	(4028 g)
10 lb	4½ kg	(4536 g)
12 lb	5½ kg	(5443 g)
14 lb	6¼ kg	(6350 g)
15 lb	6¾ kg	(6804 g)
16 lb	7¼ kg	(7258 g)
18 lb	8 kg	(8165 g)
20 lb	9 kg	(9072 g)
25 lb	11¼ kg	(11,340 g)

OUNCES TO GRAMS

Ounces	Convenient Equivalent	Actual Weight
1 oz	30 g	(28.35 g)
2 oz	60 g	(56.7 g)
3 oz	85 g	(85.05 g)
4 oz	115 g	(113.4 g)
5 oz	140 g	(141.8 g)
6 oz	180 g	(170.1 g)
8 oz	225 g	(226.8 g)
9 oz	250 g	(255.2 g)
10 oz	285 g	(283.5 g)

Ounces	Convenient Equivalent	Actual Weight
12 oz	340 g	(340.2 g)
14 oz	400 g	(396.9 g)
16 oz	450 g	(453.6 g)
20 oz	560 g	(566.99 g)
24 oz	675 g	(680.4 g)

LIQUID MEASURE CONVERSIONS

Cups and Spoons	Liquid Ounces	Approximate Metric Term	Approximate Centiliters	Actual Milliliters
1 tsp	¹/₆ oz	1 tsp	½ cL	5 mL
1 Tb	½ oz	1 Tb	1½ cL	15 mL
¼ c; 4 Tb	2 oz	½ dL; 4 Tb	6 cL	59 mL
⅓ c; 5 Tb	2⅔ oz	¾ dL; 5 Tb	8 cL	79 mL
½ c	4 oz	1 dL	12 cL	119 mL
⅔ c	5⅓ oz	1½ dL	15 cL	157 mL
¾ c	6 oz	1¾ dL	18 cL	178 mL
1 c	8 oz	¼ L	24 cL	237 mL
1¼ c	10 oz	3 dL	30 cL	296 mL
1⅓ c	10⅔ oz	3¼ dL	33 cL	325 mL
1½ c	12 oz	3½ dL	35 cL	355 mL
1⅔ c	13⅓ oz	3¾ dL	39 cL	385 mL
1¾ c	14 oz	4 dL	41 cL	414 mL
2 c; 1 pt	16 oz	½ L	47 cL	473 mL
2½ c	20 oz	6 dL	60 cL	592 mL
3 c	24 oz	¾ L	70 cL	710 mL
3½ c	28 oz	⁴/₅ L; 8 dL	83 cL	829 mL
4 c; 1 qt	32 oz	1 L	95 cL	946 mL
5 c	40 oz	1¼ L	113 cL	1134 mL
6 c; 1½ qt	48 oz	1½ L	142 cL	1420 mL
8 c; 2 qt	64 oz	2 L	190 cL	1893 mL
10 c; 2½ qt	80 oz	2½ L	235 cL	2366 mL
12 c; 3 qt	96 oz	2¾ L	284 cL	2839 mL
4 qt	128 oz	3¾ L	375 cL	3785 mL
5 qt		4¾ L		
6 qt		5½ L (or 6 L)		
8 qt		7½ L (or 8 L)		

INCHES TO CENTIMETERS

Inches ("in")	Centimeters ("cm") (Nearest equivalent)
¹/₁₆ in	¼ cm
⅛ in	½ cm
³/₁₆ in	"less than ¼ in/¾ cm"
¼ in	¾ cm
⅜ in	1 cm
½ in	1½ cm
⅝ in	1½ cm
¾ in	2 cm
1 in	2½ cm
1½ in	4 cm
2 in	5 cm
2½ in	6½ cm
3 in	8 cm
3½ in	9 cm
4 in	10 cm
5 in	13 cm
6 in	15 cm
7 in	18 cm
8 in	20 cm
9 in	23 cm
10 in	25 cm
12 in	30 cm
14 in	35 cm
15 in	38½ cm
16 in	40 cm
18 in	45 cm
20 in	50 cm
24 in	60 cm
30 in	75 cm

Index